THE DEAF COMMUN

IN AMERICA

P9-CKS-943

THE DEAF COMMUNITY IN AMERICA

History in the Making

Melvia M. Nomeland *and*
Ronald E. Nomeland

FOREWORD BY TRUDY SUGGS

McFarland & Company, Inc., Publishers
Jefferson, North Carolina, and London

LIBRARY OF CONGRESS CATALOGUING-IN-PUBLICATION DATA

Nomeland, Melvia M., 1940–
    The deaf community in America : history in the making /
Melvia M. Nomeland and Ronald E. Nomeland ; foreword by
Trudy Suggs.
       p.   cm.
    Includes bibliographical references and index.

    ISBN 978-0-7864-6397-8
    softcover : acid free paper ∞

    1. Deaf—United States—History.   2. Deaf—Education—
United States.   3. Deaf culture—United States.   4. American
Sign Language. I. Nomeland, Ronald E., 1936– II. Title.
HV2545.N66 2012
305.9'0820973—dc23   2011044165

BRITISH LIBRARY CATALOGUING DATA ARE AVAILABLE

Front cover image: Teaching a deaf-mute to talk. Training
School for Deaf Mutes (1917) photographer Lewis Wickes Hine,
1874–1940 (Library of Congress)

Manufactured in the United States of America

McFarland & Company, Inc., Publishers
  Box 611, Jefferson, North Carolina 28640
   www.mcfarlandpub.com

To Deaf people of all generations

Table of Contents

Foreword by Trudy Suggs   1

Preface   3

ONE • Earliest Known History of Deaf People   5

TWO • Origins of Deaf Learning in America   27

THREE • Historical Issues in Education   48

FOUR • Life in Deaf Communities   72

FIVE • Recognition of ASL as a Language   101

SIX • Expansion of Visual Languages   116

SEVEN • Emergence of Colorful Communication   141

EIGHT • Enlightenment of Independence   171

NINE • Personalities Through the Years   189

Epilogue: Today and Beyond   209

Notes   213

Bibliography   217

Index   225

Foreword

by Trudy Suggs

Growing up as a Deaf person born in the 1970s, I came into this world as the Deaf community was finally starting to receive well-deserved recognition for its culture, language and accomplishments. Deaf people had just been granted equal access in education, were riding on the social justice and civil rights movements of the previous decade, and had been given a fresh identity with the recognition of American Sign Language as a bona fide language. Although we were still two decades away from the Americans with Disabilities Act, we were making pioneering progress in a multitude of ways.

Even though I was born Deaf to Deaf parents, I grew up always thirsty for confirmation of what my parents told me about my culture and language. I wanted to learn about the Deaf community's leaders, ordinary people, and accomplishments, because to understand their existence helped me feel validated about being a Deaf person and verified that I, too, had a world of opportunities before me. I saw so many of my friends feeling discouraged, disengaged and dismayed because of what others told them they *couldn't* do as Deaf people.

I scoured every word of anything I could find about my community. Since most books I came across talked about Deaf people as people with an affliction or in need of rehabilitation, I chose mainly to read articles in newspapers such as *Silent News* and magazines, especially articles written by Deaf people. Such articles helped remind me that I *could* do whatever I wanted and affirmed my cultural identity. I was also fascinated by how Deaf people of generations past were oppressed and discriminated against in far worse conditions than I have ever been and ever will be, yet they continued to flourish in their careers, families, and lives.

After the Deaf President Now movement in 1988 — which took place when I was a high school freshman — the Deaf community had an even stronger collective identity. I drank every bit of it up and wrote many of my papers in high school on Deaf-related topics. Yet, as I think back, I find it difficult to identify books written by Deaf people that explored the Deaf community in a historical and informative nature, except perhaps the fictitious *Islay*. It is only within the past decade that more and more books have been published by Deaf people — and to this I ask why it took so long to happen. But never mind that; better late than never, perhaps.

Authors Melvia and Ron Nomeland have compiled a fascinating and inspiring chronological account of Deaf people's emergence as a community and people. Written in an engaging, easy-to-read manner, this book can be read in a classroom or lounging on a couch. What makes this book even better is that the authors are Deaf and come from Deaf families and are active in the Deaf community. They know firsthand the illustrious aspects of living within a society that often misunderstands the Deaf community and its culture and language.

Melvia and Ron have witnessed the evolution of Deaf people, from being perceived as misfits, needing help and needing rehabilitation, into being perceived as a wonderfully rich linguistic and cultural community. And the authors have themselves evolved through personal experiences and insights. The research they have undertaken is of an enormous nature, and yet the information in this book is hardly dry or dull. Quite the contrary; the stories and historical tidbits are splendidly fascinating.

This book is one that I will pass down to my children.

Trudy Suggs, owner of T.S. Writing Services, is a writer who is Deaf and has been an educator, advocate and administrator. She and her family live in Faribault, Minnesota.

Preface

Given how rich and deep the history of Deaf people is, we wrote this book because we wanted to highlight in an organized, interesting fashion how the lives of Deaf people have evolved through the years. Readers will learn about early awareness of deaf people in Europe and about early European influence on American Deaf people. This book also presents the growth in education and society through the years.

Our goal is that this book will educate, enlighten, and entertain parents of Deaf children, educators of deaf children, the public at large, and especially Deaf people about the rich and fascinating tidbits in Deaf history. More importantly, the book is an attempt to divulge the changing attitudes toward Deaf people from within and outside the Deaf community.

In our retirement we have spent many enjoyable hours in researching the mesmerizing history of Deaf people, the Deaf community, and American Sign Language. We reviewed over a hundred books written by Deaf and hearing researchers and linguists, recycled some materials from our teaching careers, and attended conferences and workshops. As Deaf people with Deaf parents, we wrote this book in a historical context, given our personal experiences and documented facts.

The book adopts the current custom to distinguish between the cultural and audiological representation of deaf people by using the capital "D" to refer to a community of people who share a language and a culture and the lower case "d" to refer to the audiological condition of hearing loss.

Hanging around us on an everlasting basis as we spent hours at the computer working on this manuscript, our young granddaughter, Laila, often begged to play with us. Someday she will understand. We deeply appreciate our daughter Jamie's and her partner Laura's support; they gave us quiet time and cooked meals for us as well as took Laila and our dog Calvin out of the house.

Our deep appreciation is hereby bestowed on Trudy Suggs of T.S. Writing

Services for her support of our endeavor. Trudy went further than editing support; she provided suggestions as well as challenged us to research further information to clarify some concepts. To Cathryn Carroll, Dr. Mervin Garretson, Dr. Genie Gertz, Dr. E. Lynn Jacobowitz, Dr. Barbara Kannapell, and Dr. Rachel Stone, we owe deep gratitude for their time spent in reviewing the drafts of this book, particularly in their areas of expertise, and providing excellent feedback.

For making our book thought provoking with their humorous and/or honest perspectives of Deaf culture, we thank Matt Daigle, Roy and Marjoriebell Holcomb and their sons Samuel and Thomas, Maureen Kleczka, Ruth Peterson, Shawn Richardson, and Ann Silver.

We are indebted to the Gallaudet University library for its rich collection of deaf-related books and media, and to the Gallaudet Archives for access to its valuable collections. We also appreciate the contributions of Dr. Dennis Cokely, Dr. Carol Padden, Fanny Corderoy du Tiers, SIGNews, Matthew Moore, Dan McClintock, and DawnSignPress for allowing us to include their illustrations.

This book has been a labor of love. We sincerely hope that you will appreciate learning the many fascinating tidbits and trivia that have meshed into the magnificent history of deaf people.

ONE

Earliest Known History of Deaf People

Deaf People in Ancient Times

Perhaps the best place to start in Deaf history is at the beginning of mankind, as researched by scientists. About four million years ago, human-like animals called *australopithecines*[1] appeared on Earth. They walked differently than we do and had smaller brains. Without any recorded history of deaf people — none of the hieroglyphics discovered by archaeologists ever mentioned any incident of hearing loss or deaf people — we are left with several potential situations.

During those times, it was a survival-of-the-fittest environment; each person had to fend for himself. It's likely that children born with disabilities or deformities were killed or abandoned. Still, it wouldn't be surprising if deaf people survived, given that hearing loss is often overlooked.

Deaf people often jest that the first sign or gesture was for "come here." Another possible first gesture could have been using the index finger to point at things. Deaf children are often told that it is impolite to point at people or things, but hearing children also use this gesture for a variety of reasons; they most certainly did not invent this gesture.

Gordon Hewes, Ph.D., an anthropologist at the University of Colorado, suggested that signs were probably the first language and that signs helped humans to start voice languages. He added that sign languages probably made voice language possible.[2] Eventually gestures and sounds were used to identify people, places or things. As thousands of years passed, people used fewer and fewer gestures, with their grunts eventually evolving into speech to communicate desires or ideas.

The earliest history of mankind was recorded through tools and crafts created from iron and bronze. In 4000 B.C., physical strength and manual skills were considered significant. It has been theorized that writing started during the Sumerian civilization (circa 5000 B.C.), when people drew pictures on wet clay. The clay, later sun dried, was used to communicate or record events. Eventually drawings got smaller and smaller; small drawings were then made into a form of symbols.

Deaf People in Biblical Times (700 B.C.–A.D. 400)

Based on the earliest known written records, it appears that attitudes toward deaf people and people with other disabilities were partly positive and partly negative.[3] In ancient Greek society, if a disabled or deformed child was born into a family, the father had the authority to decide whether or not the child would live. Hebrews and Egyptians, however, had significantly different perspectives.

The Egyptians treated disabled persons with respect; in fact, in Egypt, blind men often became musicians. The first mention of a deaf person, Chushim, is noted in the Torah. The Torah tells of how Chushim killed his grandfather Cain and was praised. The Hebrews considered disabilities as a fact of life, part of God's creation. Although deaf people were considered "legally incompetent," they could be taught and were therefore not idiotic. If they could not speak, they were not considered legally competent, although they might communicate via writing. It has also been observed in the Talmud, or Jewish religious writings, that deaf persons were not allowed the right to own property.[4]

Jewish scripture dictated that it was necessary to hear speech so that a person could understand and obey the Lord. Isaiah 28:23 states, "Give ye ear, and hear my voice; harken, and hear my speech." Sympathetic attitudes toward deaf people (and blind people) were noted when the Lord offered Moses a set of several laws. Leviticus recorded one of them, which reads: "Do not curse deaf people or put a stumbling block in front of the blind, but fear your God. I am the Lord" (Leviticus 19:28).

The ancient Hebrews may have been the first to distinguish between born-deaf people and those who lost their hearing later in life.[5] Although literature does not show the distinction as "prelingually deaf" and "postlingually deaf," as is said today, Hebrews said that those born deaf could not own property. Furthermore, those born deaf were perceived by hearing people as easily tricked and thus treated like children by society at large. Those who lost hearing later, especially those who could not understand language through hearing and did not speak, were given certain rights; those who could speak were bestowed with more rights and were better accepted by Hebrew society.[6] Even though the Hebrews were kind to deaf people, they did not allow deaf people to participate fully in Temple rituals.

Two early Greek historians mention a deaf man believed to have lived from 600 to 550 B.C.[7] No name is given, but he was a son of Croesus, King of Lydia. The king is believed to have said that Atys, his other son who was hearing, was his only son; the deaf son was considered lost. Atys built a reputation for himself, became as famous as his father, and was next in line for the throne. However, he met an accidental death when his friend impaled him with a spear while trying to kill a boar.

There are two versions of what happened to the deaf son. Herodotus, who wrote the story of the two sons a century later, mentioned that Croesus's army fought Persians to increase his empire. The deaf son, in seeing a Persian soldier rushing toward his father, yelled out, "O man, do not kill Croesus!" He was able to speak for the rest of his life. The other version, written by Xenophon in *Cyropaedia*, portrayed Cyrus taking Croesus prisoner. Croesus was said to tell Cyrus that he had two sons, but "they have been of no good to me, for one remained mute, and the other died in the flower of youth."[8] Croesus was no longer a king, so his deaf son did not inherit his father's crown.

The Greek philosopher Socrates in the fifth century B.C. appears to have been the first person to write about sign language. Apparently fascinated by it, he inquired of his colleague Hermogenes: "Suppose that we had no voice or tongue, and wanted to indicate objects to one another, should we not, like the deaf and dumb, make signs with the hands, head and the rest of the body?"[9] Hermogenes replied, "How could it be otherwise, Socrates?" This illustrates that deaf people existed then, and were accepted by Greek society.[10]

Another famous Greek philosopher, Aristotle (384–322 B.C.), was a pupil of Plato, who learned under Socrates. Aristotle apparently disagreed with Socrates when the former wrote in 355 B.C., "Men that are deaf are also speechless; that is they can make vocal sounds but they cannot speak." He was also recognized with producing the quotation: "Those who are born deaf all become senseless and incapable of reason." Because Aristotle believed that hearing contributed the most to intelligence, and that thought could be expressed through the medium of articulation, he was, for the next two thousand years, accused of oppressing deaf people. On the other hand, it has been said that he was quoted out of context. Apparently he was referring to the fact that a deaf child, born deaf, would not learn to speak or express himself without special training.[11]

Christianity first records philosophical acceptance toward deaf people around A.D. 30.[12] Although the church excluded deaf people from church

Aristotle, Intelligence and the Deaf. © 2003 Dan McClintock.

membership, its benevolent attitude benefited these people. The Bible mentions the word "ephphatha," uttered by Jesus Christ who healed a "deaf and dumb" man. Mark 9:25 in the New Testament reads:

> They brought to him a man who was deaf and had an impediment in his speech, with the request that he would lay his hand on him. He took the man aside, away from the crowd, put his fingers into his ears, spat, and touched his tongue. Then, looking up to heaven, he sighed, and said to him, "Ephphatha," which means, "Be opened," and at the same time the impediment was removed and he spoke plainly.... [The people said] "He even makes the deaf hear and the dumb speak."

One of the more fortunate deaf individuals was Quintus Pedius, whose name first appeared in history books around A.D. 77. Quintus' grandfather requested permission from Emperor Augustus Caesar for Quintus to study to become an artist. The fact that his grandfather was in a position of influence as a consul of the emperor probably played a vital role in Caesar's approval. At that time, deaf children born of prominent parents had more opportunities than those born into lower classes within the Roman caste system.[13] Subsequently, Quintus was considered one of the most eminent painters of Rome.[14]

Christians believed that Jesus had magical powers through God and could perform miracles. Yet deaf people were excluded from church membership, primarily based on Romans 10:17: "So faith comes from what is heard." Christians also believed that deaf people were not able to confess their sins. Saint Augustine is often credited with the view that Deaf people could not be saved because they were not able to hear the word of God. The New Testament suggested that deafness was caused by an evil spirit and deaf people could not become Christians.[15] Perhaps Augustine was merely following his church's doctrine when he commented that deafness was a hindrance to faith. Later, he became more optimistic when he disclosed that deaf people could learn and thus were able to receive faith and salvation.

Deaf People in the Middle Ages (A.D. 400–1400)

During the Dark (Middle) Ages, humans faced difficulties such as poverty, famine and diseases. As a result, there were not many advances in arts and sciences. Painters worked mostly on religious subjects.

During the early part of the Middle Ages, deaf adults were objects of ridicule and even served as court jesters. Others were committed to asylums because of their lack of speech or because their behaviors were thought to be the result of demonic possession. During the late Middle Ages, the Christian church viewed deaf people as heathens and barred them because they were unable to hear the word of God. Deaf people, in the church's eyes, lacked faith and thus could not be saved.[16]

During the sixth century A.D., Romans recognized deaf people who could not speak as a group that required special attention and protection. Interestingly enough, the Romans were careful in categorizing various types of deafness. Similar to the ancient Hebrews, the Romans noted the differences between those who lost hearing at birth and those who lost their hearing later on. Roman Emperor Justinian was a Christian and one of the most influential men of the early Middle Ages. In A.D. 528, the Justinian Code,[17] created during Justinian's reign, classified deaf people into five categories:

1. The Deaf and Dumb with whom this double infirmity is from birth;
   - Forbidden the right to control their property
   - All purchases and sales had to be arranged through a guardian.
   - Can't make wills, build properties, or free slaves
2. The Deaf and Dumb with whom this double infirmity is not from birth, but the effect of an accident that occurred during life;
   - Could have all privileges returned to them if they were able to communicate in writing
   - Are educable, can be taught, mainly in art or painting
3. The Deaf person who is not dumb, but whose deafness is from birth;
   - Could be what we call today "hard of hearing" (speech is not perfect, but still can speak)
   - May function and think like hearing persons, depending on the hearing loss
4. The person who is simply deaf, and that from accident;
   - Because s/he still uses speech, s/he follows the social and legal status that hearing people enjoy.
5. Finally, he who is simply dumb, whether born dumb or became dumb.
   - Simply put, this person is mute.
   - If can read or write, then follow the 2nd classification.

In order to survive, deaf people during that period had to depend on their parents' wealth, on working in important positions, and on their educational status (especially the boys). Otherwise, they were rejected, neglected, or abandoned.

However, during the Middle Ages, interest in teaching deaf people grew. The earliest medieval efforts at instructing deaf people were always sparked by religious zeal to provide salvation of the souls of deaf people. In 685, during Lent, a disheveled young deaf man was brought to the Bishop of Hagulstad in England. The bishop taught him the alphabet, then progressed to syllables, whole words and then whole sentences. The young man was also taught to speak. Modern-day scholars have questioned the validity of being able to learn to speak well in a short frame of time. However, the bishop, then St. John of Beverly, is today the Patron Saint of Teachers of the Deaf.[18]

Monks, as a source of information, preserved and shared some of their writings about deafness. Benedictine monks invented a system of signs and fingerspelling to circumvent "vows of silence." These signs may have been used later in attempts to teach Deaf children.

Physicians in those days considered deafness a malady and a physical condition that should be eliminated to allow a healthy life. Deaf people endured numerous experiments in the search for a cure for deafness, such as the blowing of a trumpet in the ears or pouring liquids (oil, honey, vinegar, bile of rabbits or pigs, garlic juice, goat's urine, eel fat mixed with blood) into the ears.

Deaf People in the Renaissance (A.D. 1400–1600)

The Renaissance was a time of great change and rebirth in religion, astronomy, literature and art. During this rebirth and growth, deaf people were recognized as people of abilities. They were taught to read and write, and they were able to express themselves.

A comment on teaching a deaf child was noted in the book *De Inventione Dialectica (On Dialectical Invention),* by Rudolph Agricola (1443–1485), a Dutch author. He described a deaf-mute who was taught to read and write. The book was not published until 1521, 36 years after his death.

Italian physician Dr. Girolamo Cardano (1501–1576) discovered Agricola's story and was impressed by the achievement of the deaf man. Cardano's firstborn son was deaf, and Cardano happened to focus on the eyes, ears, mouth, and brain in his medical practice. He reasoned that written words were independent of the sounds of speech; thus deaf people could understand and be taught without aural references. He theorized that a deaf individual might be taught to "hear" by reading and to "speak" by writing.[19] Cardano also recognized deaf people's ability to use reason. American professor Dr. Ruth Bender, in her book, called Cardano's findings "a revolutionary declaration,"[20] thus breaking down the long-standing belief that the hearing of words was necessary for the understanding of ideas.

During the Renaissance, because so much intermarriage in the Spanish royal families took place, a fairly large percentage of children were born disabled or deaf. Since there still were no schools for the deaf in Spain, wealthy families sent their deaf children to monasteries or convents or hired tutors for them.

Ponce de Leon (1520–1584), a Spanish Benedictine monk, taught deaf people at a monastery, with an emphasis on speech. His students included Gaspard Burges, who learned to read and write there. At that time, tightly knit families of the noble and upper-middle classes tended to keep their conquests and hold their wealth within the families, usually through intermarriages. The de Velascos were one of Spain's most powerful families. Juan de Velasco and Juana Enriquez were blood relatives and had nine children, four of them deaf. Two older deaf daughters entered separate convents. Their father, seeking a teacher for his two deaf sons, was referred to a nearby monastery where de Leon, already known for his success with Burges, resided.

There, the two younger male siblings were taught to read and write so that they could legally inherit their family's property and status.

De Leon first taught objects' written names, then their pronunciations, and then the words were practiced in association. The two brothers, Pedro and Francisco de Velasco, learned well the skills of reading and writing, and they also were said to have learned to speak. Both eventually assumed their full responsibilities as noblemen. According to Scouten,[21] de Leon was the first *bona fide* teacher of the deaf. Carved on his tombstone is the epitaph: "Pedro Ponce educated the deaf and dumb though Aristotle declared it impossible."[22]

In the 1500s, deaf artist Juan Fernandez X. Navaretta was known as *El Mudo,* Spanish for "the mute one." He was a very talented artist who could read and write. When King Philip II saw Navaretta's painting of Christ's baptism, he hired *El Mudo* as a court painter, a high honor.[23]

In 1575, the Spanish lawyer Lasso denounced an old belief that being deaf automatically meant a lack of intelligence. He also announced that deaf people should have the right to bear children.[24]

First Learning Opportunities (1600–1700)

During the seventeenth century, the opportunities for learning were greatly expanded for deaf children. Again, the fortunate deaf children were usually born of royal bloodlines or had connections to royalty.

After de Leon's death, Spanish educators Juan Pablo Bonet and Manual Ramirez de Carrion carried on his work. In 1612, two-year-old Luis de Velasco lost his hearing due to high fever. He was the son of widowed Doña Juana de Córdoba. Incidentally, he was the grandnephew of the two aforementioned brothers, Pedro and Francisco de Velasco. Bonet, a long-time secretary to the family, recalled hearing about the successful learning of the two brothers. After a search, Bonet located an articulation teacher, Ramirez de Carrión. De Carrión had served as a tutor and secretary to a deaf man, Marquis de Priego, in Montilla. Nothing has been written about de Priego, but apparently, able to afford a private tutor, he was a rich and successful man. Bonet struck an agreement with the Marquis to release de Carrión for three to four years so that de Carrión could teach Luis.

De Carrión worked with the deaf boy for four years. One can assume that Luis' knowledge of speech before becoming deaf facilitated his learning and the recovery of his ability to talk. At the age of nine, Luis had basic skills in reading, writing, and speaking Spanish. During this time, Bonet observed de Carrión's work with Luis and recorded the events. Subsequently, Bonet wrote a book on de Carrión's practices and added his own theories of teaching deaf children. He asserted that deaf children could be taught through the eyes

Ponce de Leon and Student © Gallaudet University Archives.

by learning letters in print and manual alphabet and then learning to lipread by copying the teacher's use of lips for consonants, vowels, words, and sentences.[25] The book, *The Simplification of Letters and the Art of Teaching the Mute to Speak*, published in 1620, is said to be the most influential book of the time that was about teaching deaf students.[26] Additionally, the alphabet published in Bonet's book is the basis of the American manual alphabet.

Englishman Sir Kenelm Digby (1603–1665), who had visited King Philip IV in Spain as a member of Prince Charles' entourage, was impressed by the appearance and manner of the handsome and gracious Luis de Velasco, then 13 years old. He also met Bonet. In 1644, Sir Digby wrote *Treatise on the Nature of Bodies* and mentioned his encounters with Bonet and Luis, the latter having received the title of Marquis de Fresno when he turned 18 years old in 1628. This book is said to have roused the idea that deaf people could be taught. One person whom it inspired was a physician, Dr. John Bulwer (1606–1656), who never taught deaf children but believed that one sense could take over the duties of another — the eye for the ear and the hand for the tongue.[27] In 1644, Bulwer published *Chirologia*, a book on fingerspelling; the handshapes described in the book are still used in British Sign Language. He wrote *Philocopus* in 1648, in which he advocated for the establishment of an academy for deaf people.

In England, William Holder, D.D. (1616–1698), and John Wallis, D.D. (1616–1703), were considered the first teachers of deaf people. Although they had intense interest in teaching deaf people, they could not put up with each other. In 1659, Admiral Popham and Lady Wharton hired Dr. Holder, a clergyman, to teach their deaf son; it can be again recalled that deaf children from elite society had more opportunities for education. Holder taught sounds, then combined them into syllables and finally whole words, using a two-handed manual alphabet. He described his teaching methods in a book, *Elements of Speech with an Appendix Concerning People, Deaf & Dumb*.

In the meantime, Dr. Wallis, also a clergyman and a tutor, agreed to teach a 25-year-old deaf man, Daniel Whalley, the son of the mayor of Northampton. After a year of instruction, Whalley could understand the Bible and read orally from it. A presentation of his newfound skills was made before the Royal Society and awed the members. However, the audience was not aware of the fact that Whalley lost his hearing at five years of age and therefore was postlingually deaf. Wallis read books on teaching the deaf by the Spaniard Bonet and taught reading, writing and speaking using gestures. He wrote *Grammar of English for Foreigners with an Essay on Speech or the Formulation of Sounds*.

Lady Wharton learned about Dr. Wallis' presentation and success. She decided to remove her son from Dr. Holder's tutelage after three years and place him with Dr. Wallis for instruction. Apparently this incident caused friction between the two educators for years.[28]

Another book on teaching the deaf was published in 1680, *Didascaloco-phus* (The Deaf and Dumb Man's Tutor), by George Dalgarno. The Scot was the head of one of Oxford's private grammar schools and was interested in the acquisition of languages. He published *Ars Signorum* (The Art of Signs) in 1661, which had nothing to do with sign language. After its publication, he became acquainted with the Holder-Wallis controversy and was captivated by the learning struggles and language acquisition of those born deaf. His background as a Latinist and a grammar school teacher offered him some insight in the process of learning and language acquisition.

Dalgarno may have been the first person to articulate the difficulty of blindness compared to deafness. He surmised that it was less difficult to be blind than to be deaf, and that was at least two hundred years before Helen Keller pronounced her thoughts on the same topic. Dalgarno concluded that, because of auditory input from birth, blind people had greater capacity for linguistic growth, with the ensuing talent of expression of thoughts and words. He theorized that a congenitally born-deaf child, without auditory input, did not have a similar natural vehicle of learning and thus was at a disadvantage from the beginning.

Interestingly, because of his involvement with the learning of deaf children, Dalgarno became an advocate of early childhood learning, especially for deaf people. He emphasized, in teaching deaf people, that it was necessary to be persistent "in order to lift the deaf child from his predicament of ignorance into understanding and communication."[29] The first of the six principles for teaching deaf children that he laid down was:

> Here the first piece of diligence must be ... using the pen and fingers [fingerspelling] much.... Great care, therefore, must be taken, to keep your scholar close to the practice of writing; for, until he can not only write, but also got a quick hand, you must not think to make any considerable progress with him.[30]

Dalgarno created his version of the fingerspelling alphabet, said to be the first one developed especially for deaf people, as opposed to Bonet's alphabet. It should be recalled that Bonet's alphabet was presumably used by Benedictine monks who used fingers to circumvent their vows of silence. Dalgarno's alphabet consisted of placing letters on different parts of the palm and pointing to the various spots to spell out words. The five vowels were located at the tip of each finger — the letter "a" at the tip of the thumb, "e" at the tip of the index finger, "i" at the tip of the middle finger, and so on. The placement of the vowels is still recognized and used in British countries as the two-handed alphabet.

By the end of the seventeenth century, successful teaching of deaf people was recorded in four European countries: Spain, England, France and Holland. The enthusiasm was noted by Kenneth Hodgson,[31] who wrote about "...widespread recognition of the possibilities of teaching speech and speechreading. Miracles had become practical: something to be accepted as quite within the ordinary bounds of human achievement."

Johann Amman (1669–1724) was an avid Amish physician who left Switzerland because of religious persecution and settled in the Netherlands. His teaching goals included making vowel sounds and consonant sounds, forming words and sentences, and lipreading as part of the language achievement. He described his methods in his book, *The Talking Man*, in the 1700s. He advocated oralism, and his methods of teaching deaf people influenced deaf people in Germany and France.

Henry Baker (1698–1774) opened the first school for the deaf in England. He taught his deaf niece using Wallis' theories and used mirrors for speech practice, later writing a book, *Motion of Fingers*. Baker charged high fees for deaf children's education and kept his teaching methods a secret until his death.

The first phase of the history of education of the deaf, as Eriksson[32] noted, ran from the beginning of the sixteenth century until the late eighteenth century. Some characteristics of the teaching of deaf children during that period included:

- The education of deaf children was usually arranged by the family.
- Its purpose was to teach the deaf to communicate with other people orally or in writing.
- The students were rarely taught lipreading.
- The media of instruction were speech, writing, fingerspelling and signs.
- Because teachers jealously guarded the secrets of their trade, the art of deaf education was often veiled in mystery.
- Many teachers of deaf students thought their methods were of their own invention.
- Many teachers of the deaf were priests or physicians.
- Very little of what was written about deaf education at that time contained description of actual methods.

Expansion of Deaf Education in Europe (1700–1800)

In Europe during the late 1700s, the Industrial Revolution took place, and many factories and steel mills were built. Many public schools opened for hearing children, while only a few private schools were opened for deaf children. People no longer believed that deaf people lacked intelligence. The first books in English about teaching deaf students were published. Some teachers were secretive about their methods, which slowed down the progress of education of deaf people.

This century is notable in the history of deaf education because:

- Formal, school-based education of deaf people (or the first public institution serving deaf individuals) began in England and France.
- For the first time, sign language was used consistently in a school; the school was founded by Abbé de l'Épée.
- For the first time, deaf students had a deaf teacher, Jean Massieu.
- The first known debate about sign language and speech began.[33]

In England and Scotland

Englishman Daniel Defoe is renowned for writing *Robinson Crusoe*, but he also wrote *The Life and Adventure of Duncan Campbell*. Campbell was a real-life person renowned throughout England for his psychic abilities, and he was deaf. Defoe wrote about how Campbell got his education via the British two-hand alphabet, and then Campbell learned speech.

Another Englishman, Henry Baker, had just completed his apprenticeship as a bookseller. The 22-year-old Baker was visiting relatives in Enfield when he learned about his deaf eight-year-old niece Jane Forester, who apparently had no previous learning. Baker came across Defoe's book and found out about the work of Dr. Wallis. Baker became Jane's teacher for nine years, and during that time, he became acquainted with Defoe's daughter, Sophia. He and Sophia married in 1729 after he left his teaching position. Baker became a bookseller and kept his teaching procedures a secret.[34]

A mathematician by profession, Thomas Braidwood I surprised his colleagues in 1760 when he agreed to teach a 15-year-old deaf man, Robert Sherriff, how to write. Sherriff had lost his hearing at the age of three and appeared to be intelligent. After Sherriff learned to read and write, Braidwood decided to teach him speech. Braidwood was then motivated to teach other deaf students and announced the opening of a school in Edinburgh to serve children whose parents who could afford the tuition. The school grew, and in 1783 he moved the Braidwood Academy to Hackney, in the London area. His sister's son, Joseph Watson, and his brother's son, John Braidwood I, were trained to teach deaf students; they pledged to keep the methods within the family. When Thomas Braidwood I died in 1806, his widow and John directed the school program. After the death of both, John's widow took over.

The London Asylum for the Deaf and Dumb, another school, was opened at Kent Road in 1792 to accept deaf children from poor families in London.

The Deaf and Dumb Asylum, Kent Road. © Gallaudet University Archives.

It was the first public school for deaf children in Britain. Joseph Watson, the nephew of Braidwood I, left Hackney to become its principal and served for 37 years until his death in 1829. He was said to be an excellent teacher. His son, Thomas, succeeded him and held the job for 28 years.

In 1809, three years after Thomas Braidwood's death — although he promised to keep the "Braidwood Method" a secret — Watson revealed the teaching method in a publication. The Braidwoods described their method as oral, but the students were allowed to use gestures and natural signs until they learned to talk. The Braidwoods also used the two-hand manual alphabet.[35]

In 1810, the Edinburgh Institute was founded in Scotland by the same group that started the Asylum at Kent Road. John Braidwood II, the son of John Braidwood I and a grand nephew of Thomas Braidwood I, became its principal. Two years later he was fired due to alcoholism. He later moved to the United States, where he continued his teaching career.

IN GERMANY

Germany developed a state school system for the deaf, presumed to be the earliest free public schools for deaf children. There were also state schools for the deaf in Austria, Sazony, and Prussia.[36]

The most renowned German educator was Samuel Heinicke (1727–1790), who opened a school in Leipzig in 1778. He was influenced by Johann Amman (1669–1724), author of *The Speaking Deaf.* Amman, a Swiss, had moved to Holland because of religious persecution. He was a doctor who was unable to cure a deaf patient medically; instead he began to teach speech to the child. Amman wrote another book, *A Dissertation on Speech,* which was said to have profound influence on education of deaf children in Germany.

Heinicke rejected the use of signs, believing that sign language and the manual alphabet prevented the students from learning. He used speech as the only method of teaching and as a means of communication in

Samuel Heinicke © Gallaudet University Archives.

the classroom. In 1778, he published *Observations on the Deaf and Dumb.* In advocating the pure oral method, he developed a set of eight principles of instruction, including:

- Clear thought is possible only by speech, and, therefore, the deaf ought to be taught to speak.
- Learning speech, which depends on hearing, is only possible by substituting another sense for hearing, and this can be no other than *taste,* which serves chiefly to fix the vowel sounds.
- Although the deaf can think in signs and pictures, this is confusing and indefinite, so that the ideas thus acquired are not enduring.
- The manual alphabet is useful, but, contrary to its ordinary use, it only serves to combine ideas.[37]

Heinicke's career ended with his death in 1790, and his two living sons were not interested in his efforts. His widow and two sons-in-law tried to carry on his work. For a while, Charles de l'Épée's work in France had influence upon teaching methods in Germany. However, with the latent influence of Heinicke's teachings, the oral method experienced a revival in Germany during the nineteenth century.

In France

In France, the earliest well-known teacher of the deaf was Jacob Rod-riguez Pereire (1715–1790) of Spain. It is said that he became interested in teaching deaf people after tutoring his deaf sister before he moved to France. Another version is that he started working with deaf children after falling in love with a deaf girl. However, personal documents obtained from his son and grandchildren did not mention either girl. Students at Pereire's school in Paris were sworn to secrecy about his teaching method, but "Pereire employed a one-handed alphabet for the teaching of speech, relied on a 'natural' approach to the development of language, developed auditory training procedures for individuals with residual hearing, and used special exercises involving sight and touch in sense training."[38] Pereire took his secrets to the grave in 1790.

Meanwhile, the Catholic priest Abbé Charles-Michel de l'Épée (1712–1789) was visiting a family in an impoverished section of Paris when he happened to say hello to two girls. They were doing needlework in the living

room and did not respond to him. Later he found out from their mother that the 15-year-old girls were deaf. Their father had passed away, and the girls were doing needlepoint to earn money for food. The mother was worried that her daughters did not know about God and religion. The priest had no previous knowledge of deaf people and teaching but noticed that the sisters used signs to talk with each other. He learned the signs and used them to teach the girls reading and writing.

Initially, de l'Épée used his own methods, but eventually he was partially influenced by the writings of Amman and Bonet, the latter especially in regard to the one-hand alphabet. After finding several poor deaf children in Paris during the 1760s, de l'Épée

Abbé de l'Épée © Gallaudet University Archives.

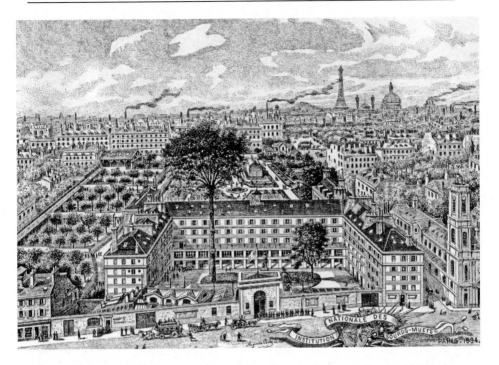

Royal Institute in Paris (note Eiffel Tower in background). © Gallaudet University Archives.

used the small income from his family to establish a school for deaf children. The National Institute for Deaf-Mutes was the first free national school for the deaf in the world.

Compared to other educators, de l'Épée was not so secretive and was willing to share his teaching philosophy. He authored two books, *Instruction of the Deaf and Dumb by Means of Methodical Signs* in 1776 and *True Manner of Instructing the Deaf and Dumb, Confirmed by Long Practice* in 1784. The Abbé had considerable interest in speech development and suggested that teaching could be best done on an individual basis. He figured that by devoting ten minutes to each of his 60 students, it would take ten hours per day to complete the task.[39] He was more concerned with other parts of teaching, especially reading and writing. De l'Épée was not opposed to the teaching of speech, but he considered it to be a slow, arduous process. He felt it was more important to attend to the overall education of his students.[40]

Contrary to popular belief, de l'Épée did not invent sign language. Rather, he copied the signs that his deaf students used and perhaps added some signs he learned from Cistercian monks who had taken vows of silence. He also created signs according to spoken French grammar. He called this sign system "signes methodiques," or methodical signs; it was also known as the French method.[41] De l'Épée wrote that the "methodical sign" was any sign used to instruct the deaf students because the signs were subject to rules.[42] The signs, however, were not identical to those used by deaf people in the Parisian community. He was almost alone in advocating that deaf children be taught through signs instead of speech.

During his 29-year tenure with the school, de l'Épée trained many teachers. Among them was another priest, Abbé Roch-Ambroise Sicard (1742–1822), who opened a school for deaf students in Bordeaux in southwestern France and wrote a dictionary of signs.

Austrian Abbé Stark, also trained by de l'Épée, founded Austria's first school for deaf students in Vienna in 1789. This establishment upset the ardent oralist Heinicke. De l'Épée invited his contemporaries — Heinicke and Pereire — to visit his school and observe the teaching methods. Both declined. Heinicke and de l'Épée then started a correspondence discussing teaching methods. In fact, some believe the infamous feuding that has marked deaf education through the ages began with the two men's correspondence.

Heinicke objected to the introduction of language through either print or writing; it was his belief that in order for a pupil to think, the pupil first had to speak. De l'Épée countered with his conviction that children needed to learn how to read and write in order to function in society. He even brought the issues of deaf education and Heinicke's philosophies before learned scholars at the Academy of Zurich. The February 2, 1783, response, "Decision of the Academy of Zurich, in an Assembly of Its Members on the Controversy Arisen Between the Teachers of the Deaf and Dumb," was that de l'Épée's approach was more effective and successful, and Heinicke was politely criticized for not trying to understand de l'Épée. Despite this affirmation of sign language, Heinicke's work and influence spread throughout Germany and has continued to this day.[43] The philosophical differences between de l'Épée and Heinicke were the start of the "two-hundred-year war" between supporters of sign language and supporters of oralism, explored in the next chapter.

The Paris school was primarily supported by gifts from individuals and grants from King Louis XVI. However, softhearted de l'Épée also used his family income to purchase food and clothing for his students. It is believed that this kindness led to his demise on December 23, 1789, at the age of 77. He had bought firewood to keep the children's rooms warm but not for his own rooms. The extreme coldness deteriorated his health to the point of death.

De l'Épée is known as the first hearing educator interested in learning from deaf people themselves. He was an innovator in several ways. First, he united deaf people by directing his instruction toward a group, rather than isolated individuals. Second, he championed the idea that public education was to be available to all children, regardless of social status. Lastly, he emphasized the importance of using sign language for instruction.[44] He nurtured an active deaf community in Paris where deaf people often visited each other and shared a common language. The first real deaf community is said to have been based in Paris, largely credited to de l'Épée.

With de l'Épée's passing, King Louis XVI appointed Abbé Sicard to become the director and principal of the National Institute for Deaf Mutes in 1790. Prior to this, Sicard had taught at Bordeaux. One of his pupils was Jean Massieu (1772–1847), who came from a family of five siblings — two

Sicard © Gallaudet University Archives

brothers and three sisters — all deaf. Their parents were not deaf.

At the peak of the French Revolution in August 1792, Abbé Sicard was arrested, apparently for his Royalist opinions. He was placed in confinement along with members of royalty and nobility and some churchmen who proclaimed their allegiance to royalty. Deaf children banded together to demand the release of Sicard. Along came Jean Massieu, "the big fellow [who] stopped immediately below the high desk of the Tribunal ... reached up and placed a document on the desk of the Tribunal."[45] The secretary then read aloud a message:

August 26, 1782

Mr. President:
   They have taken from the deaf and dumb their fosterer, their guardian, and their father. They have shut him up in prison as if he were a thief and a murderer. But he has not killed, he has not stolen. He is not a bad citizen. His whole time is spent in teaching us to love virtue and our country. He is good, just, and pure. We ask of you his liberty. Restore him to his children, for we are his children. He loves us as if he were our father. It is he who has taught us all we know. Without him we should be like beasts. Since he was taken away, we have been full of sorrow and distress. Return him to us and you will make us happy.[46]

The Tribunal quickly issued an order to release Sicard. However, in the midst of the confusion, he remained in prison. A week later, on Sunday, September 2, at three o'clock in the afternoon, he was pulled from his cell with 30 other prisoners to a courtyard where six carriages were waiting. A massacre allegedly started at the prison gate, and all the prisoners except Sicard were slain. Sicard had been rescued from the mob and hidden in the prison by a watchmaker who knew him. The next morning, over a thousand dead bodies were counted in the courtyard.

Two days later, Sicard escaped by hiding in a loft in his cell with two comrades who considered his life more important than theirs. Fortunately, all of them survived. It is said that Sicard had a few more escapes from death during the revolution and eventually was absolved of any guilt against the French Republic. He then returned to his duties as principal and director of the Institute.

Sicard was an outspoken person, and in 1797 he was banished to Guiana for supporting the Catholic Church and the Pope's authority over the national government. He fled into hiding in the Paris suburbs. During his 28 months in hiding, he wrote two books: a general grammar book and a book on how he trained Massieu. The latter was the second book to explain how to educate deaf students.[47] Massieu came to Sicard's rescue again when he petitioned Napoleon Bonaparte to reinstate Sicard to his former job.

Sicard remained at the Institute for 32 years where "...emphasis on grammar was law at the National Institution, and training for speech discouraged as time-consuming and unprofitable for deaf people."[48] For his work, Sicard received honors from Tsar Alexander I of Russia, King Bernadotte of Sweden, and King Louis XVIII of France. In 1805, when Pope Pius VII visited Paris for Napoleon's coronation, he made an official visit to Sicard and the National Institute.[49]

Jean Massieu © Gallaudet University Archives

At the turn of the nineteenth century it was Sicard who, more than anyone else in the world, brought deaf people to the public's attention. Had anything happened to Sicard during the turmoil, the direction of American education would likely be considerably different from what we know today.

Massieu eventually became the first deaf teacher at the National Institute. Sicard had brought Massieu to Paris, where Massieu was appointed as a tutor. At the age of 25, Massieu taught Laurent Clerc. According to Clerc, Massieu was a character to the point of being eccentric. At times he would carry three or four watches, books, and small articles on his person and display them to everybody. His fascination for watches and his intimacy with the jewelers in Paris is believed to have been a factor in Sicard's rescue from the deadly massacre and later from banishment during the French revolution.[50]

Massieu was much more of a thinker than a writer. He was said to have called on others to help him write business letters. However, according to Clerc, Massieu's logic was highly convincing, and he was capable of the most abstract thinking. He has been credited with the following sayings:

"Gratitude is the memory of the heart."

"Hope is the flower of happiness."

"Hearing is the auricular sight."

"A sense is an idea-carrier."

"Eternity is a day without a yesterday or a tomorrow."[51]

By the age of 45, Massieu was already famous, primarily as Sicard's student. Upon Sicard's death, Massieu, then 50, was the natural and sentimental choice to assume control of the school. His pupils, upon graduation, ended up all over the country. In fact, they directed schools for the deaf around the world — Lyon, Limoges, Besançon, Geneva, Cambray, Hartford and Mexico City. However, the administrative board did not choose Massieu to be the successor. His abstract thinking was not appreciated by the board members, who forced him to resign. He left everything — his home, his friends, his colleagues and pupils in Paris — and returned to his childhood home in Bordeaux.[52]

A year later, Massieu was hired by Abbé Pereire to be his assistant at a small school for the deaf in Rodez. Massieu fell in love with an 18-year-old hearing girl employed at the school and married her. When Abbé Pereire left to become the director of the National Institute, Massieu became the head of the Rodez school. Massieu, with his wife, a son and an infant daughter, later moved to Lille where they established the first school for the deaf in northern France, near the Belgian border.[53] He died in August 1846 at the age of 75. His school died with him, and his widow and daughter set up a millinery business.[54]

Laurent Clerc (1785–1858), who had studied under de l'Épée and Sicard, was now teaching at the National Institute. Born in La Balme and the son of the town mayor, Clerc became deaf when, as a baby, he fell into the cooking fire. He wrote, "My mother ran over and scooped me up. She had always blamed the fall — probably herself— for my broken ears and mouth."[55] After numerous fruitless visits to doctors to restore his hearing, his parents sent Clerc to the National Institute. He was 12 years old and wrote of riding in a stagecoach with his uncle for five days from home in the southern part of France to the school — a distance of at least 360 miles.

Clerc, in recalling the day when Sicard came out of his exile and returned to the school, described the event:

> We gathered in the assembly room to welcome him. Students, teachers, staff, and all the finest people of Paris were assembled.... So was the bishop and government officials, French nobility, and royalty from neighboring countries.... They crammed into the gallery above us, and the men in frilly collars and morning coats. Outside, carriages filled the courtyard.... Massieu was so excited that he couldn't sit down. He walked back and forth, hands clasped behind his back, eyes aflame....[56]

Clerc was an excellent student and quickly rose to the position of student monitor in which he was responsible for the conduct of younger students. When Clerc was 20 in 1805, Pope Pius VII visited the National Institute. Clerc remembered, "My memory of the pope's visit is flat, without excitement. He arrived the next day, flanked by a group of men, some of them in bright red clothes, all of them well-dressed and dignified."[57] On stage in the auditorium, the Pope handed over a copy of the book, *Lives of the Popes*, to Massieu, with Sicard and Clerc standing nearby. The pope asked Massieu to sign excerpts from the book, and in turn, Clerc translated them into perfectly written French.

Shortly after the Pope's visit, and before graduation, Sicard offered Clerc the position of teaching assistant. Clerc was flabbergasted as he now had the chance to stay at the school — and get paid. Politics in France were returning to normal with Napoleon's departure and the return of the deceased king's younger brother, Louis XVIII, from exile. The school now had almost a hundred students; among them, one was from America, and one was from Russia. Although Massieu had a ten-year teaching seniority over Clerc, Clerc was eventually promoted to teaching the highest-level class. Massieu was not disappointed when he shook Clerc's hand and congratulated him, remarking that the promotion would be good for their students.

After Napoleon's defeat, the French army left Russia. Czar Alexander I, whose deaf son was Clerc's student, asked for someone to start a school for deaf students in Russia. Sicard sent one of his teachers, Jean Baptist Jauffret. When learning of this, Clerc insisted on accompanying Jauffret. After several weeks, he was tersely told by Sicard that he could not go as Russia was poor and had money for only one teacher.

Almost a decade had passed since Clerc started teaching. Napoleon had escaped from prison and his army was marching toward Paris. King Louis was a close friend of Sicard and often attended the school's performances. King Louis also met personally with Massieu and Clerc when visiting. Since Sicard, Massieu, and Clerc were threatened by Napoleon's march toward the city, they decided to leave the country for a while.[58] Unbeknownst to Clerc at that time, he was embarking on a lifelong new career.

TWO

Origins of Deaf Learning in America

Earliest Deaf Americans

The 1500s were an era of exploration. New settlers came from Europe to American ports, particularly in Massachusetts. Deaf individuals have been recorded in those early days. Although the first formalization of American signing took place in 1817 when the first school for deaf students opened, signing has its roots in history dating back to the 1600s, perhaps even earlier. Linguist James Woodward's research discovered that by 1817, deaf individuals had been signing for over a century in Martha's Vineyard.[1] In this chapter, we will learn more about the evolution of Deaf education in America.

MARTHA'S VINEYARD

In 1602, Bartholomew Gosnold landed at an island lying some five miles off the southeastern coast of Massachusetts and stayed there for the summer. Upon returning to England, he named the island after his daughter, Martha, and for the profusion of wild grapes growing on the island. Records[2] also indicate that in the 1640s, the Wampanoags, a Native American tribe, and new settlers lived on the Martha's Vineyard island in peace with each other. Whaling was the main industry, and the isolated island population expanded rapidly due to a tremendously high birthrate.

Another study[3] found that there were deaf people living in the southeastern part of England in the seventeenth century. Many were poor farmers and left England to begin a new life in America. Most eventually settled in Chilmark, an isolated town in the western part of Martha's Vineyard. Families with fifteen to twenty children were common in those days. During the first generation in America, marriage "off-island" was rare, so intermarriage among

Chilmarkers was common. It is said that at one point, one of every four babies born in certain areas of the island was deaf.

According to Groce,[4] Jonathan Lambert, a deaf father of two children, was the first deaf person on Martha's Vineyard. He was born in Barnstable, located in the Cape Cod area, and moved to Martha's Vineyard in 1694 when he bought a land tract. Although he served on a military expedition to Quebec in 1690, "his life was uneventful as he was a deaf mute ... two of his children were also unfortunately afflicted with congenital deaf-mutism, the first known cases on the Vineyard."[5] By trade Lambert was a carpenter, and he and his wife had seven children, including two who were deaf. Ebenezer and Beulah lived on the island all their lives but never married.

In 1880, the second United States census showed an incidence of one deaf person per nearly 6,000 persons. However, the frequency of incidence was as high as 1 in 155 on Martha's Vineyard, as high as 1 in 25 in Chilmark and 1 in 4 in the Chilmark section of Squibnocket. Chilmark remained an isolated community for three centuries, since the town was a half day's journey from anywhere on the island.[6] Consequently, the deaf population was so integral in the community that signing was used everywhere by both deaf and hearing people. At one time, more than one-quarter of Chilmark's residents were deaf. Old-time Vineyarders viewed people signing in Chilmark simply as a difference, not a disability. Written records rarely indicate who was hearing and who was deaf.

According to Bahan and Nash,[7] there were three likely factors other than consanguinity and hereditary causes that sustained the Martha's Vineyard signing community. First, geography (or physical location) was the main factor; the island was isolated and insular, which helped contain the community. Attitude was the second factor; the hearing residents looked at deaf people as perfectly normal, and they would spontaneously sign when a deaf person came into the scene. Finally, access was the third factor. The deaf person had full communication accessibility in the community.

In the latter part of the nineteenth century, marriage patterns changed as both hearing and deaf people started to marry off-islanders. When a great number of children from Martha's Vineyard attended the American Asylum in Hartford, some of them also married off-islanders and left the island. Some islanders brought spouses from the mainland to live on the island; many did not sign. As a result, the Martha's Vineyard signing community, especially in Chilmark, slowly died out. The last known Chilmark deaf native, Eva West Look, passed away in 1952.

Chilmark Sign Language was later known as Martha's Vineyard Sign Language, and it is very likely to have been absorbed into what is now American Sign Language (ASL). Some changes in signs through history are detailed in Chapter Six.

Poole Nash, a hearing teacher of deaf students and a 1980 graduate of the School of Education program at Boston University, learned ASL when she was a counselor at a summer camp that had several deaf children. When she later visited her hearing great-grandmother on Martha's Vineyard, her great-grandmother mentioned that she knew some signs. The great-grandmother was then in her nineties. Poole, a Boston University sophomore at the time, videotaped 300 signs that her great-grandmother recalled.[8] She also recorded some signs that her grandfather remembered.

In June 2004, middle school students at the Learning Center for the Deaf and Horace Mann School in the Boston area performed a play about Martha's Vineyard at the Wheelock Family Theatre. The students studied the island's history for ten weeks, then performed *A Nice Place to Live*. The play centered on deaf and non-deaf people who lived together and how they saw the world through each other's eyes. Cay Munro, then 83 years old, was invited to a reading. Munro was the hearing daughter of a deaf father and used to live on Martha's Vineyard.[9] After becoming a career counselor for deaf people in Chicago, Munro moved back to the island to live with her son. The 20 students were surprised by her attendance and were thrilled that she communicated with them in sign language.

Initial findings about American Indian Sign Language indicate that it may have partly contributed to the development of Martha's Vineyard Sign Language (MVSL). We must remember that American Indian Sign Language (AISL) was created by hearing Indian people, and AISL was in use long before ASL. The Wampanoags (which means "eastern people," or "people of the dawn") were known to have exchanged spoken language and sign language with the pilgrims when they bartered, feasted, planted, and hunted. Moreover, Mountain Blue, Chief Sitting Bull's stepson, was deaf and communicated using sign language. In the Iroquois tribe, women and children used sign language when in the presence of warriors and elders, since using their voices was considered disrespectful. Theoretically, Native Americans may have blended AISL in with MVSL.[10]

Comparable Findings

A setting similar to that of Martha's Vineyard was discovered in the late 1990s by two linguists at the University of Haifa in Israel. The village, in an undisclosed location in Israel, consists of 3,500 inhabitants, of which nearly 150 are deaf. The number represents a percentage of four percent, higher than the average of one deaf person in a thousand. *Village of the Deaf*[11] describes how the residents in the Bedouin village communicate with each other.

Although the residents have the trappings of modern life, such as wearing T-shirts and jeans and owning automobiles, computers and VCRs, the village is located in a remote part of the desert. The hearing people speak either Hebrew or Arabic, but many of them are proficient in Al-Sayyid Bedouin Sign Language (ABSL), which is spoken only in this village among the hearing and deaf villagers. The signs started as home signs with the first generation of about ten deaf children born in the 1930s and evolved into ABSL through future generations.

Four linguists, including American Carol Padden, Ph.D., are analyzing ABSL in an attempt to demonstrate that signs are a natural product of the human brain, just like spoken language. Padden, a professor in the Department of Communication and the associate dean for the Division of Social Sciences at University of California, San Diego, was one of 23 MacArthur Fellows in 2010. The award enables Padden, a deaf daughter of deaf parents, to continue her study of ABSL.

The conditions leading to the preservation of this signing community are similar to the factors mentioned earlier: location (an isolated village), hearing people's attitudes toward deaf people, and people being deaf serving as a non-issue.

A similar situation in Nicaragua may also be the result of such isolation. A study by Ann Senghas and Marie Coppola suggested that deaf children develop their own language naturally. Deaf children attended two Nicaraguan schools where instruction was limited to lip reading and spoken Spanish, with no signing access for about 20 years. Unsuccessful instruction and lacking accessible communication left the children to seek alternate outlets. They compensated by developing their own language, with increasingly complex grammar structure. This language, now Nicaraguan Sign Language, and its development demonstrated that the children had an innate grasp of the rules needed to create a language.[12]

Earliest Attempts at Mainstream Education

Probably the first instance of mainstreaming was recorded in the early 1700s. Samuel Edge, a hearing planter in Fredericksburg, Virginia, paid double the normal tuition to have his 14-year-old deaf son, John, taught in a class of hearing children. Teacher John Harrow wrote in his diary dated June 21, 1774: "Mr. Samuel Edge Planter came to me and begged me to take a son of his to school who was both deaf and dum [sic], and I consented to try what I cou'd do with him."[13]

During the eighteenth century, there were attempts at teaching deaf children, often by parents of deaf children or by relatives. A fourth-generation American, Francis Green (1742–1809), was a Harvard University graduate and a merchant. His son, Charles, was found to be deaf at the age of six months. Their family moved to England just prior to the Revolutionary War, and in 1780, eight-year-old Charles enrolled at the Braidwood Academy in Edinburgh, Scotland.

Although Braidwood Academy was known to offer oral education, Francis was surprised to see his son master both speech and signs. Charles apparently learned signs on the sly in the school, and his father noted that Charles signed with his schoolmates. He was so impressed with his son's educational progress after three years that he published an anonymous work in London in 1783 lauding Braidwood's work. Tragically, Charles died at the age of 15 when he drowned while fishing.

However, Francis maintained his interest in deaf education. In 1790 and 1791, he visited the National Institution in Paris, where Sicard used signs as the basis of instruction. Green later founded a free school for the deaf in London; it used signs in the classroom. After marrying for the second time, he returned to Medford, Massachusetts, where he advocated for free education of all deaf children in America. In 1801, he translated de l'Épée's book, *Education of the Deaf*, into English. Green is considered the first American to have authored an account of deaf education.[14] In 1809, after collecting the names of 75 deaf individuals in Massachusetts (the first-ever American census of deaf people) in hopes of opening a school, Green died without seeing the fruit of his labors.

Marriage between cousins was a common practice during colonial times, especially among wealthy families that wished to keep the family property intact. Thomas Bolling, who married his first cousin Elizabeth Gay, had three deaf and one hearing offspring. John, Mary, and Thomas, Jr., received their schooling at the Braidwood Academy in Edinburgh and were Charles Green's schoolmates. First John went to Braidwood in 1771, and his siblings followed in 1775. However, because of the Revolutionary War, the children could not return home until the war's end in 1783.[15]

Within three years of Green's death, Col. William Bolling, a Virginia father of two deaf children, attempted the first American school for deaf children in 1812. He was the hearing offspring of Thomas and Elizabeth Bolling and had married his first cousin, with whom he had two children who were deaf. Bolling was hesitant to send his children overseas and was delighted that John Braidwood II, a grandson of Thomas Braidwood, had moved to America.

Braidwood II was the head of the family school in England for two years prior to his departure for America. Upon his arrival in the United States in

February 1812, he was approached by Dr. Mason Cogswell of Hartford and William Bolling of Virginia. Dr. Cogswell had a deaf daughter, Alice, and Bolling had two deaf daughters. It is not known what happened to Dr. Cogswell's request, but Braidwood turned down Bolling's offer as he did not want to go to the Virginia rural countryside. Instead, Braidwood initially advertised founding a school for deaf children in Philadelphia but soon changed his mind. He then planned to start a school in another urban center, this time in Baltimore.[16]

In the fall of 1812, Bolling bailed Braidwood out of a New York City jail, apparently for debt that probably was a result of his drinking and gambling. Bolling hired Braidwood to teach his children at Cobbs, the family's Virginia plantation. Unfortunately, Braidwood was a disastrous choice. His sole motivation in teaching was to make money to support his drinking and gambling. The school lasted only one-and-a-half years, solely due to Braidwood's poor management. The school closed in 1817, and Braidwood died two years later.

Interestingly, Martha Jefferson, the sister of the third United States president, Thomas Jefferson, was married to Bolling's brother, John. In January 1816, before the University of Virginia's founding, Thomas Jefferson received a proposal from the Bolling family to have the Cobb school affiliated with

Cobbs School, the first school for the deaf in America. © Gallaudet University Archives.

the university. The offer was declined as Jefferson believed that the objectives of the school and university were not related — the university as science, and the school as "merely a charity."[17]

Pioneers in Signing Deaf Education

Several schools for deaf children were established in the late eighteenth century and the early nineteenth century. But they did not last long for various reasons. The first permanent school that still stands today was the Connecticut Asylum for the Education and Instruction of Deaf and Dumb persons, which opened in 1817. This founding was the result of an incredible partnership involving the father of a deaf child (Dr. Mason Cogswell, 1761–1830), a minister (Rev. Thomas Hopkins Gallaudet, 1787–1851) and a deaf native French teacher (Laurent Clerc).

THOMAS HOPKINS GALLAUDET

The first of 12 children, Thomas Hopkins Gallaudet (THG) was born to a firmly religious family. He entered Yale at the age of 14 and graduated three years later in 1805 at the top of his class. One summer day during 1813 in Hartford, Connecticut, 26-year-old THG saw a nine year old, Alice Cogswell, and her siblings playing with THG's younger sisters and brothers. Alice had been deafened at the age of two by spotted fever (cerebrospinal meningitis). THG observed Alice's difficulty in following her playmates' conversations. He empathized with the language-less deaf girl, so he summoned her. Using a stick, he scratched the word HAT in the dirt and pointed to his hat. He patiently encouraged her to trace the letters. After understanding, Alice wanted to know her own name. In that one afternoon, he was convinced that she had the capability to learn just like the hearing kids.

THG and Alice's father, Dr.

Thomas Hopkins Gallaudet © Gallaudet University Archives.

Mason Cogswell, a prominent Hartford physician, discussed the lack of education for Alice and other deaf children. Dr. Cogswell gave him a copy of Sicard's *Théorie des Signes* (1808) that he had obtained from the National Institution for Deaf-Mutes in Paris. That night, THG learned the manual alphabet from the book, and the next day he and Alice began her education. Excited by the prospect of learning, she wanted to know the names for everything; she learned quickly. The neighboring children joined in learning signs and fingerspelling.

Dr. Cogswell, following up on Francis Green's census of deaf children, determined that there were more deaf children in Connecticut. The total was said to be 89, plus his daughter, but Dr. Cogswell believed that there were over four hundred deaf children in New England. He decided that it was more favorable to establish a school in America rather than shipping his daughter on a month-long journey halfway across the world. He asked THG to go to Europe to learn teaching methods for deaf people and raised sufficient funds with the support of ten of Hartford's city fathers. Initially, THG did not want to go, given that he did not speak French well. Even though he obliged in going to Paris, his original intention was to study Braidwood's oral methods.

At the time, the diminutive THG — his passport listed his height as five feet and six and a half inches — departed for England at a time when the United States and England were battling each other in the War of 1812. THG sailed from New York on May 25, 1815, on a small ship called *Mexico*. Among his shipmates on the month-long journey were the well-known author, Washington Irving, and several British army officers returning to their homeland.

On June 25, THG arrived in Liverpool and proceeded to London to visit the famous Braidwood Academy. Schools for the deaf in London and Birmingham were operated as family businesses. In fact, they had an ironclad monopoly on deaf education in Great Britain. The administrators did not wish to share their knowledge with prospective teachers unless financial terms were negotiated. The administrators also insisted that THG worked in that school for 11 hours daily for several years in order to learn the family's "secret" method. THG refused such an agreement.

As fate had it, Sicard, the *Theory of Signs* author, was in town with his two Deaf assistants, Massieu and Clerc. They were refugees from Napoleonic France, and Sicard had succeeded Abbé de l'Épée as the National Institution for Deaf-Mutes director. Gallaudet learned about the trio's upcoming series of lectures and demonstrations on the methods used to educate French deaf children. Gallaudet attended the demonstrations and was impressed by the use of signs in addition to the speech and lipreading methods. He was invited to the National Institution's teacher preparation program at no charge.

While in Europe, THG maintained correspondence with Dr. Cogswell. THG wrote: "I should wish, and I yet hope, to combine the peculiar advantages of both the French and English modes of instruction, for there are considerable differences between them."[18] Dr. Boatner, the author of *Voice of the Deaf,* remarked that it was the first time THG had used the word "combine" in connection with the two methods.[19]

At that time, France was recovering from the turbulent period of the French Revolution and Napoleon's rise and fall. It was not safe for THG to go to Paris given Sicard's imprisonments, although he was welcome to visit the Paris school. THG chose to instead go to Edinburgh to seek help from the original Braidwood school. The school headmaster was willing to help, but he was under a contract to not release the carefully guarded teaching methods. THG stayed in Scotland from August 1815 to February 1816, where he spent his free time lecturing in churches, attending lectures, visiting bookstores, and studying French.

On March 12, 1816, when it was safe to travel in France, THG finally arrived at the Royal National Institution for the Deaf-Mutes. Sicard enthusiastically welcomed him. THG had full access to all classes, from beginning to advanced, as well as private lessons in methodology. He studied sign language with Massieu and Clerc. After two months, diminishing funds convinced him that it was time to return to America. Aware of insufficient time to master all of the techniques and the sign language training, he persuaded Sicard to allow Clerc to accompany him and stay for three years with the goal of establishing an American school. THG and the 28-year-old Clerc left the port of Le Havre, France, in June 1816. For 52 days on the *Mary Augusta,* THG continued polishing his signing skills while Clerc learned English from THG.

On August 9, upon arrival in New York, they immediately set out to gain public support and raise funds for the new school. Although THG was of slight stature, his literary and oratorical prowess was instrumental in winning state and federal support. After seven months of fundraising, with $17,000 in contributions, America's first successful school for deaf children opened in rented quarters in City Hall on Main Street in Hartford on April 15, 1817. The Connecticut Asylum for the Education and Instruction of Deaf and Dumb Persons was renamed American School for the Deaf in 1885. Seven students enrolled on opening day, with the youngest pupil being ten years old and the oldest being 40. Four of them later became teachers. THG was appointed school principal and remained in that capacity until 1830.

There exists an intriguing but very much appreciated parallel between the Abbé de l'Épée in France in the 1700s and the Rev. Thomas Gallaudet in America in the 1800s. Each man encountered young deaf girls who led to the

Connecticut Asylum in 1817, later renamed the American School for the Deaf. © Gallaudet University Archives.

establishment of the first schools for the deaf in France and in the United States.

Sophia Fowler was the 14th student to enroll at the deaf school; she was 19 years old. After she completed her schooling, THG proposed marriage and they were married, immediately after her graduation in 1821. They were parents of eight children, and their sons are remembered for carrying on their interest in deaf people and deaf education.

After his retirement on April 6, 1830, THG worked against slavery and served as a chaplain of the Retreat for Insane; he also wrote children's books (Biblical stories) as well as articles relating to the needs for secondary education, industrial schools, colleges for women and continuing education. THG is recognized today for importing a method of teaching deaf people, opening the first permanent school for the deaf in America, and helping other states establish schools for the deaf. During his later years, THG had a passion for secondary and postsecondary education for deaf individuals. Deaf children at that time typically remained in school only four or five years. His death in 1851 left Sophia a widow at age 53; his youngest son, Edward, was only 14 years old.

Deaf people in the nineteenth century, with the assistance of the National

Association of the Deaf (NAD), raised funds to erect a statue in 1887 at Gallaudet University in honor of the centennial of the birth of Thomas Hopkins Gallaudet. The statue's sculptor, Daniel Chester French, who was not deaf, also sculpted the Abraham Lincoln Memorial statue in Washington, D.C.

LAURENT CLERC

Laurent Clerc is documented as the first deaf teacher of the deaf in America. To reiterate from the preceding chapter: Born Louis Laurent Marie Clerc to a father who was a village mayor and justice of the peace, Clerc became deaf at the age of one year when he fell into a fireplace. In his 12th year, he entered the Royal National Institution for the Deaf-Mutes in Paris. Jean Massieu was Clerc's first deaf teacher and became a lifelong friend. Within eight years, Clerc had completed the school's courses, so he was promoted to teaching. Sicard, the Royal National Institution for the Deaf-Mutes director, would sometimes take Clerc to perform for hearing people. Clerc demonstrated how he could read, write and communicate in sign language. At that time, sign language was mysterious to the people. In one performance, Clerc read a newspaper and signed what he read to another deaf teacher. The deaf teacher translated Clerc's signs into written French on a blackboard. With this, audience members saw the connection among signing, reading and writing.

Clerc was teaching the highest class in 1816 when THG visited him and began a lifelong friendship and partnership. At the Connecticut Asylum for the Education and Instruction of Deaf and Dumb Persons, Clerc became the head teacher.

In May 1819, he married Eliza Crocker Boardman (1792–1880), one of his first pupils. Eliza, who lost her hearing in early childhood, came to school in June 1817 from Whitesborough, New York. Married for 50 years, they had six children, none deaf. Two did not survive infancy.

The only known living descen-

Laurent Clerc, the first deaf teacher of the deaf in America. © Gallaudet University Archives.

dants of Laurent Clerc include non-deaf Sue Galloway of Oklahoma, a sixth-generation offspring. She is a librarian at the Oklahoma School of the Deaf. Laurent Clerc Holt, a seventh-generation descendant of Laurent Clerc, also non-deaf, has been a social worker in a Vermont hospital for 25 years. Among Holt's possessions is Clerc's traveling desk that Clerc used during his 52-day voyage across the Atlantic Ocean. Holt flew to Paris in July 2003 to participate in the Fifth Deaf History International Conference and to help open the Laurent Clerc Museum at Clerc's birthplace in La Balmes-les-Grottes, France.

At the Hartford school, Clerc helped promote deaf education by training many teachers. Clerc used the French sign language for instruction; *Langue des Signes Française* (LSF) was much revered by Clerc. Later in his life, Clerc was reported to have grieved over the fact that LSF was being modified and that other signs that he did not teach were assimilated into ASL.

Clerc retired at the age of 73 after 50 years of teaching in two countries. In 1864, Clerc addressed an audience of dignitaries at the opening of what would become Gallaudet University, in Washington, D.C., during Edward Miner Gallaudet's presidency. At the age of 84, Clerc died in Hartford. His skills in literacy in both French and English showed everyone that deaf people could be educated. There is a bronze bust of his likeness at the American School for the Deaf and a reproduction statue on the Gallaudet University campus with a eulogy: "The Apostle to the Deaf-Mutes of the New World."

Clerc, who believed he would stay in America for three years only, ended up staying for 52 years, visiting his home country only three times.

While Clerc was the first deaf teacher in America, he was not born in America. The first American-born deaf teacher is believed to be Wilson Whiton. He was admitted to Connecticut Asylum as its third student when he was just 12 years old in 1818. He taught at his alma mater for 47 years.

Sue Galloway, descendent of Laurent Clerc. © Gallaudet University Archives.

ALICE COGSWELL

Fortunately for Alice Cogswell (1805–1830), her family residence was located next to the elder Gallaudet residence in Old Hartford, their houses separated by a garden. In contrast to the popular belief that THG "discovered" her by accident, as mentioned previously, she actually often played with THG's younger siblings. Cogswell was 12 years old when she became the first student to enroll at the Connecticut Asylum at Hartford.

Cogswell was reportedly a model student. After three years of schooling, she demonstrated rather advanced abstract thoughts for a 15-year-old girl, through composition, of which a part reads: "What is hope? It is to aim the good thing with moderate wish and smile but it is not a violent emotion. What is admiration? It is to elevate with sweet feeling to see the beautiful and elegant objects and it differs from wonder."[20]

After completing school in 1823, Cogswell returned to live with her father, to whom she was passionately devoted. Nothing is known of her adult life until 1830 when Dr. Cogswell died. His death proved too much of a shock to Alice, who never recovered. She died ten days later at the age of 25 years.

On the campus of the American School for the Deaf stands a statue of Gallaudet and Alice Cogswell. In Hartford, two busy streets intersecting with each other are named "Asylum Avenue" and "Cogswell Street."

American School for the Deaf was the first permanent private school for deaf people, dependent upon contributions from supporters, while Kentucky School for the Deaf, opened in 1823, was the first state-supported school for the deaf. Twenty-four schools for deaf children were founded by Deaf persons between 1817 and 1911.[21]

Origins of Education in Washington, D.C.

It is interesting to note how history intertwines its players by coincidences and fate. Samuel Morse is recognized as the inventor of the telegraph, and he happened to have a deaf wife. It was said that Morse conversed with his wife by tapping out Morse code in her hand. Morse's friend and business partner was philanthropist Amos Kendall, who served during the Jackson and Van Buren administrations as postmaster general. The original telegraph line in America was strung from the Library of Congress through Kendall's estate in northeast Washington to Baltimore; on this line, the first telegraph message was transmitted in 1844. Kendall became acquainted with deaf people through Morse's wife and holds a pivotal role in Gallaudet University's history.

AMOS KENDALL

Amos Kendall was a Dartmouth-educated journalist, but his political connections led him to Washington, D.C., in the late 1820s. He held several federal government positions. After leaving politics during his middle years, Kendall invested substantially in the newly invented telegraph and was Morse's legal manager and business partner. Morse and Kendall became wealthy as a result of their investments.

In 1855 or 1856, Kendall was one of many Washingtonians approached by a man soliciting donations to establish a school for the deaf and blind children in the area. A man of cloth, P. H. Skinner came to Washington, D.C., with five deaf children, and found ten more children in the area. He tried to raise funds to educate them, claiming that he knew how to teach them. Kendall offered to help Skinner with a house and two acres, and entered a bill in Congress to incorporate the Columbia Institution for the Deaf and Dumb and the Blind. The bill also provided an allowance of $150 a year for each local child.

The school was opened on G Street Northwest, near George Washington University, in Washington. After a time, Kendall learned through a friend that the children were badly neglected and living in miserable conditions. Kendall, with a board member, rushed to the school, but it could not be opened either from the outside or inside. They broke down the door, and the kids were found to have been unattended for some time. Kendall gained guardianship of the five original children from New York, and the local children were returned to their homes.

Dr. Harvey Peet, the principal and superintendent of the New York Institution for the Instruction of the Deaf and Dumb, referred the Rev. Thomas Gallaudet's son Edward Miner Gallaudet to Kendall.[22] Gallaudet was then only 20 years old and a recent graduate of Trinity College in Hartford. He had taught at the

Amos Kendall © Gallaudet University Archives.

Sophia Fowler Gallaudet © Gallaudet University Archives.

Connecticut Asylum while studying at Trinity. However, Peet convinced Kendall, then in his late 60s, that Gallaudet's youth would be tempered by the counsel and guidance of his widowed mother, Sophia Gallaudet.

With some money from the government, Kendall donated two acres of his estate in northeast Washington to establish housing and a school. At that time, Florida Avenue, a filthy road, was Boundary Street. The other street surrounding the land, West Virginia Avenue, was a railroad track.

When Gallaudet visited for the first time, he was accompanied by Kendall and a driver, and taken to the Kendall estate in a horse-drawn carriage. After entering through the gate, the carriage passed several houses and then approached a meadowland. The carriage continued up a hill toward the woods and circled through the trees before finally stopping at the mansion that sat upon a terraced lawn surrounded by huge oak and maple trees. White-haired with prominent sideburns, Kendall exclaimed, "Welcome to Kendall Green!"[23] The name Kendall Green has remained to this day and is the site of Gallaudet University and the Laurent Clerc Center, which includes elementary and secondary schools. Gallaudet accepted the task of managing the school with the stipulation that he could establish a college for deaf students, a dream he had.

The elementary school opened June 13, 1857, with 12 deaf children and six blind children. Gallaudet was appointed the superintendent, and his mother, Sophia, the matron. Kendall was the school board president. One of Gallaudet's strongest supporters, Kendall was a devoted friend until his death in 1869.

Rose Cottage in 1857 was the first building on the campus and is known as the Cradle of Gallaudet. © Gallaudet University Archives.

Edward Miner Gallaudet

Gallaudet was also a teacher. He asked Congress to help fund the establishment of a college. As related in *Voice of the Deaf*, Gallaudet prepared a bill that he placed with a senator, also the chair of the Committee on the District of Columbia. The bill was passed in the Senate without difficulty, and then the House without discussion. It was signed by Abraham Lincoln on April 8, 1864. Kendall was upset because Gallaudet did not consult him or the school board until after the fact; he was concerned that Gallaudet was pushing matters along too quickly. Even so, Kendall recommended that Gallaudet be named president of the institution "*...in all its departments*, including the Corporate and the Board of Directors."[24] In doing so, Kendall relinquished his position as board president but remained on the board.

Gallaudet eventually was named college president while simultaneously serving as Columbia Institution superintendent. In 1864, the National Deaf-Mute College's first graduation ceremony awarded John Carlin, a deaf New York artist, with the first honorary master's degree for his advocacy of education for deaf people. Eight students were enrolled at the college that year.

Gallaudet reckoned that he had learned sign language even before he learned to talk. In 1867, he spent six months in Europe to learn more about the oral method of deaf education. When he returned, he shared his observations that training in speech and speechreading should be included in deaf

Edward Miner Gallaudet © Gallaudet
University Archives.

education and that the college should establish a "normal" department to train hearing people to become teachers of deaf people. In 1891, the Normal Department was inaugurated, using the combined method.

After retiring at the age of 73, Gallaudet remained actively involved with the institution's welfare throughout his later years. He even busied himself with civic-related activities such as getting the city's streets paved and working to establish a vocational school for black children. After the death of his second wife, Susan, he was so affected emotionally that he moved back to Hartford where he witnessed the American School for the Deaf's centennial celebration.

Sophia Fowler

Sophia Fowler was raised on a farm in the New Haven, Connecticut, area. She and her sister, Parnel, were deaf, and their deaf cousin Ward lived across the road. Sophia was 19 years old, and her sister 28, when THG met both at a fundraising event in New Haven. Both sisters immediately enrolled at the American school.

Upon finishing school, Sophia received a surprise marriage proposal from THG. They raised four sons and four daughters, as mentioned earlier, all hearing. The oldest son, Thomas, married a deaf woman, and they had seven children. The younger Thomas became an ordained Episcopalian priest and founded Saint Ann's Church of the Deaf in New York City during the 1850s, where services in sign language continue to be offered today. The youngest of Sophia's and THG's children, Gallaudet was the president of the Columbia Institution and later the National Deaf-Mute College. Both sons were the only offspring that followed their parents in their work with deaf people. Although deaf, Fowler was well accepted by Hartford society and was said to be fluent in written English.

Upon THG's death in 1851, Gallaudet brought Fowler to Washington , where she served as matron of the Columbia Institution for the Deaf and

Dumb and the Blind for nine years. While in Washington, she assisted Gallaudet in various ways, including lobbying the United States Congress for favorable legislation. She is considered one of the first deaf lobbyists, and she made many friends in Washington, D.C., among them many Congressmen. On campus, she was known as "Queen Sophia,"[25] and Fowler Hall was named in her honor.

The original school on Kendall Green has experienced several name changes:

1857: Unnamed private school

1865: Officially named by Congress as the Columbia Institution for the Instruction of Deaf and Dumb

1885: Renamed Kendall School

1970: Renamed Kendall Demonstration Elementary School

In 1864, Gallaudet became president of the first and only liberal arts college for deaf people in the world. The college went through different names also:

1865: Columbia Institution's college program changes its name to the National Deaf-Mute College

1894: Renamed Gallaudet College

1986: Renamed Gallaudet University

LIKE FATHER, LIKE SON

Sometimes it can be rather confusing about which Gallaudet — the father, Thomas Hopkins Gallaudet (THG), or the son, Edward Miner Gallaudet (EMG) — did what at which point in time. The table below clarifies a few key events.

	THG	*EMG*
Date of Birth	December 10, 1787	February 5, 1837
Place of Birth	Philadelphia, PA	Hartford, CT
• Original Employment Interest	• Yankee trader ("door salesman") • Merchant • Minister	• Banker • Teacher at American School for the Deaf
• Age and Accomplishment in Deaf Education	• 29 years old, served as founder and principal of the American Asylum for the Deaf and Dumb for 13 years, 1817–1830 (CT)	• 18 years old, served as tutor and teacher • 20 years old, worked as superintendent at Columbia Institution for the Deaf and

	THG	*EMG*
	• Helped found schools in NY, PA, OH and others	Dumb and Blind for 7 years, 1857–1864 • 27 years old, became president of National Deaf-Mute College for 46 years, 1864–1910 (DC) • Established graduate training program for teachers
Communication Mode in Instruction	French Sign Language and American Sign Language	Combined system (integrated oral method and manual method of instruction)
Wife	• Sophia Fowler (deaf) in 1821 when THG was 33 years old.	• Jane Fessenden (hearing) in 1858 when EMG was 21 years old; Jane died in 1866, leaving EMG with three children. • Susan Denison (hearing) in 1868 when EMG was 31 years old.
Children	8, all hearing	7, all hearing
Date of Death	September 10, 1851	September 26, 1917
Place of Burial	Hartford, CT	Hartford, CT

Gallaudet University was named after Thomas Hopkins Gallaudet, not his son, Edward Miner Gallaudet. Gallaudet University may be the only university in the nation to have statues of father and son on the same campus. As mentioned previously, the Gallaudet statue was created by Daniel French. Pietro Lazzari, an influential Italian artist and sculptor, sculpted Edward Miner Gallaudet in 1969. Lazzari was the father of Nina Lazzari, who attended Kendall School and graduated from Gallaudet University in 1967.

Pioneers in Oral Deaf Education

Although in America many schools used sign language as a method of teaching and communicating, there were other schools that chose the oral method.

The New York Institution for the Improved Instruction of Deaf Mutes was founded in 1867 by Bernard Engelsman, who taught pupils in Germany without the use of signs. He moved to America in 1864 and as a strong believer in oralism, established the school in New York City. Three years later, the school was renamed the Lexington School for the Deaf. Engelsman is credited with originating oral education in America.

Gardiner Hubbard, whose daughter Mabel was deafened at the age of four from scarlet fever, disagreed with using sign language to teach. Playing a pivotal role in the founding of the Clarke School for the Deaf, he soon had the school moved. With financial support from a wealthy man in Massachusetts, the school went to a new location in Northampton, Massachusetts, in 1867, and continues to be an oral school. For many years — until the latter part of the twentieth century — only oral education was permitted in the state of Massachusetts as a result of Hubbard's efforts. Mabel later married Alexander Graham Bell, who received the patent for the telephone in 1876. In 2001, the United States Congress recognized Antonio Meucci as the original inventor of the telephone. Bell had 18 patents in his name and 12 additional patents with his collaborators.

The Lexington School and the Clarke School, like many of schools at that time, were boarding schools. Boston's Horace Mann School, established in 1869, was the first day school in America. It was started as the Boston School for Deaf Mutes and was renamed in 1877 after Horace Mann (1796–1859), who published a report on oral education in Germany and England and advocated the oral method for classroom instruction.[26]

ALEXANDER GRAHAM BELL

Alexander Graham Bell (1847–1922), widely known as the inventor of the telephone, was born in Scotland to a deaf mother. However, in deaf education, Bell is one of the most notorious, if not the most recognized, supporters of the oral method. Like his father, uncle, and grandfather, Bell was a speech teacher. His father, Alexander Melville Bell, developed Visible Speech, consisting of written symbols that presented the anatomical formation of individual speech sounds. Bell learned diction and elocution from his father.

Bell moved to Canada in 1870 with his family and later moved to Boston where he was affiliated with the School of Oratory at Boston University. He also taught at Boston Day School in 1871 and visited the Clarke School and the American Asylum that year. He opened a teacher training school in Boston in 1872 and then received a patent for the telephone in 1876. The following year, Bell established the Bell Telephone Company, with Gardiner Hubbard as a trustee. Hubbard's daughter, Mabel, became Bell's wife after she was one of his students at Boston University. Bell, at the wedding ceremony, presented his bride all but ten shares in the Bell Telephone Company.

Both Bell's mother and wife used speech and speechreading as their only means of communication. It has been said that Bell was working on a device to help his mother hear better when he invented the telephone. The two ironies were that Bell never telephoned his mother or his wife and that the invention put deaf people at a disadvantage for many decades.

In 1878, after a yearlong honeymoon in Europe, Bell moved to Washington, D.C. Two years later he helped organize, and became the first president of, the American Association to Promote the Teaching of Speech to the Deaf, which is now known as the Alexander Graham Bell Association for the Deaf and Hard of Hearing. The Volta Bureau, the home of the organization, was built in 1893 on the corner of 35th Street and Volta in Washington, D.C., and still stands at the same location today. Since its inception, the association has had one primary purpose: "to promote the use of speech, speechreading, and residual hearing for hearing impaired persons." Bell also helped found the National Geographic Society and served as its president from 1896 to 1903.

A man of varied interests, Bell was involved with the earliest American eugenics research. Eugenics is the science of the production of desired offspring by control of inherited qualities. Although Bell worked in the field of deaf education his entire life, was the child of a deaf woman, and married a deaf woman, he seemed to consider deaf people defective. His main belief was that if deaf children signed, they would not be fluent in English; he also believed that marriage between deaf people resulted in the birth of more deaf people. He advocated sterilization of deaf people and the prohibition of deaf people from becoming teachers, and he published several books and articles about prohibiting marriages between deaf persons. Bell was highly regarded in the field of eugenics at that time, being the chairman of the board of advisors to the Eugenics Record Office for six years and serving as the honorary president of the Second International Congress of Eugenics in 1921.

With such a paternalistic attitude, common in the society at that time, Bell's declared goal was to eradicate the language and culture of deaf people, imposing upon them to integrate into the hearing society. Even so, Bell was known as a warm person and a family man who loved his grandchildren. He was said to be proficient in sign language and was a friend of Helen Keller for many years.

Recall that Bell was against the idea of marriage between a deaf man and a deaf woman because they might bear deaf offspring, which to him was a travesty. Bell could not comprehend why deaf people were satisfied with their "condition," considering themselves normal and seeing nothing wrong with having deaf children. In the end, he did not publish his research or materials, because he was unable to account for the fact that deaf parents did not always have deaf children. In fact, research has shown that 90–93 percent of deaf children are born to hearing parents.

Bahan[27] suggests that Bell was trying to solve the "deaf problem" and equated it with the "Jewish problem" during World War II. Some imply that Bell and Hitler both wanted to wipe out persons they considered "defective."

THREE

Historical Issues in Education

Relationship Between Edward Miner Gallaudet and Alexander Graham Bell

Edward Miner Gallaudet and Alexander Graham Bell differed in age by a decade and in birthplace by an ocean. Gallaudet was born in Connecticut in 1837 and Bell in Scotland in 1847, both to deaf mothers whose differences in attitudes about their hearing losses were like day and night. Gallaudet's mother, Sophia Fowler, received no education until her nineteenth year and used only sign language to communicate. Bell's mother, who apparently was postlingually deaf, never lost her hearing entirely. As an experienced speechreader, she also used an ear trumpet to listen to sounds. Naturally, the mothers had some influence on their sons' views. Bell later married a deaf woman who also did not sign, while Gallaudet was married twice, both times to hearing women.

Gallaudet and Bell, alike in many ways, were each actively engaged in the Washington-area society and shared the same circle of friends. They founded the Cosmos Club, an exclusive club open only to men in Washington; the club now accepts women as members. However, from time to time they found it impossible to reconcile their differences about deaf people, which eventually led to heated arguments about deaf education. Their long-standing communication dispute was the subject of a 1987 book, *Never the Twain Shall Meet*, by Richard Winfield.

Although Gallaudet is credited with the establishment of the Normal Department at Gallaudet College, Bell almost shot down this proposal.[1] Gallaudet told Bell of his desire to establish the normal department and suggested that Bell give lectures to the program's students. However, in preparation for testifying before the House Appropriations Committee on January 27, 1891, Gallaudet was informed that Bell would speak to the same committee. Bell spoke for 45 minutes in opposition to the program, while Gallaudet spoke for only 13 minutes. Fortunately, Gallaudet got a $5,000 appropriation. Unsatisfied, Bell shared his thoughts and presented petitions from oral schools for the deaf to the Senate Appropriations Committee. The amount was trimmed down to $3,000, and Bell claimed success — as did Gallaudet. According to Gallaudet's papers, the controversy stemmed from Bell's mistaken notion that Gallaudet wanted the program to train *deaf* teachers, while what Gallaudet had in mind was actually to train *hearing* teachers.

The teacher training program at the university's internationally acclaimed Department of Education did not accept deaf trainees for almost a hundred years. In 1962, Mervin Garretson, Ph.D., became the first Deaf graduate-level professor; that same year, the first deaf students were also accepted. Prior to his appointment, he was, at the Montana School for the Deaf and Blind, the first stone–Deaf ever to become a principal at any school for the deaf.

At the time of Garretson's appointment, most faculty members in the Department of Education were able to sign a little or not at all. Department meetings were conducted orally. A hearing colleague, Lou Fant, who had deaf parents in South Carolina, took on the role of interpreting the meetings for Garretson, doing so begrudgingly as he could not participate in the meetings. Garretson and Fant brought this matter to Dean George Detmold, who demanded that everyone be required to sign.[2]

Garretson also recalls that in his first three years there, he taught only the Deaf graduate students. At the end of the third year, hearing graduate students petitioned to take his classes, and his classes became integrated.[3] How times have changed; from 1980 to 1996 most of the graduate courses that the author, Ron, taught in the Departments of Education and Educational Technology were integrated. Although Ron signed exclusively, most of the hearing students were able to understand him and did not require interpreters.

Another disagreement stemmed from Bell's rejection of Gallaudet's suggestion that the Volta Bureau be a part of the Convention of American Instructors of the Deaf (CAID). Bell had founded the Volta Bureau in 1887 (later renamed the Alexander Graham Bell Association of the Deaf), and in 1890, the American Association to Promote the Teaching of Speech to the Deaf (AAPTSD). Gallaudet started CAID in 1850, as a professional organization for teachers of the deaf, with the goal of maintaining the combined method, using both speech and signs. Some teachers joined both organizations, but oralists aligned themselves with AAPTSD, and combined method supporters with CAID. Initially, Bell was receptive to the idea of the merger. In 1892, the CAID executive committee voted for the merger. Philip Gillett, principal of the Illinois School for the Deaf, was the AAPTSD president and was a friend of both Bell and Gallaudet. Yet the following year, Gallaudet was surprised to learn from Gillett that AAPTSD decided to postpone the merger.

Gallaudet believed that Bell was behind it and had won the power struggle over Gillett. The merger was never finalized.[4]

On May 5, 1880, during the Presentation Day program at Gallaudet, "Prof. A. G. Bell illustrated his address by diagrams on the blackboard, and a chart of the system of visible speech."[5] Despite his differences with Gallaudet, he was surprised with an honorary degree "in recognition of his important services in the cause of deaf-mute education, and his well-deserved renown as a scientific discoverer."[6] It was Bell's first of many honorary degrees. It is also notable that this honorary degree was awarded a few months prior to the 1880 International Congress on Education of the Deaf in Milan, Italy.

1880: When All Hell Broke Loose

Dating back to the beginning of the human race, people's outlooks on deaf people have been mostly negative. To recount: Aristotle believed that deaf people were uneducable. St. Augustine said, "Faith comes only through hearing." Roman law forbade the inheritance of family fortunes for those who could not speak. This paternalism lingered until the 1500s. Spanish pioneers of teaching speech to deaf people, including Spanish monk Pedro Ponce de Leon, Manual Ramirez de Carrion and Juan Pablo Martin Bonet, had some positive impact upon other parts of Europe. Two hundred years later, Abbé de l'Épée founded a school for deaf people that advocated the method of teaching through sign language. Around that time, another school of thought emerged in favor of oralism, with supporters like Amann, Heinicke and Braidwood. But it wasn't until 1880 that these methods came to a clash that affected deaf education for more than a hundred years.

In September 1880, educators from around the world convened at Milan, Italy, for the second International Congress on Education of the Deaf. The discussion among educators became so intensified that those who attended the conference anxiously voted to outlaw the use of sign language. Only one of the 164 representatives, which included Gallaudet and his antagonist Bell, was deaf: James Denison, the principal of the Columbia Institution in Washington, D.C. As a consequence of this majority vote, passed resolutions, as listed in *The Conquest of Deafness*,[7] included:

- Resolution 1: That the oral method ought to be preferred to that of signs for the education and instruction of the deaf and dumb. Voted 160 to 4 in favor.
- Resolution 2: That the Pure Oral Method ought to be preferred. Voted 150 to 16 in favor.

Other resolutions passed included:

- That the most natural and effective method by which the speaking-deaf may acquire the knowledge is the "intuitive" method ... consists in setting forth, first by speech, and then by writing....
- That the deaf and dumb taught by the Pure Oral Method do not forget after leaving school the knowledge which they have acquired there....
- That in their conversations with speaking persons they make use exclusively of speech.
- That the most favorable age for admitting a deaf child into a school is from eight to ten years.

Bell also attended the Milan conference, and it is difficult to understand why, despite his having accepted an honorary degree from Gallaudet only four months earlier, Bell continued his support of oralism in education and supported the Milan resolution.

The Congress also recommended that governments ensure that all deaf and dumb people be educated and that the teachers of the Oral System should publish their special works on the subject of oral education. Last, but not least, it was recommended that new pupils coming into a school be segregated from the older pupils, so that instruction could be given in speech to the newer ones.

In 1900 at the Fourth International Congress on the Education and Welfare of the Deaf in Paris, educators proposed a resolution to introduce the combined system that they hoped would replace the oralism resolution of 1880. In spite of a more favorable deaf-to-hearing delegate ratio (200 to 100), the proposed resolution failed.

All countries except the United States formally adopted oralism as the language of instruction for deaf students. Soon after the conference, many schools in Europe, including the Paris school that de l'Épée founded, changed from manual to oral programs. For the next hundred years, the oral method of teaching dominated in Europe.

Post-Milan Attitudes

Because of the vast Atlantic Ocean that separated America from Europe, the ban on sign language did not affect America until the early 1900s. During that time, the percentage of deaf teachers in America declined, and at the same time, a rapid growth of oral programs was noted. The aftereffects of the Milan resolutions led to a separation between the oralists and the manualists in the United States.

Schools in the United States gradually adopted oralism. In 1882, only 7.5 percent of the 7,000 pupils were taught orally (or without signs or finger-spelling). The percentage of pupils taught in oral education programs, even those at residential schools, increased to 47 percent by 1900. It was reported that the year 1919 was the peak of oral influence — nearly 80 percent of deaf students were instructed without any manual language.[8]

Non-deaf teachers who knew sign language were considered dangerous by oral program administrators. Teachers who were deaf were not allowed near small deaf children out of fear of contamination by their signs among the naive youngsters.[9] Deaf teachers were perceived as "unfit" to teach since they could not hear their students' voices or teach speech.[10] In the 1850s, nearly half of the teachers were deaf, but the numbers dropped to one-quarter around the 1880s. During World War I, one-fifth of the teachers were deaf, and by the 1960s, only one-eighth were deaf, while all superintendents were hearing.

Many deaf teachers were reassigned to teach students considered oral failures, or assigned to the vocational departments. However, many superintendents treasured the deaf teachers because they served well as role models for students. Deaf people expressed concerns that the beauty of sign language might be lost, especially with the dwindling number of deaf teachers.

By 1913, and again in 1915, the National Association of the Deaf (NAD) found itself fighting to prevent the passage of a law implementing oralism for all students at the Nebraska School for the Deaf. NAD discovered that this mission was impossible because of powerful oral advocates such as Bell, who bankrolled the Nebraska state legislature into passing this legislation.[11] That prompted deaf leaders, through NAD, to raise funds for producing a series of "the new technology — moving pictures" to safeguard "the language of signs," as it was called at that time. The project consisted of 18 sign language films. The main purpose was to record examples of great signers, both deaf and non-deaf, of that era. It was also anticipated that, by preserving signs on film, the signs would not deteriorate over a period of time like what was happening in Europe.

George W. Veditz © Gallaudet University Archives.

Until these films were made, there

was no recorded visual history of sign language. These films featured the stalwarts of Deaf America of that time —1884 Gallaudet graduate and the seventh NAD president, George Veditz; the third faculty member hired by Dr. Gallaudet who taught for 47 years, Dr. Edward M. Fay; 1869 Gallaudet graduate and former Laurent Clerc student who became the first Deaf Gallaudet professor, John B. Hotchkiss; 1872 Gallaudet graduate and first NAD president Robert McGregor; and Gallaudet president Edward Miner Gallaudet, who was 75 years old that time.

The 1913 NAD film, *Preservation of the Sign Language*, narrated by George Veditz, is by far the most inspirational and memorable film in deaf history. One of the most-oft quoted Veditz statements is:

> As long as we have deaf people on earth we will have signs and as long as we have our films we can preserve our beautiful sign language in its original purity. It is my hope that we all will love and guard our beautiful sign language as the noblest gift God had given to deaf people.[12]

Unfortunately, not all 18 films are in existence today; most of the films, running between eight and nine minutes each, were damaged. The surviving clips have been copied onto videotape and DVD formats. If it were not for Veditz's preservation of ASL on film, we might have no documentation of the signs as they were produced back then; the signs were eloquent and somewhat different in style from today's signs. All were made during the late 1800s, when Bell had strong passion for the removal of sign language from education.

As a result of the Milan conference and particular influence from oral schools, some existing schools for the deaf moved toward oralism, while most of the other schools adopted the combined method of instruction. Because of disagreement with the oral method, proponents of the combined system provided instruction in both sign language and speech as needed. Usually these schools provided oral education in the lower grades, and a combination of speech, signs, and fingerspelling in the advanced grades and vocational classes.

THE AUTHORS' EARLIEST EXPERIENCES

Author Ronald recalls his days at the Minnesota School for the Deaf in Faribault, which he attended from kindergarten in 1942 through his junior year in 1954. No signs were used at all during his first two years in a dormitory housing the youngest students. To make matters worse, he came from a deaf family whose members did not either speak or lipread at all, even though his parents were graduates of the school's so-called oral program. Instruction up to the sixth grade was done orally through the use of lipreading and speech; however, some teachers would sign or fingerspell on rare occasions if a student did not catch a particular word or understand the concept. Ronald was emotionally more at ease when he could understand the instruction carried on through the "combined method" used in the advanced department (grades seven through 12). The hearing teachers would sign and speak simultaneously, while the deaf teachers would sign, some with mouthed words and others with closed mouths.

Some of the larger schools — with enrollments of 400 or more — maintained dual programs. Students were assigned to the oral department or the manual department. The students usually lived in separate dormitories and had classes in separate classroom buildings. Usually they mingled only through sports or during social events. This author, Melvia, attended the Texas School for the Deaf in Austin, which had such a dual program.

In September 1946, Melvia, aged six, and her seven-year-old sister, Claudia, first came to Texas School for the Deaf where there were two separate buildings for the oral department and the manual department. All classes in the primary department at that time used an oral-oriented approach. Although being the children of deaf parents who did not mouth words and used sign language—again, her parents were the products of an oral program, but her mother had been in the manual department — Melvia and her sister remember no negative experiences, only fond memories, with the teachers in their first two years.

In their third year at the school, Melvia and her sister had a very strict teacher, Miss W, who always had lipreading drills at the end of each day. With a row of large pictures posted side by side at the top of the wall around the classroom, she would point to a pupil and utter a short description of a picture. When the pupil pointed to the correct picture on the wall, Miss W would nod at the pupil with pleasure. When Melvia and Claudia had their turns, they erred approximately 90 percent of the time. Miss W showed her displeasure visibly, making both sisters tense.

One December day, their mother and older hearing sister, Dollie Faye, were in the dormitory packing up for Melvia and her sister to go home for Christmas. The dormitory and the classrooms were in the same building. On that day, Melvia faced her turn for the usual lipreading drill, which was very frustrating for her because Miss W would not give up. Miss W spoke several words to describe another picture if the author failed to choose the correct one. Several pictures were described, but the author still did not point to the correct one. Miss W blew up and signed, "Oh, you, stupid!" She then turned to the best speechreader in class and had the student demonstrate her skills by getting every answer correct.

Humiliated, Melvia cried and looked at Claudia, who told her to go to their dormitory room where their mother was. She left the classroom and ran to her dormitory room and fell in the arms of her mother, sobbing. After explaining the problem to her mother and Dollie Faye, they accompanied Melvia to the classroom. Melvia's mother, with Dollie Faye interpreting, expressed her concerns to Miss W. The teacher profusely apologized and gave Melvia a hug with arms that were as thin as a rail. After Christmas, the two sisters were transferred to a manual class, much to their happiness.

Padden and Humphries[13] reported that by the late 1800s, the oral movement overtook most schools for the deaf in the country, with nearly 40 percent of all deaf students reportedly educated orally. By 1920, the number increased even more dramatically, to 80 percent. Lou Ann Walker,[14] a hearing child of deaf parents, also mentioned the rise of the oral method in her book; her figures showed that in 1915, 65 percent of all schools were oral, with 35 percent using the combined method. However, by 1976, the figures were reversed, with 35 percent of the schools being oral, the rest the combined method.

During the reign of oral programs (circa 1900s, up until the 1960s), deaf students signed behind the teacher's back in classrooms. When caught, the students were usually punished. The types of punishment included slapping their hands, slapping their arms with a ruler, or sending them to the principal's office. In public places, deaf people would sign in "whispers" — making small signs not visible to passersby. Often Deaf people were embarrassed to sign in public because of how they had been conditioned in schools. In those days, signing was viewed as a stigma, a taboo.

The prevalent viewpoint in those days was that the ability to talk was a passport for deaf people to succeed in the hearing world. To publicize the success of this ability's value, schools would host demonstrations for groups such as service organizations. Students with intelligible speech were chosen to demonstrate the phenomenon of acquiring speech and the success of oral training. What the audience usually did not know was that typically, the participants had lost their hearing later in life or were hard of hearing. Author Ron also recalls how his deaf parents were excited that he and his sister learned how to talk and had them speak several words to their hearing friends, such as "Merry Christmas." The siblings outgrew this behavior at nine or ten years of age.

The resolution to ban sign language and to foster the oral approach of teaching deaf students remained in America for the next 80 years, until the late 1960s. For deaf people in America, these decades are often considered their Dark Ages.

Segregation

Segregation in the annals of America took several forms. Other than segregation by communication as described earlier, segregation by gender and race were the most prominent, and this practice also existed in educational settings for deaf students. In residential schools, boys and girls usually sat in separate areas of the classrooms and dining hall, if not in separate rooms. On Saturdays, boys and girls would go to town to shop and go to the movies — but never together. Instead, they would go on alternate weekends.

Women were barred from attending Gallaudet College until 23 years after its opening in 1864. Six women were admitted on an experimental basis in 1887, and the college's doors were opened to them permanently the following year. President Gallaudet, who was by then semi-retired at the young age of 49, was initially reluctant about having women attend the university, with "...considerable apprehension that the college education of the sexes together might lead to unsatisfactory results. I had never been warmly in favor of co-education."[15] Facilities for the women were non-existent then, so the women lived in Gallaudet's on-campus residence, House One.

The board of directors had voted to allow Gallaudet to spend half of his time in Hartford and the other half in House One with the "young ladies." A few months after the THG and Alice Cogswell statue was dedicated, Gallaudet moved back to the campus full-time. He wrote, "In September 1889 I resumed the full occupancy of my home on Kendall Green, which had been given up to the young women of the college for two years, and my family returned from Hartford. The young women of the college were furnished accommodations in the east building of the institution."[16]

Although Percival Hall, president of Gallaudet College from 1910 through 1945, stated that "...there is no legal restriction, as far as I can see, against a colored person entering Gallaudet College,"[17] black students were not admitted until the 1950s. Hume Le P. Battiste, Class of 1913, was said to be the first black student to be admitted and to graduate. However, this claim is controversial, since he was also allegedly an Indian or a Creole; this has not been confirmed by his alma mater, the Mt. Airy School for the Deaf in Philadelphia.[18] As a result, the honor of being the first black student admitted to Gallaudet College may actually belong to James Gilbert from the Ohio School for the Deaf. In 1954, Andrew J. Foster was the first black person to graduate from the college and in 1970, was also the first black person to be awarded the Doctor of Humane Letters from Gallaudet University.

Interestingly, at Columbia Institution (Kendall School), located on the Gallaudet campus, there was no restriction on admitting black students to its elementary and secondary program. In the late 1890s, several African-American students shared classrooms with other students, but they had separate sleeping facilities. In September 1905, 14 students were transferred to the Maryland School for Colored Deaf-Mutes, known as the Overlea school because of its location near Baltimore. It was not until 1952 that the *Miller v. D.C. Board of Education* case stipulated that Kendall School accept colored students living in District of Columbia.[19]

The school was reorganized into "separate, but equal" programs: Division I, for white students, with classrooms and dormitories in existing facilities, and Division II for African-American students. During the first year, there were no facilities for African-American students, so classes were held in the first floor in the college's gymnasium (affectionately known as Ole Jim) on the opposite side of the campus. Three portable blackboards served as partitions dividing four classrooms. The children were taxied between home and school daily. The building for Division II was completed in the spring of 1953 and included classrooms and dormitories. However, the 1954 *Brown v. Board of Education* decision entirely integrated the school. The new building still had classrooms and dormitories, but was transformed into an integrated program in the Primary Department. Integrated older students remained at the older facility.

A BLACK DEAF AMERICAN'S OLD-TIME EXPERIENCE

Until after the Civil War, there were no schools for deaf children who were black. After schools were established for them — the first in 1869 in North Carolina, and the second one seven years later in South Carolina — for many years, they were usually separated from the white pupils — either in their separate schools, or if in the same school, in different buildings on the same campus, or even on different campuses. The black pupils lived in separate dormitories, had different teachers and administrators, separate infirmaries and even separate graduation ceremonies. Padden and Humphries[20] pointed out that black students were integrated by being moved to white campuses, but never were white students moved to black campuses. The authors also noted that many African-American teachers did not move with their students, usually because there were no jobs for them at the newly integrated schools. A consequence of this was that much of the oral history of the black schools was left behind.

Most schools serving black students in the south were jointly for deaf and blind students, such as North Carolina School for the Negro Deaf and Blind and Florida School for the Negro Deaf and Blind. In the early 1950s, segregated schools were founded in 13 states. The majority of those schools emphasized vocational training and skills. Instead of aptitude basis, students were placed in vocational training programs according to grade, age, and mental ability. Students left the school with marketable skills and usually found employment in stable professions such as barbering and tailoring for boys and beauty culture for girls. Students were required to take state examinations in their training fields, and upon passing, placed in apprenticeship for a year. Some eventually became shop owners.[21]

After the Civil War ended, many records of black pupils were lost or destroyed when their schools closed. After the 1954 *Brown v. Board of Education* ruling, the West Virginia School for the Deaf and a few others were the first to open to African-American students. Ernest Hairston, currently the Chief of Captioned Media at the Department of Education in Washington, D.C., and his schoolmates moved from the West Virginia School for the Colored Deaf and Blind in Institute to the white campus in Romney in 1955. This author's father, Emery Nomeland, secured a position at the West Virginia School for the Deaf in 1955 because a similar position became vacant with the retirement of a black teacher. Most schools took longer to integrate — in fact, as late as 1963, eight states still had separate schools for black deaf children.[22]

The practice of distinctions and separations within the school systems had been existent since the late 1800s. At first the pupils were separated by gender, then by race, teaching methods, and most recently, language. Even with the Supreme Court's support of desegregation, problems arose among schools relating to administration, the recruitment and inclusion of additional staff, and physical plants and transportation. With black students being admitted into previously predominantly white schools, black deaf children, for the most part, lost their cultural identities.

Albert Couthen, a retired school administrator, recalls that he did not know anything about black culture, black history or black issues when attending the integrated American School for the Deaf in Connecticut in the late 1950s. Coming from a black hearing family, he said, "The deaf schools didn't teach us, and neither did my family. My family is beautiful, but [they were] all hearing ... so I didn't develop my black identity until much later."[23]

Carolyn McCaskill-Emerson first attended a racially segregated school in Alabama and was one of the first black deaf students integrated into Alabama School for the Deaf in 1968. She recalled knowing very little about black history, but she learned from her family and reading the few books that were available in the library. She never saw herself represented in the school's curriculum as a black Deaf person.[24]

Padden and Humphries wrote, "It is now against the law to segregate African-American and white children, but the practice of separating deaf children on the basis of other characteristics continues today."[25] As discussed previously, another type of separation was practiced by some schools where deaf pupils were placed in different classrooms based on type of teaching methods (oralism, manualism or combined) This, surprisingly — or perhaps not so surprisingly — continues to be practiced, especially at programs where children with cochlear implants are segregated from those who do not have cochlear implants.[26]

Home Sweet Second Home

In the nineteenth century, deaf pupils usually traveled to school in the fall and remained there until the school year ended in the spring. Fortunate ones would go home during Christmas recess. Travel between home and school was slow, arduous, and lengthy. It has been recorded that students living in Kentucky had to travel by stagecoach to Connecticut to attend the American Asylum for the Deaf, until 1823 when the state established the Kentucky School for the Deaf in Danville. It was the third school to open in the United States, and the first school located west of the Appalachian Mountains.

Some of the earliest schools for the deaf were so separate and remote that they had their own cemeteries. Kansas School for the Deaf, Pennsylvania School for the Deaf, and South Carolina School for the Deaf all had cemeteries either on or adjacent to the campus. Students who died while at school and could not be returned home were buried there. Not only their lives belonged to the schools, but also it would seem, their bodies.[27] Texas School for the Deaf never had a cemetery on the school campus, but it purchased Lot 4 in Section 2 at Oakwood Cemetery in Austin for $41. In 1876, a 16-year-old female student was the first to be buried in the cemetery; at least eight students are known to be buried there.[28]

Schools for the deaf in southern states such as Virginia, Tennessee, Kentucky, Mississippi, Missouri, Georgia and Louisiana were closed during the Civil War so that the Confederate or Union Armies could use the buildings as forts or hospitals.

During their earlier years at residential schools, both authors had similar experiences of staying at school the whole year except for the two-week Christmas break. Ronald lived a hundred miles from his hometown, and Melvia about 150 miles, but in those days, such distances were overbearing. For Ronald and his sister, travel was highly restricted during World War II when gas was rationed and tires were not made of rubber. Travel was more accessible after the war, and students were able to go home for Thanksgiving and Easter breaks, and sometimes, for the weekend.

However, the truth was that a majority of the students preferred to stay at schools rather than to go home for a variety of reasons, mostly because the schools offered a family-like atmosphere that promoted togetherness. For those who came from backwoods country, schools were swanky hotels with hot and cold running water, ceramic toilets, and comfortable beds. More important, the students were able to communicate with their peers — something they often could not do at home with their non-signing parents or siblings. At home, they often ate alone in a roomful of people who spoke vocally to each other, leaving them out. At school, there were activities to keep the students occupied, such as sports, movies, literary society meetings, and scouting. Religious services were usually available for different denominations, and, before the middle of the twentieth century, there were the drearily boring Sunday afternoon chapel sermons.

By the 1960s, residential schools were encouraged to send their students home every week. At the beginning, students were sent home every other week, but today, practically all residential students go home every weekend, with the exception of special weekend activities such as sports or the prom. Some schools have a fleet of buses equipped with television, so students can enjoy open-captioned television movies as they travel home. In some states, some students even fly home every weekend. One reason for this change was that states found that it was cheaper to send students home over the weekend than to maintain the dormitories, food service, and other ancillary personnel, especially with the federal enactment of the 40-hour workweek law. Another factor had to do with the perception of preserving family relationships. Fortunately, with increased familiarity of deafness and greater sensitivity toward communication accessibility, more non-deaf family members have been willing to learn fingerspelling or sign language.

Going Down in History: Deaf Rights

Many of the legal assumptions, attitudes and prejudices against Deaf people were brought to America from Europe, stemming from fictitious opinions formed by misguided philosophers, priests, scholars and physicians. Although America was founded by brave souls who fled from the Old World, mostly to escape religious persecution in Europe, they still carried a latent bias toward minority groups. For almost 400 years, the attitude of "benevolent" hearing people insulated not only deaf people, but also Native Americans, African-Americans, Asians, and others from their self-respect and rights.

- An attitude that continues to affect Deaf people is paternalism, which in those days was often experienced within their own families and in educational settings. Discrimination against deaf people has come from individuals, groups or even schools. An example: Civil service in 1908 excluded applicants possessing "...conditions that would bar persons from examinations including insanity; ... epilepsy; ... blindness; total deafness; loss of speech; ... heart disease; ... and diabetes."[29]

- Signing in school was banned in the late 1880s, and, consequently by 1919, "schools reported that nearly 80 percent of deaf students received their instruction and communicated with their teachers without any manual language."[30]
- The right to drive automobiles was threatened by some state legislation during the 1920s and 1930s, when roads began to become crowded with automobiles. Motor vehicle laws were created in some states to ban granting licenses to deaf drivers for the "safety of motorists." The winning case against the discriminatory legislation has been specifically credited to the National Association of the Deaf's committee, the Automobile Bureau. Nowadays, it is well known that deaf drivers are safe drivers.[31]
- In 1988, two deaf persons were passed over for a hearing person to secure the presidency of Gallaudet University. The then-board chair was rumored to have said, "Deaf people are not ready to function in the hearing world."[32]

In approximately 1910, Veditz said he "despised hearing people who listened more carefully to others speaking on behalf of the Deaf but not to Deaf people themselves."[33]

In the early 1970s, this author, Ronald, applied for the principal position at his alma mater, the Minnesota School for the Deaf (now Minnesota State Academy for the Deaf). The school superintendent required responses from the four deaf applicants to a set of seven questions, such as how a deaf principal could deal with the secretary, who could not sign, and how a deaf principal could work with hearing parents of deaf students. Although the author possessed a master's degree in school administration and a doctorate in instructional technology, both from hearing universities, and was then serving as an administrator at another school, he was passed over for a less qualified hearing person. He filed a lawsuit against the school in 1975, which was eventually settled out of court.

The NAD president at that time, Mervin Garretson, Ph.D., vividly recalls the lawsuit that was filed through the efforts of the NAD Legal Defense Fund:

> ... Fred Schreiber and I held a press conference on this, upsetting the entire educational community in the USA! When the [Minnesota] Department of Human Rights responded with a statement finding no fault and supporting Mr. Brasel, as president of the NAD, I insisted that we appeal the decision in civil court. The ultimate resolution of the case was an out-of-court agreement and the eventual resignation of Brasel as superintendent and the opening of administrative jobs to deaf people all over the United States. For example, Harvey Corson was appointed superintendent of the Louisiana School for the Deaf soon after this case was resolved.[34]

Last, but not least, the punch line was that Ronald's hearing neighbor was shocked that "a deaf person could not be the principal at a deaf school that serves deaf students." In addition, Donald Moores, Ph.D., a college professor who is currently the editor of *American Annals of the Deaf* and has authored several books on deaf education, said, "Approximately one-half of superintendents of schools for deaf children are themselves deaf or hard of hearing. This is a tremendous change. As recently as the late 1960s, not one superintendent was deaf."[35]

March 1988 found coalitions in the Deaf community fighting for the right for a deaf person to be the president of Gallaudet University. The university, which had never had a deaf president in its 124-year history, had selected Dr. Elizabeth Zinser, a hearing person, over two qualified deaf candidates to become the new president. As Jack Gannon[36] summed it up:

> DPN didn't "just happen."
> It was an event waiting to happen.
> And, what a long wait we've had!

Students, alumni and faculty protested by taking over the campus. The "Deaf President Now" (DPN) movement lasted for one week, with multiple rallies, press conferences, and marches. After eight days and the resignations of Dr. Zinser and Jane Spillman, the chairman of the Board of Trustees, I. King Jordan, Ph.D., was named the first deaf president of Gallaudet University.

One of the movement's many positive aftereffects was that it captured world attention and created increased awareness of deaf people. The Reverend Jesse L. Jackson[37] even expressed his thoughts adeptly when he declared, "The problem is not that the students do not hear. The problem is that the hearing world does not listen." The exposure toward millions of Americans via the national media helped cultivate optimistic attitudes in the public. In the meantime, deaf youth, who were already less dependent on hearing persons as a result of increased self-awareness and technological advancements, increased their self-confidence with the protest's success.

Although the protest received the attention of the world, Benjamin Bahan, Ph.D., emphasized in 1989, "We only won one battle. The War is Not Over!"[38] He described the continuing plight of the Deaf education system, noting that nationally only ten percent of teachers of Deaf children were themselves Deaf. He also noted that there was a need for more Deaf administrators at schools and programs serving Deaf students.

Eighteen years later, a repeat of the students' and faculty's protest occurred when the selection of Jane Fernandes, Ph.D., a deaf woman, by the Gallaudet University board of trustees was disputed. This time the uprising centered on Fernandes' questionable 11-year track record as an administrator and a leader on the campus, a track record that included votes of no confidence by her current and former faculty member groups.

The students' and faculty's discontentment was noted right away after the selection was announced on May 1, with the establishment of a "tent city," where tents were pitched on the front part of the campus in protest. Since the events happened so close to the end of the academic year, the opposition appeared to be short lived. However, at the NAD conference in Palm Desert, California, in early July, the protestors sponsored rallies and gatherings. The tent city sprouted up again on October 2. During that following weekend — when the board reiterated its decision during a fall regular meeting — the simmering flames were relit. A full-scale rally forced the suspension of classes for a week. Alumni from all over the world overwhelmingly supported the students and faculty with demonstrations at over 70 sites. The protest lasted for four weeks until the board, under tremendous pressure from many groups, finally withdrew the appointment of Fernandes on October 29.

On December 10, on Thomas Hopkins Gallaudet's 219th birthday, Robert Davila, Ph.D., was appointed as interim president to serve a minimum of 18 months while the presidential search committee reopened its nationwide search. He served a total of three years until December 2009, when the current president, T. Alan Hurwitz, Ph.D., was selected. Both Davila and Hurwitz are deaf.

PERCEPTION OF STIGMA/DISCRIMINATION

Groups such as African Americans, Hispanic Americans/Latinos, American Indians/Native Americans, and gay/lesbian people regularly suffer oppression on a continuous basis. *A Journey into the DEAF-WORLD* identified four common characteristics usually found in minority communities and explained how these characteristics relate to the deaf community[39]:

- A group that shares a common physical or cultural characteristic such as skin color or language: Deaf people possess a common characteristic, that is, their primary source of information is vision. Deaf Americans also share a common language, ASL.
- Individuals identify themselves as members of the minority, and others identify them in that way: Deaf people indeed identify themselves as Deaf.
- There is a tendency to marry within the minority: Deaf persons marry Deaf persons nine times out of ten.
- Minority members suffer oppression: Deaf people suffer oppression, either intentionally or unintentionally, by individuals or groups.

Deaf people, based on the characteristics listed above, are similar to other minority groups that are perceived as inferior by the "majority," or the hearing population. Bahan[40] recalls a humorous incident when he ordered food at an upstate New York roadside diner by pointing to items on the menu. His waitress served the order with a note she wrote: "I have a deaf brother who went to wonderful school up north. Now he speeks wel, you know you should lern to speak. Its nevar to lat. Aftar al you lif in a hearing world." As he read the note, Bahan vowed that it was his world, too, and that he did not have to be told that deaf people needed to speak, although the brother had "succeeded." He added that hearing people needed to learn to respect deaf people's need to communicate in sign language, so both worlds could co-exist.

FAITH HEALER

In Tom Holcomb's *Revival Preacher Praying for Open Ears*, the picture represents a real-life experience that author Melvia had. When she was five years old, she was brought to a local revival where a minister hollered in a prayer to help solve the attendees' health or physical problems. After the service — which of course was not interpreted — the author's older hearing sister brought Melvia and her deaf sister to a line to be saved. After waiting for what seemed to be hours, it was the girls' turn. When Melvia finally faced the minister, he put his little fingers deep into her ears and shook her head as he screamed for God's help to make her hear. When he was done, Melvia was told to speak, "Mom" — a word easily pronounced even by people who

Revival preacher praying for open ears. © 1994 DawnSignPress. Illustration by Frank Paul, reproduced with permission from *Deaf Culture, Our Way.*

can't speak. To the audience, it was a huge miracle to hear her voice. They sang praise to the minister and to God. He smiled and glowed. Saved? There was no difference in her hearing, but the author has never forgotten the sharpness of the minister's fingernails.

EUGENICS IN THE AMERICAN DEAF COMMUNITY

Eugenics is a Greek word that means "well born." The heart of eugenics research is centered on hereditary improvement of the human species through controlled selective breeding.

More than 400 types of hereditary deafness have been identified through genetic studies. Most of the types are recessive, meaning that both parents possess the gene for deafness. A common recessive gene is Connexin 26 (Cx26) found in America and Europe, especially in England and Spain. One out of 30 non-deaf Americans is a carrier of Cx26.[41]

Most people, of course, still marry based on love, but it remains to be seen if genetic counseling will someday become a factor in selecting mates. Genetic technology has pros and cons, such as people making choices about the "kind" of children they want, society pressuring deaf people and parents of deaf children to make choices about having children, and health insurance companies and employers dictating limitations upon deaf and hearing parents with high chances of having deaf children. Fortunately, specific laws in many states have been developed to protect people's right to choose and to prevent genetic discrimination.

In modern times, there have been positive media reports about genetic engineering, which holds potential in steering family planning for future generations. Unfortunately, one of its goals is to eliminate what the engineers called a "negative" genetic effect — deafness. Many are surprised to learn that Alexander Graham Bell was renowned in the eugenics field during the early 1900s. His main interest, as described previously, was to prohibit marriages between deaf people, in order to prevent deaf offspring. Once again, it is ironic that 93 percent of deaf children have hearing parents.

AUDISM

Racism? Sexism? Audism? The difference is that the word "audism" is not yet in the dictionary, although efforts are underway to change that. The word was coined by Tom Humphries, Ph.D., in 1977, when he was seeking an appropriate word to include in his dissertation. He combined the Latin word *audire* (to hear) with *-ism*, representing a system of practice, behavior, belief or attitude. Humphries defined the word as "the notion that one is superior based on one's ability to hear or behave in the manner of one who hears."[42]

A racist is a person who believes his race is superior to other races. A sexist person is someone who believes his/her sex is superior to the opposite sex. Thus, an audist — usually a hearing person — considers himself superior to Deaf people. This attitude has been prevalent throughout time, with the influence from the medical profession being dominant, and paternalism toward Deaf people existed at school, at work, and in society. For example, in the past, deaf drivers were considered unfit to drive automobiles. Yet, so-called audists drive around with windows closed, radio on full blast, and talking non-stop on a cell phone or texting while at the wheel.

It was in 1992 that the word "audism" was first seen in print. Harlan Lane, Ph.D., in his book *The Mask of Benevolence: Disabling the Deaf Community*, credited Humphries with the word.[43] Ever since, the word has created controversy among deaf people and also hearing people who work with deaf people. Some deaf individuals have even behaved like audists, especially when they consider themselves superior to others because they have intelligible speech.

However, there exists a thin line between audism and ignorance. Ignorance occurs when a hearing person wonders why a hearing person marries a deaf person; conversely, it is audism when a hearing person discourages such union because the hearing spouse is superior to his/her mate. Audism can be subtle or blatant, as Humphries suggests, but an understanding of audism can help deal with the anger and frustration of basic intolerance in our society for anyone different in the slightest way. This intolerance is typically caused by "...a lack of understanding about how deaf learn which leads people to assume that they will learn best in the same way as hearing people and to seek methods that try to duplicate the hearing experience for the deaf person. This is ignorance about the impact that deafness has on one's life which leads people to believe that deaf people are inferior both in intelligence and ability and thus should be treated accordingly...."[44]

DEAFHOOD

A relatively new term, "Deafhood," has gained attention in America since the early 1990s. Paddy Ladd, Ph.D.,[45] of England, who also studied in America, suggested the word as a result of the deaf community's dissatisfaction about the term *deafness*. *Deafness* most likely originated within the medical field and focuses on hearing loss as an abnormality or handicap, and on pathological conditions. *Deafhood*, instead, refers to a process of creating or accepting an identity, rather than a state that focuses on people's existential stances.

Deafhood is a complex concept that finally began capturing people's attention during the early 2000s. As of the writing of this book, Deaf people everywhere are hosting Deafhood panels and workshops, learning more about the process involved. Deafhood is defined as a state of mind where Deaf people achieve their fullest and strongest Deaf selves and is a positive approach to re-affirming Deaf people's potential and place in society, history and the world.[46]

Attitudes: Recognizing the Past

Regardless of pride or acceptance of our individualities, a look into Europe's past will help us understand how attitudes started and carried on over the years to the United States. The stigma persisting today is that being deaf or having no speech skills is equivalent to a lack of intelligence. Before the advent of written language, speech was the main means of communicating thoughts, and, as a result, people who did not speak were cut off from mainstream society, although not by choice. Deaf people were considered peculiar, imbecilic, even cursed, or inhabited by evil spirits; these considerations still exist in many parts of the world. Prejudice is still prevalent even in modern-day countries like the United States.

Observe how some of the most noted figures in the early history contributed to those attitudes throughout our history.

- **Ancient Times.** Although attitudes toward the deaf and other disabilities were mixed, the thinking, mostly influenced by philosophers, was that deaf people were hopeless since they were not able to hear; therefore they were senseless and unable to express themselves appropriately.
- **Ancient Greece.** Deaf and disabled children were killed, as they were considered "non-human" or even barbarians.
- **Ancient Rome.** Justinian law recognized the differences among the deaf people by creating five classifications of deafness and muteness.
- **Biblical Times.** The Hebrews and the Romans recognized the differences among deaf people by identifying those who were born deaf and those who became deaf later. With Romans 10:17, which reads, "So faith comes from hearing the message, and the message that is heard is what Christ spoke," deaf people were generally excluded from church membership.
- **Nineteenth Century.** Although educational opportunities became widespread in America, the 1880 Milan conference and Alexander Graham Bell's crusade to phase out the deaf race were examples of the pathological view that deafness needed to be "fixed."

- **Twentieth Century.** Paternalism toward deaf people continued. Throughout Hitler's regime during World War II, sterilization was performed on several thousand deaf Germans. "When the Nazis took over in 1933, they burned many books on teaching deaf and handicapped children. Deaf people would soon discover they were among the many groups persecuted by the Nazis. They were ordered not to have children, and many were sent to concentration camps. During World War II, 150,000 disabled people were put to death under Nazi rule; 1,600 of them were deaf."[47]

Traditional and Pioneering Views

To better describe how deaf people are seen by hearing people, the following table presents a comparison of the two prevalent views over the years. For many years, the traditional view was based on studies that focused mostly on the medical or pathological aspects; the view has shifted to more positive aspects, perhaps attributed to modernistic analysis focusing on cultural or humanistic aspects.[48]

Traditional Studies (Pathological/Medical Perspective) (1600–1900) Europe and Early America	Pioneering Studies (Humanistic/Cultural Perspective) Late in the 20th Century, Specifically After 1960
People most interested in deafness and deaf people were: • Philosophers • Politicians/law makers • Physicians/doctors • Educators • Theologians/religious people	People most interested in deafness and deaf people are: • Historians • Educators • Researchers/linguists • Advocates • Deaf people themselves
Educators and physicians dominated historical writings about deaf people: • Describing and remedying the disabilities caused by lack of auditory ability. • Deaf students' educational shortcomings, describing in great detail what deaf people usually could not do instead of presenting a picture of what they did or thought or how they lived.	Researchers/linguists and historians shared many facets about deaf people: • Chronicling history based on deaf people's experiences, rather than only studies of how medicine or education applied to them. • Studying the linguistics of sign language. • Embracing the diversity of deaf people.
Common beliefs: • Deafness was a curse from God.	Common beliefs: • Deafness occurs from a gene in one

Traditional Studies
(Pathological/Medical Perspective)
(1600–1900) Europe and Early
America

- A congenitally deaf person who lacked intelligible speech also lacked a soul and perhaps all ability to reason.
- Deafness was pathological.
- Deaf individuals were problems of society.

Pioneering Studies
(Humanistic/Cultural Perspective)
Late in the 20th Century, Specifically
After 1960

or two parents or in a generation, other than illness or accident.
- Deafness can be inherited from either deaf parents or hearing parents.
- Being deaf has nothing to do with one's intelligence, abilities, and social skills.

In his closing speech at the Deaf Studies IV conference in 1995, Dr. Harlan Lane advised that the concept of *disability* came from France in relation to body function. If people could work, they contributed to society. Those who could not work were considered disabled, so they got support.[49]

The late Gilbert Eastman, an author of at least three books, wrote in 1996:

> Deafness is not a disease,
> Deafness is not a disorder,
> Deafness is not a punishment.[50]

Trends in Education of the Deaf

"U.S. deaf history rests a great deal on the European history, and the durability of ASL and deaf culture can be traced to the institution that de l'Épée built..." when he established a deaf school in Paris, France, in the 1750s.[51]

Since the 1970s, the deaf educational system in America has moved from residential/boarding schools to mainstreamed settings. Some residential schools have closed due to various reasons, whether financial, dwindling numbers or other factors. Between 1900 and the 1950s, there was a residential school for the deaf in almost every state, some states having two or more. In the 1940s, there were 312 schools for deaf students in the United States, and 65 of them were public, residential schools with an enrollment of approximately 4,800 students out of approximately 20,367 students identified as deaf or hard of hearing.[52] During the academic year of 1973-1974, a total of 28,639 students, or 54 percent of the deaf school population, were reported to attend residential or day schools. The rest either attended home schools or had other schooling.[53]

Researchers Mitchell and Karchmer[54] reported that over the past quarter century, the percentage of deaf and hard of hearing students attending special schools declined by more than half. The number of students attending special classes — as defined by those who attend regular mainstream schools less than 60 percent of the time — also declined. Both account for 35 percent, as compared to 65 percent who attend regular educational settings.

Mitchell and Karchmer estimated that "...at least 80 percent of schools serving deaf and hard of hearing students have three or fewer students with hearing loss or deafness," and 53 percent of schools serving deaf and hard of hearing students enroll only one such student in that school. Furthermore, it pointed out that "nearly one of every five (19 percent) deaf and hard of hearing students in special education is a 'solitaire.'"[55]

Some note the positive benefits of this shift in educational settings, such as being closer to family at home rather than away for extended periods of times (note: residential schools nowadays typically require students to go home every weekend). There are also negative aspects, such as a lack of critical mass and a sense of isolation.

This may be best expressed by Gina Oliva, Ph.D., a retired Deaf Gallaudet University professor and a voice of experience. In her book, *Alone in the Mainstream: A Deaf Woman Remembers Public School*, Oliva takes a look at her public school days during the 1950s and 1960s. Her school did not teach sign language, and she wrote that her school days were mostly "lonely" and that many of her colleagues expressed similar feelings or experiences. Oliva said she wrote the book in hopes of helping make hearing people, especially parents of today's deaf and hard of hearing children, understand what it is like being solitary in school.

As mentioned, some schools for deaf students have closed in the last ten years. That may be bad news, but it seems that there is a silver lining in the clouds. In response to deinstitutionalization, deaf schools that used to serve an entire state have become more regionalized, organized to serve large urban areas. Some areas have established charter schools for deaf students. With the dwindling numbers, some deaf schools have experienced a revival in enrollments.

More and more schools for deaf students around the nation are raising academic requirements to be on par with those of public schools. Many are not considered "institutions" in the traditional sense but rather are similar to boarding schools. In other words, schools for the deaf may be resurrected in a different form in the future.[56]

With increased awareness of diversity in today's nation, especially in educational settings, schools are expected to expose students to multicultural education. As McCaskill-Emerson, Ph.D.,[57] puts it, most schools use a Eurocentric curriculum that does not adequately prepare students to live in a multicultural society. Children of color know much about the history, values, and culture of European Americans but lack knowledge of their own cultures. Exposure to deaf culture is in the same boat. Deaf studies and awareness of diversity have been added to the curriculum in many schools, especially those with large deaf and multicultural school populations. Introduction to Deaf culture has been added to many programs teaching ASL.

FOUR

Life in Deaf Communities

American Deaf Community

The historical review of deaf people in the first three chapters offered a fascinating glimpse of the deaf community's early years around the world. The chapters also examined how events were intertwined throughout the years with many twists of fate. For example, when Thomas Hopkins Gallaudet went to England, his original intent was to study the Braidwood method of educating deaf people. But he ended up going to France and bringing Laurent Clerc to America. Suppose Laurent Clerc had gone to Russia as he originally desired and had declined the offer to come to America.

It may be difficult to visualize what the deaf community would be today if not for such events. If Amos Kendall had not taken guardianship of the neglected five children abandoned by H. H. Skinner or did not establish the Columbia Institution for the Instruction of Deaf and Dumb, he might not have had the opportunity to establish a college-level program on Kendall Green. Gallaudet University, during its first century of existence, served as the beacon of higher education of deaf people across the nation. Subsequently those people have played vital roles in shaping the deaf community. The following chapters will present a kaleidoscope of the deaf community, its colorful expressions, and sign language, all of which have matured and evolved during two centuries of existence in America.

Deaf? Hard of Hearing? Hearing Impaired?

Before delving further into the deaf community, let us pause to review some simple adaptations of descriptions of deaf, hard of hearing, and hearing impaired that were suggested in the 1988 book, *Let's Learn about Deafness*.[1] This book was designed for parents of deaf children not familiar with hearing loss and also for non-deaf children in schools. The purpose was to help them to understand and become familiar with deaf children who were mainstreamed in their classes. The book listed different attributes of each category:

DEAF

- Deaf people cannot hear many sounds.
- It is as if the ears are "broken" and do not work well. Sometimes the hearing cannot be fixed.
- If you have a toy that is broken, you cannot use it well. Maybe you can get it fixed. But most broken ears cannot be fixed.
- For some deaf people, hearing aids do not help at all.
- Deafness is like watching television with the sound turned off. You cannot hear what people are saying. You might be confused about what is happening on the screen.
- Some people who cannot hear at all have good speech.
- Some people who cannot hear do not use speech. They prefer to communicate in sign language and writing.

HARD OF HEARING

- Hard of hearing people can hear many sounds, but not all sounds.
- Hearing aids are often helpful for hard of hearing people.
- People who wear hearing aids usually cannot hear everything. If you see someone wearing a hearing aid, don't think the person can hear everything you say.
- Being hard of hearing is like watching television with the sound turned low, so that you can barely hear.
- Or it is like trying to play with a toy car that has two wheels missing. You can play with it, but it does not work as well as a car with all four wheels.
- Some hard of hearing people with hearing aids understand only a few words; others understand many words.
- Some hard of hearing people have good speech; others do not speak clearly.

HEARING IMPAIRED

- Hearing impaired is a word used to describe all people with hearing problems. Deaf people are hearing impaired and hard of hearing people are also hearing impaired.

• Some deaf people prefer to be called hearing impaired. Other deaf people may want to be called deaf. Most hard of hearing people want you to call them hard of hearing.

"Hearing impaired" was the "politically correct term" during the 1970s and was used to describe everyone with any degree of hearing loss, ranging from a mild loss of acuity to profound deafness. The medical profession — recall the "traditional" and "pioneering" views, outlined in Chapter Three — preferred, and still prefers, to use "hearing impaired" to placate the parents of children with hearing loss, or other individuals who lose their hearing. However, this label has provoked a backlash from the deaf community, mainly because the "impaired" label suggests a malfunction, substandard, defect, or disability. Many deaf and hard of hearing people prefer a more respectful term such as "deaf" or "hard of hearing" that does not provide negative connotation.

During the eighteenth century and the early nineteenth century, "semi-mute" was used to describe deaf people who were born hearing but lost hearing during infancy. During those days, medication such as sulfa drugs and penicillin were non-existent, so many children lost their hearing to common childhood diseases such as whooping cough and scarlet fever. They usually acquired language and speech prior to their illnesses, so they possessed understandable speech throughout their lives. Today, most deaf children are born deaf— most often due to illnesses during pregnancy, such as German measles, or hereditary reasons. Medications may also cause hearing loss. Generally, more children are born either deaf or lose their hearing in infancy before acquiring language and speech.

Currently the accepted phrases are "deaf" or "hard of hearing."

The accompanying illustration *A Century of Difference* on the following page shows a deaf artist's perception of the various labels that the hearing population has used throughout the last century.

From the 1800s to the Present

According to *Megatrends*[2] author John Naisbitt, the story of America can be told in three words: agriculture, manufacturing, and information — the three eras that Americans have lived through. This chapter will present an insight into the American deaf community's evolution. During America's early days, the population consisted of mostly independent individuals who depended on farming to make a living. People tended to be more isolated and spread out in the country. Deaf children and adults were also typically isolated, probably more isolated than their hearing peers. Some deaf children never

A Century of Difference © 2002 Ann Silver. All rights reserved.

had schooling and stayed on the farm throughout their lives, typically communicating with homemade signs.

More fortunate ones might have gone to school — sometimes only for a couple of years, or staying until graduation. Some left school early to help out on the farm or went back to the family farm upon graduation. They might have become isolated again or never bothered to maintain contact with their deaf or school friends the rest of their lives. Others completed their schooling and received a diploma, a vocational certificate, or a certificate of attendance.

As manufacturing progressively became dominant in America, cities grew larger; more people congregated in the cities. A similar phenomenon occurred with deaf people, who moved to the cities where they could conveniently mix with their friends. Usually vocational training at schools for the deaf made deaf people's skills more marketable to employers. The two world wars presented golden opportunities for deaf people, who could not fight for the United States but could successfully contribute to the war efforts. Many were hired at factories and plants to replace men who were off fighting the war; employers found deaf people to be very capable.

Even today, there continue to be large deaf populations in certain towns around the nation: in cities and towns where companies are known to hire deaf people, or in towns where deaf schools are located. In the present information age, deaf people, as well as those in the hearing community, have become more independent. They have convenient access to information via various means of technologies, which will be described in Chapter Nine. As a result, the deaf population may no longer have a strong grip on its own society, and the sense of belonging appears to be more fragmented.

The Community and the Deaf Community

A community is created when a group of people with common interests is drawn together. These people tend to share a basic pattern that includes common languages and experiences, such as the African-American community, the Asian-Pacific community, and the Hispanic/Latino community. When they are in their own communities, they feel at home and respected.

The Deaf community can be defined as a group of deaf and hard of hearing individuals who share a common language, common experiences and values, and a common way of interacting with each other and with hearing people.[3] The degree of hearing loss typically is not an important factor. Participation in the Deaf community is usually by those who consider themselves deaf and are accepted by the community. Knowledge and use of ASL is another factor but not necessarily required.

Because there were limited opportunities for interaction among early Americans, it is doubtful if there existed a formal Deaf community prior to 1817, with the exception of Martha's Vineyard. Many historians point to residential deaf schools as the beginning of a formalized Deaf community, where common language and experiences provided the foundation of the deaf community.

DEAF CLUBS

There is a lack of reliable recorded information about the Deaf community's social life until after World War I. The deaf American community seems to have evolved from the state schools for the deaf. Since most states had only one school for the deaf, many deaf children lived for at least nine months each year at the residential schools. Upon leaving school or graduation, quite a number of them migrated to large cities where they became part of a close-knit community characteristically populated by former students of the same school. The residential schools, indeed, fostered relationships that led Deaf people to the establishments of Deaf clubs existing even today, where Deaf people govern, socialize, communicate in ASL and organize Deaf sports.[4]

Consequently, clubs in those days were established to provide culture and social opportunities for deaf people with similar backgrounds. The clubs often had "silent" in their names, such as Akron Silent Club, but deaf people themselves called such organizations "deaf clubs." Most met in rented halls, usually on the second floor above stores, that were close to streetcar or bus lines. In some cities, club members raised funds to purchase or build their own clubhouses. Most of the clubs were open every weekend, usually Friday evening and all day Saturdays. On Sunday evenings, they were also open for captioned movie showings. Some clubs were open every evening, or even 24 hours, seven days, especially during World War II, when defense workers gathered to socialize and share news after work.

Deaf Minnesotans are fortunate to have a dedicated clubhouse donated by a wealthy Deaf man. The large, historical Charles Thompson Memorial Hall, constructed in 1916 and a state landmark site, stands today at 1824 Marshall Avenue in St. Paul. A renowned Deaf architect, Olof Hanson, drew plans for the building that contains four floors, including an assembly hall with a seating capacity of 250. The club events continue to draw crowds from around the state and even neighboring states. Author Ron recalls as a youngster traveling with his family from his rural hometown to attend social functions at Thompson Hall.

Author Melvia, who grew up in Houston, recalls many good memories about a deaf club owned and run by the Houston Association of the Deaf. Strategically located one block east of the 2200 block of North Main Street, the L-shaped building on a corner was easily accessible to both buses and cars. She lived two blocks from the club, and her deaf parents were club members.

The whole family went to the clubhouse during the summers, when school was closed. Club activities included monthly business meetings, with annual elections for officers and building committees. Functions included parties, special celebrations, banquets, sports, and card games. During Christmas, children would be treated with gifts and candy from Santa. The most popular attraction during the 1960s through 1980s was captioned films. With open captions or subtitles, Deaf viewers were able to enjoy full-length Hollywood films, such as *Shane, Gone with the Wind,* or *Lawrence of Arabia,* presented through 16mm projectors.

One's residence also could be as good a place as the clubhouse. Friends often paid surprise visits to homes of deaf families — those with several deaf family members — and stayed hours and hours to socialize. Melvia remembers, as a child, sitting and watching deaf adults talk until all hours of the night.

She also recalls that her family's First Baptist church denounced the club-goers, saying they were sinners in the eyes of God. When her family visited the club, they had mixed feelings: delight in seeing old friends and pangs of guilt.

Like the hearing community, Deaf people have their share of sub-community groups, such as bridge or poker groups, quilting bees, and scrapbooking groups. Author Melvia's bridge group, the Bridgettes, has met almost every month for 45 years and has performed volunteer work such as coordinating lunches and contributing to needy organizations. Ron has played poker with two groups every month for almost 50 years, although the two poker groups now have consolidated to one as a result of age and changing demographics. In many states, there are Deaf individuals who gather for scrapbooking activities, Red Hat Society activities, and other hobby-related activities. The Deaf Seniors of America national conference has always provided a luncheon meeting of the Red Hat Society members, who make a conspicuous splash with their fancy hats and garb, in red and purple.

RELIGION

Although religion has played a central part in colonists' lives since America's founding, it was not accessible to deaf people probably until the middle of the nineteenth century. It has been mentioned that Thomas Gallaudet, Thomas Hopkins Gallaudet's eldest son and Edward Miner Gallaudet's brother, started a Sunday school class for deaf people in New York City. He was then a teacher at the New York Institute for the Deaf. Concerned with the lack of religious opportunities for deaf people, he forsook his teaching career to become an Episcopalian priest and founded St. Ann's Church for the Deaf in New York City. He is credited as the originator of sign language in religious services for deaf people.[5]

Deaf Heritage reports, "In 1906 the Baptists entered the foray between the devil and the deaf with its one-man army in the person of John W. Michaels."[6] Michaels convinced the Southern Baptist Convention that an estimated 45,000 deaf people had no access to Baptist religious services, and he was appointed the first missionary to deaf people. Spreading the gospel, he was said to have established 19 religious classes in 11 states by 1914. By the 1960s, over 240 classes existed from his efforts.

Several denominations, such as Lutheran, Methodist, Latter Day Saints, Baptist, and Catholic, eventually provided services for deaf people, although their efforts varied. During the middle years of the twentieth century, itinerant ministers who traveled to various communities served deaf churchgoers. For example, those representing the three synods of the Lutheran Church drove from their home churches in large cities to small towns and conducted services once a month. Sometimes a minister preached two or three sermons in different towns the same day.

Usually, churches with deaf congregations were led by hearing people. Often, especially with the younger pastors, their sign language left much to be desired. In larger cities, religious services might be interpreted for deaf parishioners; the interpreters were often untrained, yet they considered themselves God's devoted saviors rescuing the unfortunates from the devil. Even so, some of them did become quite proficient, and it has been said that religious interpreting was the forerunner of today's interpreting profession.

The Episcopal Church, in 1884, was the first church to have ordained a deaf person, Henry Syle, as a priest. Henry Syle (1846–1890) was born of a missionary in China, but poor health forced his move to America where he lived with his aunt in Alexandria, Virginia. He lost his hearing due to scarlet fever at the age of six. As a young man, he expressed to Thomas Gallaudet of St. Ann's Church a desire to enter the priesthood. Although there was no known deaf priest at that time, the Rev. Gallaudet encouraged Syle in his endeavors.

Before teaching at the New York Institute for the Deaf, Syle enrolled at Trinity College in Hartford, Connecticut, and later St. John's College in Cambridge, England. However, due to poor eyesight, he failed to complete his studies. While in New York, Syle participated in correspondence study with Yale College and in 1869, completed the four-year bachelor's degree program in one year. He eventually earned two master's degrees, one from Yale in 1872 and later, from Trinity College.

In 1874, Syle moved to Philadelphia where he worked for the U.S. Mint as an assayer. He came across a number of the town's deaf churchgoers whose pastor was the Rev. Francis J. Clerc, Laurent Clerc's son. Syle's desire to become a priest was revived. He was ordained as a deacon in Philadelphia in 1876. After studying for priesthood and passing examinations in Latin, Greek, and Hebrew, in addition to the history and doctrine of the Episcopal Church, he also overcame protests from the church authorities, "...who argued that only the one perfect in all the five senses of the body should be considered fit for the ministry."[7] In 1883 he was ordained as a priest. By 1900, there were seven ordained deaf priests, and by 1930 the number had grown to 22.

Either by choice, or by failing to overcome the barriers, not many deaf persons entered the ministry up to the mid–20th century. An unknown Methodist minister was ordained in Illinois in 1894. In 1977, the Reverend Thomas Coughlin became the first ordained Deaf Roman Catholic priest in North America.

NATIONAL FRATERNAL SOCIETY OF THE DEAF

Looking back to the late 1800s, we find it difficult to conceptualize that deaf people were not able to purchase life or disability insurance. "Insurance companies in those days considered deaf people high risks and accident-prone, and they believed, mistakenly, that the deaf had shorter-than-average lifespans,"[8] explained *Deaf Heritage*. Those deaf persons accepted by insurance companies often were forced to pay exorbitant premiums for accident or death benefits.

In 1901, a group of 13 young men with extraordinary foresight met at the Michigan School for the Deaf in Flint and established the Fraternal Society of the Deaf with the immediate purpose of the organization being the provision of insurance protection and social opportunities. The organization was renamed the National Fraternal Society of the Deaf in 1907 and began its operation as a *bona fide* insurance business. Later, sickness and accident coverage were made available to patrons.

Similar to fraternal lodges, NFSD ran an organization consisting of local divisions that provided social opportunities for deaf people in their communities and published a bi-monthly informative publication called *The Frat*. In 1929, almost seven thousand members were affiliated with 111 local divisions, and the organization continued to expand up to 13,000 members in the 1980s. In 1937, women were first permitted to establish "social auxiliaries." The number of local social auxiliaries grew to 39, with membership of approximately 1,500. In 1951, NFSD permitted women to purchase life insurance.

In many smaller cities or towns, where local clubs did not exist, there were frequent events hosted by the "Frat." Events such as annual "Frat picnics" or "Frat dinners" were common. In reality, such occasions were the *de facto* social gathering of deaf people where social ties grew strong among the members. These divisions would sponsor projects, such as food or clothing drives to aid needy populations. In the fall of 2001, NFSD, partnering with NAD and Deaf Seniors of America, initiated a "United We Stand" drive to aid the victims of the September 11, 2001, disaster in New York City and maintain funds for future similar catastrophes.

For many years, NFSD honored outstanding high school scholars and sponsored an annual selection of outstanding high school athletes in sports such as football, wrestling, boys' and girls' basketball, track and field and volleyball.

In January 2005, NFSD ceased to exist as a fraternal benefit society and stopped selling insurance due to dwindling membership; it also merged with the Catholic Order of Foresters. Early in 2007, NFSD announced that its board of directors decided to cease operations as of January 1, 2007. Shortly after its closing, NFSD's final director, Al Van Nevel, passed away.

Since its original goal of ensuring that deaf persons were given insurance coverage was accomplished, NFSD officially went out of business in March 2010. With the establishment of two foundations, NFSD's legacy of charitable giving will continue with the Dr. Frank B. Sullivan Memorial Foundation and Al Van Nevel Memorial Fund, which were created to support education, seminars and workshops for Deaf youth. Cultural archives and memorabilia have been donated to the Gallaudet University Archives.

THE WORLD WARS

Although not at front lines, the deaf community was vigorous and visible during World Wars I and II. Before the wars, many factory jobs were not available to deaf people, because employers were afraid of the so-called burden of not being able to hear and the "risks" this posed to the company. At the outbreaks of the two World Wars, big towns and cities suddenly mushroomed with deaf people seeking factory jobs manufacturing mostly military products. Historical accounts indicate high satisfaction rates from employers for performance quality and deaf employees' dedication, especially since they were not as easily distracted by noises like hearing workers.

Akron, Ohio, was the place to go during World War I. A large number of deaf workers moved to Akron from around the country to obtain work, primarily at Goodyear. In fact, it is said that between five hundred and one thousand deaf persons lived in one square mile.[9] Young and socially active, numerous deaf employees held skilled technical and professional positions, such as management and office work. At the end of the war, many positions were closed, and deaf workers were laid off. The number rebounded after the Pearl Harbor attack that led to World War II. Goodyear and Firestone hired approximately a thousand deaf Americans. Close to five thousand deaf workers across the nation,[10] including author Ron's mother, worked at war plants throughout the country.

During these wars, deaf Americans' patriotism came out in full force. Many planted vegetables in what were called "Victory Gardens" to feed the armed forces, as well as knitted scarves and socks, sweaters, and blankets. Even students at deaf schools and Gallaudet College were actively patriotic. Girls at Maryland School for the Deaf produced approximately 18,000 surgical dressings for Red Cross, and students at the Virginia School for the Deaf and Blind sold over $2,200 worth of war stamps and bonds.

Deaf organizations also participated in war efforts. NAD coordinated a Victory Fund with assistance from state-level associations and raised approximately $7,700 to present to the American Red Cross for the purchase of three "clubmobiles" (ambulance station wagons) and defense bonds. On each club-mobile's door beneath the Red Cross logo were the words, "Presented by the Deaf of USA, Through the NAD."[11]

Post-War Doldrums

More often than not, life got tough for deaf people after major wars. They were laid off when the defense plants that produced goods for the war closed down or lost their jobs to returning members of the armed forces. Some of them were even demoted to lower-paying jobs. Author Ron recalls that his family lost its apartment to a family returning from the service just after World War II. The landlord was holding the absent family's furniture in the second bedroom while the author and his family slept in one bedroom and the living room. As soon as the war ended, the landlord evicted the author's family for "making too much noise" as an excuse.

The eviction is an example of what usually happened at the end of the wars. Soldiers returned home or to their jobs and displaced whoever stood in for them. A more serious problem was that the factories that produced materials and supplies for the war ceased to produce, causing mass layoffs. The crisis was more pronounced after World War II, when there was an alarming increase in deaf peddlers who solicited donations from the public. The image of deaf peddlers, many deaf people felt, tarnished the image of honest and hard-working deaf people.

To dodge vagrancy laws, peddlers sold inexpensive tokens in exchange for "contributions" instead of panhandling like any other beggar on the street. They were usually found at places such as railroad stations, bus depots, and downtown bars where they would pass out small cards explaining that they were deaf and had trouble finding jobs. The back of the cards characteristically had an illustration of the manual alphabet with a short note: "Learn to Communicate with the Deaf!" After handing out the cards to patrons, the peddlers would then make a second round of the room, picking up coins or the rejected cards. On a good day during the late 1940s or early 1950s, a peddler could make between $25 and $30 per day, tax-free. Some peddlers obtained short-term licenses, so they were able to sell various goods legally and pay taxes.

The debate about "wiping out" peddlers probably reached its highest and most emotional point among deaf organization leaders after the war. Deaf children were taught the evils of peddling. Some local organizations countered the proliferation of peddling by distributing alphabet cards with the message "THIS CARD IS FREE. Respectable deaf citizens do not beg nor peddle. They have good jobs and neither need nor want charity."

Today peddlers still make their rounds, but their places of operation have been upgraded to airports and shopping malls. Their tokens include first aid bandages, combs, pens, sewing needles, scissors, or even religious bookmarks.[12] In the 1960s some peddlers would make $100 a day; a peddler in Arizona claimed that he made $800 on a typical Friday and Saturday.[13]

In the summer of 1997, New York police found 62 persons, including some children, from Mexico, who were living in poverty in two small apartments. These deaf persons were brought to the city illegally to beg for money, and none of them knew any English or ASL. Later, in the middle of August, 11 more were arrested in New York, four in Chicago, and several in other cities. Some had been selling trinkets as long as ten years under the control of "kings" who refused to pay them and threatened them. Many of the bosses were also deaf and used intimidation to enslave the peddlers. A group of the peddlers reported the slavery to New York police, and hearing interpreters translated between ASL and English, while deaf interpreters translated between ASL and Mexican Sign Language.

The peddlers were in the country illegally and were subject to deportation. Mayor Rudolph Guliani's administration put the peddlers in a motel and found housing for them. They also arranged schooling for some of them and found jobs for them. Nearly 40 of them decided to stay. The youngest Mexican was 17 years old at that time, and he attended Lexington School for the Deaf where he met his future wife. Now he works as a janitor at the Statue of Liberty and Ellis Island, and he and his wife have a two-year-old daughter.[14]

The typical employment opportunities for deaf people in the 20 years after World War II were as laborers or skilled workers (i.e., printers, carpenters, bakers, upholsterers, tailors, and tire factory workers). It should be mentioned that excellent vocational training in residential schools often provided the occupational prerequisites for deaf people to work in one of the trades. Tire factory jobs became popular among deaf persons during World War II. Key-punching was a popular option for women after World War II. Since the early 1970s, employment possibilities flourished, especially professional endeavors such as doctors, dentists, lawyers, school and college administrators, and teaching at all grades from preschool through college.

ATHLETICS

After the 1945 establishment of the American Athletic Association of the Deaf (AAAD) in Akron, Ohio — incidentally, one of the cities that many deaf individuals relocated to for jobs during the war years — many deaf clubs sponsored basketball teams that competed in one of the seven regional tournaments, with the winners advancing to the national AAAD basketball tournaments. The eighth team in the tournament was usually the host club. The Akron Club of the Deaf hosted the first national basketball tournament in 1945. In the 1950s, deaf clubs began to sponsor fast-pitch softball teams, but in the 1960s, slow-pitch became more popular.

AAAD is currently the USA Deaf Sports Federation (USADSF), the umbrella organization for over 20 individual and team sports. USADSF sponsors competitions for both men and women on local, regional, and national levels, most of which occur annually. The organization has maintained its Hall of Fame since 1952 and has recognized a Deaf Athlete of the Year since 1955.

USADSF is affiliated with the International Committee of Sports for the Deaf (ICSD). ICSD was founded in 1924, and in 1935 the first two Americans participated in the World Games for the Deaf, currently the Deaflympics. USADSF coordinates Deaflympics and Pan American tryouts for United States athletes.

ICSD membership is currently composed of 104 federation nations and four regional confederations, including the Pan American Deaf Sports Organization (PANAMDES) of which the USADSF is a member. Like the Olympics, the Deaflympics are held every four years.

USADSF hosted the 1965 Summer Deaflympics in Washington, D.C., the 1985 summer games in Los Angeles, the 1975 Winter Deaflympics in Lake Placid, New York, and the 2007 winter games in Salt Lake City. Over 600 athletes and officials participated in the 2007 competition. In September 2009, more than 4,000 deaf athletes and officials from 77 nations participated in the 21st Summer Deaflympics in Taipei, Taiwan.

THE VANISHING "DEAF CLUB"

As mentioned earlier, Deaf clubs were the ideal places to see old friends or make new ones, or be entertained. However, during the late 1990s and early 2000s, Deaf clubs lost their standing as the centers of the adult deaf community. As a result of declining membership and support, the majority of clubs have folded, and some clubhouses have been sold. For example, the Houston Association of the Deaf clubhouse was sold during the summer of 2006. There are several possible reasons for the dwindling membership. In the past, deaf clubs satisfied emotional and social needs; nowadays deaf people have a wider range of entertainment available to them, especially through captioned television or rental movies. Instead of going to the club each week to watch the latest captioned film, deaf people can now simply rent DVDs from the local video store, or lately, from vending machines or even on the Internet, and enjoy the movies in their homes.

Another factor may have been the availability of teletypewriters (TTYs). Prior to the 1980s, a very few deaf persons had telephones in their homes. The advent of TTYs — old teletype machines converted to devices that deaf people could use to type to each other using telephone lines — changed the landscape, making it more convenient for deaf people to talk instead of meeting each other in person. With the Internet, the need to meet in person has eroded even further, since deaf people can easily interact with each other or with hearing people via e-mail, instant messaging, or video conferencing.

Another popular theory for deaf clubs' decline is that residential schools no longer educate the majority of deaf children. At least 75 percent of deaf children now attend public school, either in special programs for deaf children or in regular classrooms with the assistance of interpreters. These children do not have the close relationships among their deaf peers like those forged at deaf schools in the old days.

However, Padden and Humphries[15] think differently. They surmise that the decline started in the early 1960s, before "telephone access exploded in the 1980s, *after* clubs had started to see their membership numbers decline." Moreover, closed caption decoders for television did not become available for sale until 1978. They theorize that during the 1960s, more deaf adults sought out professional opportunities other than the old standbys of the teaching and printing professions. They entered into a diverse range of employment, such as counseling, social work, administration, government, education or private practice. They had their own offices and formed what Padden and Humphries refer to as the middle class. The middle class members possessed similar interests as others in their professions, so they were less likely to attend deaf club functions. In addition, deaf persons no longer had to go to deaf clubs for consultation on personal or business matters.

LIFE AFTER CLUBS

A new and current trend is that Deaf people gather in a variety of places on a regular basis, be it at shopping malls, restaurants for breakfast or lunch, bars for happy hour, or coffee at coffee shops or bookstores. For instance, a food court in Richmond, Virginia, not only offers a place where deaf people can socialize with each other but also gives hearing individuals an opportunity to learn sign language. In Washington, D.C., a group of deaf professionals meets to interact at one of the drinking spots one evening every month. A website, www.deaf-coffee.com, offers a list of "deaf chat coffee" sites in the United States. There are also deaf professional "happy hours" in many cities around the country.

UTOPIA AND DEAF PEOPLE

Throughout the years there have been ongoing debates of a "Deaf Utopia" where Deaf people could live together and communicate effortlessly with each other. At Martha's Vineyard, even though a majority of the population could hear, the ability of each person to mingle and sign with deaf persons came close to being an ideal community for deaf people. As mentioned, two factors accounted for this phenomenon — isolation from the mainstream and inter-marriages among relatives. The last deaf person on the island passed away in the 1950s.

Writer John James Flournoy (1810–1879), a graduate of the American Asylum for the Deaf in Connecticut, suggested in the 1850s the creation of a community where only deaf people could reside. He proposed to Congress that land be set aside in the western territories for deaf people. In his quest, he mentioned that Laurent Clerc supported the venture. However, Clerc, then 72 years old, rebutted this claim at a meeting of the New England Gal-laudet Association for Deaf-Mutes, saying that his early beliefs had been mis-interpreted. Clerc said he had suggested that some of the land in Alabama given to the American School for the Deaf by the federal government be used as "headquarters" for the deaf and dumb. He had no intention of supporting a separate deaf state.[16]

Due to negative feedback from the deaf population, in addition to Clerc's rebuttal, Flournoy's vision did not materialize. Yet this type of vision became commonplace among many authors. Similar visions were suggested in the form of books: *Island of Silence* by Carolyn B. Norris, published in 1976, and *Islay* by Douglas Bullard in 1986.

In 2003, Marvin Miller, a fourth-generation deaf individual, and M. E. Barwacz, his hearing mother-in-law, purchased real estate in Salem, South Dakota, about 80 miles northwest of Sioux Falls. They proposed Laurent — in honor of Clerc — as the name for this new town for sign language users. In the early spring of 2005, planners, architects and potential residents met to draw detailed blueprints for the town, which could accommodate at least 2,500 people. As of October 2005, a total of 151 families had expressed interest in residing in Laurent.

Early in 2007, it was announced that Miller and his family were relocating to Indianapolis. The $10 million that had been promised by an investor never materialized, and it was one of the factors that led Miller and Barwacz to declare bankruptcy and dissolve the Laurent Company. The non-profit Lau-rent Institute continues to exist, and the founders are considering new strate-gies for building the town in a new location.

To play with words a bit: it has been suggested that our planet EARth is inhabited by persons who hEAR. Far away in the galaxy there is a planet called EYEth where all inhabitants are deaf. They use their eyes and hands to communicate and possess their own language, culture and traditions. One humorous story[17] has all children in EYEth who are born hearing being fitted with an implant. Those who are not able to learn sign language are sent away to live on EARth among hearing people. With the clever use of words in entertaining the readers, the authors point out that the story is "an analogy to the experiences that some Deaf people have recounted for decades."[18]

Post-Secondary Educational Opportunities

In both deaf and hearing communities, deaf people have been assuming positions of power in new fields. As author Lou Ann Walker puts it,

> There are more white-collar Deaf workers than ever. Suddenly there is an increase in Deaf government officials in high positions, in Deaf stockholders and accountants and lawyers. Deaf activists are working toward setting up more rest homes for elderly Deaf people. They are creating programs so that hearing parents of Deaf babies can meet Deaf adults and see that there is a real future for their children....[19]

The authors believe that this is mostly influenced by the availability of increased opportunities in post-secondary education for deaf youth. Prior to the 1970s, advanced educational opportunities for deaf people were very limited. Probably a better term would be that the opportunities were beyond reach. It can be surmised that a number of deaf people were interested, yet they felt that opportunities were beyond their reach. Some were denied admission to graduate programs because they were deaf and perceived as unable to take the advanced coursework. Those who earned master's degrees were typically those who became deaf after acquiring language or possessed intelligible speech.

Another major barrier was the lack of resources for deaf students taking courses. Back then, professional interpreting services were not readily available. Author Ron was with Gallaudet University for three years when he saw the need to advance himself professionally by earning a master's degree. In 1964 he enrolled in the Industrial Education program at University of Maryland and was joined by two other teachers, all of whom completed the program and received master's degrees in Industrial Education — without interpreters, albeit with limited assistance from note-taking by hearing classmates. One professor in the department even mentioned that in his class, the three deaf fellows produced the best paper, the best project, and scored highest on the final examination — yet they all got a B for the course, just because they did not adequately participate in class discussions.

During the 1960s, opportunities for post-bachelor education began to proliferate. A serious need for training of administrators to manage schools and programs serving deaf people was identified. A master-level training program in school administration and supervision was established at California

State University, Northridge (then known as San Fernando Valley State College) in 1962. The concept started with an idea by Mary Switzer, the commissioner of the federal Vocational Rehabilitation Commission, and Spencer Tracy's wife, the founder of the John Tracy Clinic. The comprehensive program, with an eight-month classroom and internship stint, could be completed during the spring semester and two summer sessions. For those established in their jobs, the schedule was a major incentive. Monthly stipends from a federal grant were another incentive, especially for those who did not get paid during their leave.

The Leadership Training Program in the Area of the Deaf (LTP), was limited to non-deaf candidates at its onset. Class enrollment was originally limited to ten individuals, but later increased to 15. In 1964, two deaf professionals were admitted to the program for the first time, and later the enrollment consisted of two-thirds non-deaf and one-third deaf students. The program was a trendsetter within deaf education for two major changes: first, it was established at a college that had no previous track record with deafness. Second, the program, by recognizing the potential of deaf persons in administration roles, offered training opportunities to prospective Deaf candidates who wanted to become school or program administrators. The program closed in 1990 after the federal funds were exhausted.

Vocational training was a staple at residential schools for the deaf and offered preparation in trades such as woodworking, printing, upholstery, shoe repair, and tailoring. Some schools offered automobile body or automobile mechanics classes. Trades taught during the early days in some schools included coopering and harness making. *American Annals*[20] listed a total of 57 schools for the deaf, and all but three had vocational departments. Girls usually learned ironing, sewing and cooking. It is believed that Thomas Hopkins Gallaudet and Laurent Clerc brought the concept of vocational training to the United States.[21] Clerc was said to have learned "...to draw and to compose in the printing office of the Institution till 1805."[22]

Although the schools offered excellent vocational training, there were some educators who, since the turn of the twentieth century, advocated a post-secondary trade or vocational training. In June 1965, President Lyndon B. Johnson signed into law a bill establishing the National Technical Institute for the Deaf (NTID) to "...be located in a large metropolitan industrial area..." that would "...be affiliated with a major university for the administration of its program."[23] Twenty-eight colleges and universities applied to establish NTID, and the Rochester Institute of Technology in Rochester, New York, was awarded the contract in 1966. The program opened in 1968 with an enrollment of 71 students.

Currently over 1,500 students are enrolled at NTID, and close to 1,900 students at Gallaudet. Including over 200 deaf students at California State University, Northridge, and many others, it can be conservatively estimated that at least ten thousand deaf youths are in post-secondary programs in at least 75 programs across the country, in either deaf programs or programs with supportive services for deaf students.[24]

Not to be overlooked are the expansion of teacher training programs and interpreter training programs. At least 65 programs across the country offer teacher training programs, mostly at master's degree level, graduating over 600 candidates in 2009.[25] There are at least 70 interpreter preparation programs, at associate, undergraduate, graduate and doctoral levels. Increased opportunities, especially in interpreter training programs, bring about favorable circumstances for a deaf person to pursue higher degrees at his or her choice of programs and locations.

The Deaf Community

The study of the American "deaf world" poses questions: What is the deaf world? Who are the people?

It can be said that the "deaf world"— another phrase for "deaf community"— is composed of mainly Deaf users of sign language. The authors of *A Journey into the DEAF-WORLD* remind readers that "Deaf people in the U.S. use the sign DEAF-WORLD to refer to these relationships among themselves, to the social network they have set up, and not to any notion of geographical location."[26]

For years, deaf people considered themselves part of the "deaf world." During their college years and early adulthood the authors recall the frequent use of the sign DEAF-WORLD by deaf adults. In the years up to the 1980s, "deaf world" was used mostly, but today it is more likely a person says "Deaf community." Although Deaf individuals live and work in the hearing world on a daily basis, many look at the "deaf world" as a place where they can enjoy social events, athletics, entertainment and gatherings with peers they feel most comfortable with.

Interested hearing individuals who sign may be part of this world — such as interpreters, parents of Deaf children, and so forth. Even so, they often may feel unwelcome, or even choose to not fully participate. For example, hearing teachers or rehabilitation counselors who work with Deaf people may choose to socialize outside office hours with hearing counterparts, family and friends.

However, the "Deaf community" is more inclusive and encompasses a wider range of membership, such as parents of deaf children, hearing children of deaf parents, and professionals working with Deaf people. Padden[27] explained that a deaf community may include persons who are not themselves deaf but actively support the goals of the community and work with deaf people to achieve them.

The year 1961 was probably the earliest turning point in the deaf world's annals. Specifically, the *Workshop on Community Development through Organizations of and for the Deaf*, more commonly known as the Fort Monroe Workshop, was the first national workshop to bring together a large group of deaf leaders. Participation was by invitation only, and a total of 69 were invited. Of the 57 attending, 11 were hearing people.[28] Attendees included six printers, five Linotype operators and nine teachers, and the rest were from other fields, including a principal, an aircraft sheet metal mechanic, an architect, a tax attorney and a rubber worker. There were only five female participants.

The workshop, held in Hampton, Virginia, represented "...a sharp break in traditional paternalism; a benchmark in the evolution of the independence of deaf people," wrote the late Boyce Williams of the Office of Vocational Rehabilitation in the Department of Health, Education, and Welfare.[29] Many needs and concerns of deaf people were identified, and ideas led to "a positive impact on the lives of deaf people and the deaf community for years to come...."[30] Although the event's significance has diminished with the passage of time, a major outcome was the identification of a need for a united body to represent deaf people. This led to the formation of a coalition of 18 organizations, the Council of Organizations Serving the Deaf (COSD) in 1967, made possible with seed money from Social and Rehabilitation Services at the Department of Education, Health and Welfare.

Serving as a clearinghouse and contact point for information and advocacy, COSD sponsored nine annual forums. These forums were the conduits through which issues were brought up and identified as action potentials for the headquarters. Federal support dried up in 1973. Unable to maintain its mission with limited funds, COSD was disbanded in 1977.

Recognition of Deaf Culture

The earliest known notion of a Deaf culture was suggested in 1965 by William Stokoe, Ph.D., in *The Dictionary of American Sign Language*.[31] The book was the result of the first attempts in analyzing and categorizing sign language by applying linguistic principles. Based on his observations, Stokoe ventured to describe "social" and "cultural" characteristics of Deaf[32] people who used sign language; "American Sign Language" was not yet widely used.

With the growth of self-awareness and self-actualization, deaf people started to look at their surroundings and existence in society. Stimulated by the recognition of "social" and "cultural" characteristics, some began to explore and document their roles in the community. One can also assume that the 1960s civil rights movement helped prompt the intensification of empowerment among deaf people.

As the 1960s faded into the new decade, awareness grew about the deaf community's uniqueness. The 1970s, as an aftereffect of the 1961 Fort Monroe Workshop, started to witness a turning point. Deaf people shed their traditionally timid and passive roles to assume more assertive roles in their affairs. This transformation happened to coincide with the nationwide rebellion of the American non-deaf youth against society.

In the course of this turbulent period, deaf people started to challenge themselves. More and more deaf people become empowered in pursuing education and therefore became more qualified for professional roles that were more challenging than the then-standby occupations of printing for men and keypunching for women. They began to move into positions requiring decision-making responsibilities. Deaf people, in a way, fostered the unearthing of latent capabilities among themselves. With this increased self-actualization, the emphasis was not to look at hearing loss as a deficiency or pathological condition but as defining a cultural entity.

Eventually, empowered deaf identity-seekers' perspectives became associated with the views of a culture. Probably the best way to describe this transformation is offered by Harvey Corson in his keynote address at the 1991 Deaf Studies for Educators conference:

> Deaf people have a "different center," a world view of our own. It is a world view that, depending on age of onset, type of deafness, and experience, can differ in some personal ways. But as members of a group, as a culture, we share many similarities. Our world view — our center — is visually-based. It is a center that has been passed from one generation to the next by hand, through American Sign Language.
>
> Our world view is shaped by what we have learned through Deaf experience and what we have been taught both formally and informally. As Deaf people, how we see ourselves and view the world, what we have learned and have been taught, have changed in profound ways. The center has shifted — from disability to ability, from handicap to culture, from silent individuals to a vibrant community, from primitive gestures to American Sign Language.[33]

The major drive in the 1990s was an awareness of Deaf culture and the establishment of Deaf studies as a vital and university-level area of inquiry. Their features were explored and analyzed in a series of nine Deaf Studies Conferences sponsored by Gallaudet University. International focus on Deaf culture was shared by at least 12 thousand international participants at the 1989 Deaf Way Conference and the 2002 Deaf Way II Conference, both held in Washington, D.C.

Deaf Identity

Jack Gannon,[34] in reference to personal identity, explains that each of us has many cultural identities that are part of our heritages. The identities, Gannon says, are an outgrowth of our roots, our ancestry, our religious beliefs, our families, and our upbringings, which have been handed down through the generations. Our cultural identities give us values, which vary and reflect the things we cherish. They tell us who we are, where we are from, and where we are going.

Personal identity may emerge from an acceptance of either medical or cultural perspectives. Most Deaf people consider hearing loss as nothing negative, except for perhaps some minor inconveniences established by the majority. Furthermore, personal identity and language choice made by a Deaf person cannot be separated. This means the person will choose which language or variety of languages — ASL, or English — to use, depending on with whom and in which situation. Kannapell[35] states that in order to study a language, one must understand the people who use it and that if ASL is taken away from a person, her/his personal identity as a member of Deaf culture is lost. In other words, to reject a language is to reject the Deaf person.

Historically, Deaf people have acquired Deaf culture through two ways. Those born to Deaf parents typically acquire sign language from their parents and learn the culture through normal interaction with their families and the wider Deaf community. The Deaf children then carry linguistic and cultural knowledge into schools (especially deaf schools), where they play major roles in transmitting the culture and language to their peers. The other way is at state schools that provide the initial introduction to the deaf community through these Deaf children of Deaf parents, and teachers and other staff.

Due to the shift toward school integration since the 1970s, educational settings have changed in ways that now make the positive acquisition of Deaf identity less accessible for deaf children. This is seen especially in programs or settings where a small number of deaf children are taught. Consequently, those children have limited opportunities to mingle with their peers and learn from them, and they lack Deaf role models.

Thus, it seems only appropriate that the family of a deaf child be encouraged to work with deaf people to create positive attitudes and realistic expectations. The deaf child's feelings and perceptions, most of which are formed at home, can have a significant impact on educational performance and achievement. Families are encouraged to take advantage of the plethora of resources relating to deaf people. Families often find it worthwhile to learn sign language in order to communicate with deaf people or ensure that the deaf child's communication and visual needs are met. Meeting deaf adults also provides valuable insight into the deaf community's dynamics.

ADDITIONAL CHARACTERISTICS OF DEAF CULTURE

Deaf culture possesses the common structure of any culture, including behavior developed over many years. Padden advises that culture can be defined as a set of learned behaviors of a group of people who have their own language, values, rules of behavior, and traditions.[36]

It may be helpful to know the characteristics of a culture by reviewing each category and listing traits relevant to Deaf culture. This is not an exhaustive listing; rather, the information presented here may enhance understanding of the basic commonalities among deaf people. The major feature of Deaf culture lies in its language, which will be discussed in depth later. Some of the other learned behaviors include:

Values (Beliefs)

- Respect for ASL as the primary means of communication.
- Respect for eyes and hands.
- Full visual access to information through signs, posters, and visual announcements.
- Full access to captioned videos and movies.
- Availability of qualified interpreters.
- Visual signaling devices (doorbell, phone, alarms).
- Support of Deaf professionals or organizations.

Rules of Behavior

- Maintaining eye contact/gaze during conversation.
- Getting attention by tapping on shoulder or arm, waving, stomping on floor, switching on/off ceiling light or lamp, or throwing soft objects toward the receiver.
- Avoiding situations as standing in front of a bright window, gum chewing, smoking, holding an object while carrying on a conversation. These "visual noises" distract the receiver from reading signs and fingerspelling.

Traditions

- Clubs, private gatherings, community events.
- Sports, table and board games.
- Oral history, Deaf humor, ASL poetry, folklore, storytelling.
- Mime, plays and skits.

Norms

- Including a variety of information in introductions, such as background, education and family ties.
- Dating or marrying other Deaf people.
- Sharing news that often travels quickly (this existed even before the Internet or other technology existed).

Tapping on another's body in order to get attention (instead of yelling) might get a deaf person in trouble. Deaf persons often pat or tap people without looking and are given surprised looks by strangers who wonder why they are being touched. Most of time, the consequences — after explanation — are humorous.

Hazards of Deaf Culture © 1994 Heriberto Quinones.

PERSONALIZED NAME SIGNS

When the authors were born, their Deaf parents gave them name signs. For Melvia, her parents decided on an /MM/ handshape spelling sideways twice in signing space in front of the signer to represent the initial letters of her first and last name. Ron was christened with the name sign containing an /R/ handshape tapping on a single location on the chest. The authors also gave their Deaf daughter, Jamie, a twisting /J/ handshape name sign.

One receives a name sign from peers, family or school personnel. A name sign is of great value to a Deaf person because, without it, he or she would have no effective means for identifying himself/herself. Possessing a name sign actually marks a deaf person's participation in the Deaf community.[37] However, there are some exceptions. If the name is short with only two or three letters, or can be spelled smoothly or flowingly, the name may be spelled. For example, it is often easier to spell J-O-E than to create name signs. Longer names like M-A-R-Y and W-A-L-L-Y may also be easy to spell.

Sam Supalla[38] identified two broad categories of the ASL name sign system used exclusively among Deaf people. Name signs are created to describe a person (descriptive name sign or DNS) or arbitrarily (arbitrary name sign or ANS). For example, the name signs of both authors are arbitrary since they do not describe any physical characteristics. Eighty-one percent of American name signs are ANS.

In the United States, name signs appear to have been used as far back as the founding of the first American school for deaf students. Thomas Hopkins Gallaudet, Laurent Clerc, and Edward Miner Gallaudet had name signs (see illustrations below). It is not known if name signs were used in Europe, or if Clerc brought his name sign to America from France.

| Clerc's Descriptive Name Sign | T.H. Gallaudet's Descriptive Name Sign | E. M. Gallaudet's Arbitrary Name Sign |

Left: Clerc's descriptive name sign. *Middle:* THG's descriptive name sign. *Right:* EMG's arbitrary name sign. Sign illustrations by Paul Setzer, reproduced with permission from *The Book of Name Signs*, DawnSignPress.

Handshapes, location, and movement are governed by linguistic rules. For an ANS sign, the initial letter of a person's name — such as a /C/ handshape for Charlotte — may shake sideways in the signer's natural space; be tapped on a single location on the body such as the shoulder, chin or arm; or be used in a dual location on the body.

DNS signs are derived from distinctive physical appearances or behavior, e.g., hairstyle, a birthmark on a cheek, or even slow walking. DNS signs can be either negative or positive. Name signs for Gallaudet and Clerc fit into the DNS category. THG wore glasses, so the GLASSES sign was used, probably also because his last name began with the letter G. The sign for Clerc was because he had a scar on his cheek caused by a burn during his youth. The sign for Edward Miner Gallaudet, however, is classified as an ANS sign because the initial letter M was used to represent his middle name.

In getting acquainted with each other, first and last names are typically fingerspelled. Sometimes a person will volunteer his name sign during an introduction, or either person will learn of the name sign through a third party. Addressing deaf persons by their sign names communicates a sense of familiarity.

An interesting use of name signs was related by the late Dorothy Miles, who attended a school for the deaf in England. She explained in the play *The Third Eye* that the students knew each other by the number of the coat hooks assigned to them. She claimed that even after the students had finished schooling, they still remembered each other for years by their unique numbers instead of their name. Similar sign-naming on basis of locker numbers has been noted during the early days at Lexington School for the Deaf.[39]

Three-Fingered Salute

A well-known gesture, the I-Love-You (ILY) sign was first expressed in 1905.[40] Somehow, this symbol died away afterward. Instant fame for the ILY sign was resurrected in the mid–1970s after several presidential candidates, such as Gerald Ford and Jimmy Carter, flashed the sign to the deaf community. Nowadays, many feel that the symbol has become so overexposed that some catalogues or some conference exhibits show nothing but the ILY symbol in the forms of jewelry, mugs, key chains, magnets, T-shirts, and the like. Some deaf people collect ILY products, while others are sick of such products. Yet many do use the ILY handshape to greet or bid farewell to their loved ones either in person or via videophones.

ILY sign courtesy of Ruth Peterson.

VIEWPOINTS ON DEAF CULTURE

Artist Ann Silver, who is Deaf, explains in the exhibit brochure for *20 Deaf Artists: Common Motifs*, "Centuries ago we were a box of crayons, not human beings." She further elaborates on her illustration of the two sets of crayons, saying the then "pathological, medical, and audiological viewpoints" represent the "anomalous descriptors" bestowed on deaf people. Interestingly, the "seeing" crayon represents deaf people who depend on sight for input, as compared to hearing people who depend on their ears. The "CODA" crayon is an acronym for (hearing) Children of Deaf Adults. As a whole, the newer set of crayons represents a greater diversity in the deaf community.

Shane Feldman, a former editor of *NADmag*, recalls being offended when being told he wasn't part of Deaf culture. Feldman attended a mainstream program and then attended the Model Secondary School for the Deaf for two years before graduating from a public high school. He also attended the National Institute for the Deaf and Rochester Institute of Technology. One of his friends described him by signing "hearing" on the forehead, indicating that he was more like a hearing person or "thinks hearing." As a result, he surveyed persons of various backgrounds about Deaf culture and shared their opinions in an issue of *NADmag*.[41]

Feldman concluded that the comments showed different perspectives on Deaf culture and that there were no right or wrong answers. Experience, age

Deaf identity crayons: then and now. © 1999 Ann Silver. All rights reserved.

and background seemed to account for the differences in perspectives. However, it can be determined that even with differences, they share common language, values, rules of behavior, and traditions.

It is interesting to note that Deaf culture exists even in countries where there is no formal organization of deaf people and where deaf people have social lives or informal meetings, as viewed by renowned Deaf sociologist Yerker Andersson, Ph.D. Through his lifelong involvement in international affairs, Andersson expands on the fact that deaf people adapt for survival in society to meet their unique human needs. In sociology, Deaf culture and sign language are considered "cultural universals" since they exist in all or most of the countries around the world, even if sign language differs from country to country.[42]

DIVERSITY IN DEAF CULTURE

Like other cultures, Deaf culture cannot be narrowly described or defined, since the characteristics and traits of Deaf and hard of hearing people are so varied. Diverse factors include age, economic class, race, ethnic background, geographic origin, religious background, gender, abilities, hearing status, vision status, language, personal and family influences, education, and cultural influences. In sum, it has been suggested by Oscar Cohen, Ph.D., a former superintendent of a school for the deaf, that "Deafness make one no less a member of a racial, linguistic, or ethnic group."[43]

Although today's society has begun to recognize and embrace cultural diversity, a question about a Deaf or hard of hearing person who may also have an ethnic identity has surfaced and been debated: do they consider themselves as Deaf people first, or as members of their ethnic groups first? In a 1989 study, 87 percent of a sampling of 60 members of the black Deaf community in Washington, D.C., identified themselves as Black before Deaf.[44] The interesting part was that a majority of the 13 percent who identified themselves as Deaf first came from Deaf families and were more integrated into the Deaf community than the others. On the other hand, respondents who identified themselves as Black first felt that their ethnic identity was more visible than their Deaf identity and wanted respect for their ethnicity before their deafness. However, all respondents agreed that there exists a Deaf culture. As Carolyn McCaskill-Emerson eloquently described it,

> Our deafness is the common thread that brings us together to make a beautiful quilt. The beautiful quilt is made up of deaf and hard of hearing people who are African American, Native American, Hispanic American, Asian American, and European America. We each have a culture within the large culture.[45]

The study supports the notion that heavy influence comes from the family's ethnic culture. It is understandable that American Deaf people in general share common interests and values based mostly on vision. But when it comes to the culture(s) they acquire from their families, Deaf people cherish and are proud of their identities. African American, Hispanic/Latino American, Asian American, and Native American cultures are major cultures within the Deaf community. Scandinavians, French people, and Germans also celebrate with their own ethnic groups. Non-cultural groups that share common particular interests while embracing Deaf culture traits include women; gay/lesbian/bisexual/transgendered people; hard of hearing, deaf-blind, and late-deafened people; and even senior citizens. A look at the deaf community gives a great sense of the larger American community.

With the increased awareness of diversity in today's nation, and especially in the school populace, it behooves the school to expose its students to multicultural education. As McCaskill-Emerson, Ph.D.,[46] puts it, most schools use a Eurocentric curriculum that does not adequately prepare students to live in a multicultural society. Children of color know much about the history, values, and culture of European Americans, but lack knowledge of their own culture. This is also true of Deaf culture. Deaf studies and diversity awareness have been added to the curriculum at many schools, especially those with large deaf and multicultural school populations. Introduction to Deaf culture courses also have been added to ASL curricula.

Evolution of the Deaf Community

Like everybody else, Deaf people have specific needs and yearn for a sense of belonging. Informal and formal possibilities are available through belonging to various groups in various forms, especially at the local level — such as being an interested visitor, through partial or full membership, or through subscriptions to newsletters and publications.

Changes in the Deaf community have evolved over the years. Those attending residential schools created lifelong friendships nurtured at school. They were more likely to live in high-density settings, e.g., large cities, where they maintained close touch with their peers through deaf clubs, deaf picnics, and other gatherings such as through church. Through a sense of belonging to a group, the lives of deaf people were centered on their local deaf clubs. Deaf strangers coming from other towns often sought deaf clubs as places of sanctuary and access to guidance from the local folks. In many places, club-houses were owned and maintained by the deaf club members themselves.

However, because of deaf people's diversified backgrounds in the late 1900s, a new breed has emerged. It appears that modern-day generations have different perceptions of societal obligations and are more individualistic as an outcome of having easy access to information.

FIVE

Recognition of ASL as a Language

From Gestures to Sign Language

Sign language may have preceded voice languages by millions of years. Most anthropologists believe that spoken language evolved from gestures or signs rather than directly from speech. As mentioned in the first chapter, anthropologist Gordon Hewes argued that about four million years ago the first human-animals, *australopithecines*, communicated with each other using their hands — possibly to give directions or to ask for help in locating things such as tools. Australopithecines lived in southern and western Africa and likely did not have any speech; rather, they screamed, grunted, and babbled.

Michael Corballis, a psychology professor at New Zealand's Auckland University, wrote that gestural communication was much more effective than vocal communication among pre-human ancestors for two reasons: (1) gestures are silent, so as not to alert prey of one's presence, and (2) gestures provide information in a spatial manner, such as pointing and describing shapes.[1] He further explained that vision in animals, like monkeys, is much more developed than other senses, including hearing. He mentioned the research on three signing gorillas — Washoe, Tatu, and Koko — who were successfully taught several hundred signs representing objects or actions. Koko had a sign language vocabulary of over 1,000 words, mostly in ASL.[2]

Stokoe began his exploration of the origins of sign language with a quotation from Democritus, a Greek philosopher who lived from 460 to B.C. 370: "Everything existing in the universe is the fruit of chance and necessity...."[3] Stokoe then used that quotation to trace the development of language in humans, from gesture to language to speech. He further elaborated that chance brought human ancestors down from the trees to the ground, freeing their hands for gesture, and then sign language, a progression that came from the necessity to communicate. The gestures then evolved over thousands of years into spoken language.

In Latin, the term *language* means tongue. Stokoe disagreed and insisted that "...[language] is a cognitive system linked to some kind of physical system ... language is not something done by the mouth. Language is something done by the brain, and the mouth happens to be one way it can come out."[4]

VISUAL-GESTURAL LANGUAGE

As noted in Chapter One, the use of gestures most likely preceded the use of signs by thousands of years. Gestures are enhanced by facial expressions, which add different shades of meanings. Baker and Cokely[5] wrote that ASL is a *visual-gestural* language created by Deaf people. They further stated that ASL grammar involves the use of the signer's eyes, face, head, body posture, hands and arms.

Stokoe, in his foreword to Eastman's *Mime to Signs,* suggested, "That is how sign language began. It is not just another language with rules and vocabulary to memorize. Sign language is a way of expressing with the body instead of voice, what one has to say along with the appropriate feelings...."[6]

A unique characteristic of ASL is that it is capable of expressing three-dimensional ideas. Fingers and hands play roles in expressing details. They:

- represent three-dimensional shapes (ball, cone, cylinder and box) to add depth and definition
- demonstrate change in size, such as an expanding or deflating balloon
- describe height, width, interior or exterior space
- describe people and objects in action

Eastman advised that, when talking with Deaf persons, mime or gestures are not used, although they are valued. Rather, words and ideas are best expressed through sign language.

SPOKEN AND SIGNED LANGUAGES

Although language has evolved from gestures to spoken language, spoken and written languages have become people's major communication means. However, written language has a chief advantage: it can be recorded easily for posterity, akin to drawings on cave walls or cuneiforms. Spoken and written languages have become more sophisticated the longer humans have lived on the earth.

As the saying goes, "Knowledge is power." The following presents a parallel between spoken language and signed language as illustrated in Bob Johnson's *Tree of Language.*[7]

Although people around the world speak and sign in different languages,

languages are similar in structure, e.g., spoken words have consonants and vowels, while signed words have holds and movements.

Spoken word in any language includes consonants and vowels influenced by

- where the tongue is
- where the lips are
- if the voice is on or off.

Signed word in any language include holds and movements:

- handshape
- position of hand
- orientation of hand.

Sign Language Engraved in Deaf History

As discussed in an earlier chapter, signs were already used in America long before the 1817 establishment of the American Asylum of the Deaf and Dumb in Hartford. Fortunately, documentation exists of signs used on Martha's Vineyard prior to 1817. This information, shared by Nancy Jo Frishberg at the 1995 Deaf Studies IV conference in Massachusetts, indicates that some signs were similar to ASL, but the expressions have evolved over the years.[8] She referred to her previous study[9] and an interesting observation by Baker and Padden[10] that some signs that used to require one hand now require two hands, while others are now produced with one hand. As Baker and Padden explain, signs are to be seen — thus, ASL signs are developed according to the boundaries of the human visual system.

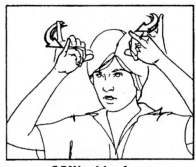 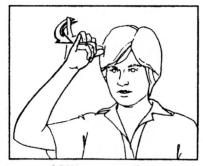

COW: older form   **COW: present form**

COW (older and present forms) © 1978 Carol Padden.

Historical Changes in ASL and MVSL [11]

In ASL, one-handed signs below the neck tend to become two-handed.

- In ASL, the sign for MAD used to be one-handed and became two-handed.
- In MVSL, the sign for MAD was one-handed.

In ASL, two-handed signs in contact with the face tend to become one-handed.

- In ASL, the signs for DEVIL and COW used to be two-handed and are now one-handed.
- In MVSL, DEVIL and COW were two-handed.

Sign production tends to become more fluid by dropping parts of a sign.

- In ASL, the old sign for BIRD was BEAK+WINGS; now it is signed BEAK.
- In MVSL, ASL's old form BEAK+WINGS was maintained.

In the process of producing signs more fluidly, sometimes MVSL and ASL took divergent paths.

- In ASL, the old sign for HOME was signed EAT+SLEEP. However, modern ASL uses a fluid movement of similar handshapes to create one sign instead of two.
- MVSL retained only the SLEEP portion for HOME.

POSSIBLE HISTORICAL SOURCES OF MODERN ASL

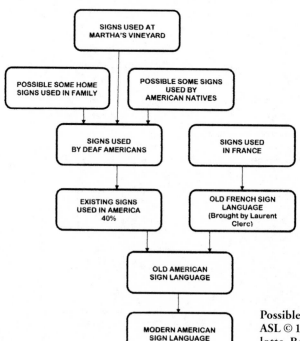

The illustration on the left, adapted from the original chart by Baker and Cokely,[12] shows how ASL has evolved over the years.

Early research by linguist James Woodward[13] concluded that 60 percent of the signs used in America during the early 1800s originated with French signs brought to Hartford by Clerc. The study determined that the other 40 percent came from unknown sources. Woodward based his

Possible Historical Sources of Modern ASL © 1980 Dennis Cokely and Charlotte Baker-Shenk. Reprinted with permission.

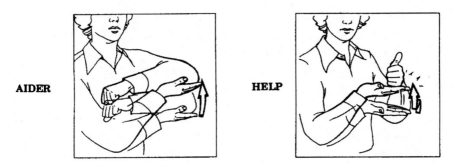

AIDER-HELP © 1980, Dennis Cokely and Charlotte Baker-Shenk. Reprinted with permission.

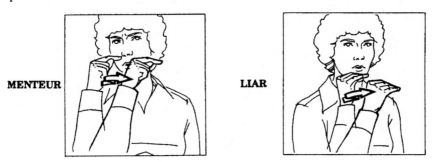

MENTEUR-LIAR © 1980 Dennis Cokely and Charlotte Baker-Shenk. Reprinted with permission.

findings on the study of "sign cognates" to identify the relationships between French and American signs. Two examples are shown above.

Information about Martha's Vineyard Sign Language, as described in Chapter Two, was published for the first time in 1980 by Nora Ellen Groce. It is safe to assume that most of the remaining 40 percent of the signs came from Martha's Vineyard, in addition to home signs within families and signs used by Native Americans, as shown in Figure 3.

Interestingly, one of the oldest signs that Deaf people have unconsciously refused to give up is the sign for INSTITUTE (both hands form an "I" handshape and tap

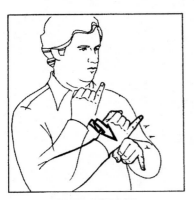

STATE-SCHOOL © 1980 Dennis Cokely and Charlotte Baker-Shenk. Reprinted with permission.

STATE-SCHOOL

the "I" handshape upon a closed fist). Many people still sign that to represent a residential school for deaf students although the word *institution* is not identified with schools for the deaf anymore.

LANGUAGE AND SIGN LANGUAGE

When laws were passed shortly after the Civil War making education compulsory, one of the underlying motives was to establish English as the majority language so that it would be a unifying influence on the diverse cultures present in the United States at that time. Large numbers of immigrants were arriving from Asia and Europe with their own languages and customs. Most freed slaves were illiterate and had to be educated to assimilate into society. Compulsory education and English language were viewed by many as the means for saving the Union by homogenizing all these diverse elements among American citizens.

The result, at least, was a partial success. The Union survived but at the cost of many cultural traditions. Many Indian tribal languages and customs were suppressed, as were the languages spoken by many immigrants. Alexander Graham Bell, a highly influential figure of that period, considered sign language a foreign language that should not be taught in the public schools. Sign language for deaf students was one of many casualties.

LEARNING IN OLD SCHOOLS

A common experience within the Deaf community was when Deaf children, especially those from hearing families, entered school not knowing they had names. Students learned sign language among themselves, or those who came from homes with deaf parents or siblings brought signs.

Author Ronald recalls vividly the time he entered the school at the age of six. He amazed older dormitory kids with his ability to sign from the first day; he had learned it from his deaf parents and sister prior to entering school. Ronald was more surprised to notice that none of his dormitory peers knew how to fingerspell. The dorm counselors had little or no sign skills, so Ronald introduced fingerspelling to his peers. Two years later, after he moved to an older boys' dorm, fingerspelling was no longer used nor encouraged in the younger dormitory as there were no newer role models to emulate.

Sign language, although it was the main form of communication among students (and some dorm counselors and teachers), was not formally taught in the classrooms at all. The irony is that in the classroom they were often first taught — remember they were Deaf children who never learned to speak — to pronounce and speak their name, then to print their name, then later given a name sign before finally learning how to fingerspell their names.

In addition, for years, Deaf-school children were required to memorize the definitions of noun, verb, adjectives, adverbs, and other parts of English grammar. They were also drilled on the correct usage of English grammar. Many older deaf people recall the use of Barry Five-Slate, Fitzgerald Key or Wing's Symbols as a crutch to help them develop written English. Some also remember sentence diagramming. Yet no classroom time was ever devoted to ASL.

Fortunately, today's practices have changed: the bilingual approach utilizing both ASL and English is used in most classrooms, although many still lack bilingual education. Students typically learn their name sign first, then fingerspell their names before learning how to write and/or pronounce their names.

EARLIER BOOKS ON SIGN LANGUAGE

Until Stokoe's work, people were not aware of the fact that ASL had its own grammar, structure and vocabulary. It wasn't something they considered. The authors recall their parents calling their communication "signing." Static pictures in early sign language books — such as J. Schuyler Long's 1910 *The Sign Language: A Manual of Signs* and John W. Michaels' 1923 *Handbook of the Sign Language of the Deaf*— emphasized the production of correct signs to accompany words; they were early sign language dictionaries.

Back in those days, correct formation of signs was the main topic whenever signs were discussed, until the 1960s when sign language was discovered to possess certain characteristics and patterns. Initially, signs were thought of as communication that could not be dissected and as lacking internal structure or individual components. Later, researchers discovered that signs had characteristics such as phonology, morphology, and syntax, and much more. This discovery, however, initially met with much resistance, even from Deaf people themselves.

Birth of ASL Research

The concept of "linguistics" pertaining to sign language was unheard of. Yet an unassuming man dared to analyze the language of Deaf people.

During the early 1960s, the study of structural linguistics became more commonplace among American colleges and universities, although it was still a raw, pioneering field. This emerging field originated in Europe as a part of a movement to compare languages of the world. Ordinarily in linguistics, (spoken) languages were described according to design and sound structures, the organization of morphemes and vocabulary, and sentence structures. European linguists argued that by coding these structures, languages could be more easily compared, and histories of language families could be tracked over time.[14] Stokoe, hired to chair the Gallaudet University English department in 1955, was fascinated by the sign language used by his students. A hearing person, he had no previous experience with sign language, nor was he exceptionally fluent in the language. Yet he was convinced that sign language contained highly developed linguistics. With a grant, he established the Linguistics Research Laboratory in 1957.

The Gallaudet community, as well as the Deaf community, was initially not supportive of the project or any sign language research — in fact, many considered the work a waste of time and money. Stokoe's grant was mentioned in the *Washington Star*, a now-defunct daily newspaper. Two letters to the editor protesting the award were printed on March 26, 1960. Helen E. Waite, who authored a book on Helen Keller and Anne Sullivan, was "...appalled ... for the purpose of teaching his new sign system of a single language for the deaf! Sign language should be as extinct as the dodo bird!"[15] The second letter came from a granddaughter of Alexander Graham Bell, who wrote, "...cruel that education in teaching speech and reading of the lips to the deaf should

Dr. Carl Cronenberg (left), Dr. Dorothy Casterline and Dr. William Stokoe. Photograph © Gallaudet University Archives.

go backwards.... There is no need for the deaf to have a sign language or to be isolated in a gesturing silent world of their own."[16]

This didn't faze Stokoe, who, along with two Deaf colleagues from the English Department, Carl Cronenberg, Ph.D., and Dorothy Casterline, Ph.D., filmed Deaf people signing. They analyzed the signs for patterns over several years. The team discovered that signs naturally followed specific rules. Furthermore, similar rules in signing were identified among other people who did not participate in the study.

EARLY FINDINGS

In 1960, Stokoe published his findings in a book, *Sign Language Structure: An Outline of the Visual Communication Systems of the American Deaf.* His research showed that sign language was a complete and complex language distinct from English. He claimed that sign language, although in a visual mode, was more than gestures and that it was a true language in itself. A subsequent publication, *A Dictionary of American Sign Language*, was authored by Stokoe, Casterline and Cronenberg in 1965. In the dictionary, signs were listed not only by their translations in English, but also by their internal structure — the combination of handshapes, locations, and movements, which they described as:

(a) Handshape: how the fingers are extended and bent in a particular sign — in the hand, or fist — or does it have some fingers extended, etc., called *tab* (or *tabula*).

(b) Location: where on the body or in space is the sign being made? On the cheek, the chest, in front of the body, etc., identified as *dez* (or *designator*)

(c) Movement: how does the hand (or hands) move? In a circle, up-and-down, forward, etc., identified as *sig* (or *signation*).

Stokoe and his team identified 19 handshapes, 12 locations and 24 movements present in sign language. Yet, instead of being praised for his efforts, he was reviled and ridiculed by many within the Deaf community. The dictionary drew criticism and anger because he, as a hearing man and an outsider, invented "new" terms such as "chereme" for gesture, "tab" for handshape, "dez" for location and "sig" for movement.[17] People were also unaccustomed to the new term, "American Sign Language."

A probable reason for the negativity was the social and intellectual climate of people, both deaf and hearing, during the 1950s and 1960s that did not click with Stokoe's work. People simply thought sign language was an extension of English and resented a hearing man's seemingly arrogant work. Yet

Stokoe did not quit; he continually discussed his work by lecturing and writing other books. During the 1970s, people's attitudes began to change — perhaps as an extension of the country's freethinking culture. People began to realize that there indeed existed a Deaf culture, one that centered on sign language, or now ASL. Stokoe's work provided a firm base on which later investigations of ASL were made.

Stokoe's influence can be summed by the words of a former research assistant, who is now a Department of ASL and Deaf Studies professor at Gallaudet University. MJ Bienvenu, Ph.D., says, "I remember the day when I finally realized ASL is indeed a language — the day my life changed. It is hard to imagine me signing ASL all my life but needing a person like [Stokoe] to recognize that it is a language. It takes a genius to be objective and notice things so obvious and so close to us, and that's what [Stokoe] was, a genius."[18]

Stokoe and his colleagues created groundbreaking work that started a ripple effect giving birth to additional theories and ideas for a new group of researchers and linguists throughout the world. They, in turn, have discovered additional patterns and continue to expand this information in related fields such as ASL linguistics, Deaf studies, and sign language interpreting. Additionally, upon being recognized as a true language, ASL has merited respect within the educational field as a bona fide language in schools and colleges. Stokoe, who retired in 1984 and passed away in 2000, is now considered the "Father of American Sign Language Linguistics."

THE SALK INSTITUTE

An early supporter of Stokoe's research came from Ursula Bellugi, Ed.D., and her husband Edward Klima. They were invited by Jonas Salk to set up a small research unit at the Salk Institute in San Diego. Previously, they had visited with Washoe, the signing chimpanzee, in its habitat in Reno, Nevada, had studied language acquisition among hearing children, and decided to research language acquisition among deaf children of deaf parents.

Bellugi, after two years of research, was convinced that ASL had its own grammatical properties.[19] Bellugi and Klima adopted Stokoe's model of the three parameters (handshape, location, and movement), and suggested that there were additional features. The early years of research at the Salk Institute were focused on ASL's morphological processes. Bellugi's and Klima's 1979 *The Signs of Language* was acclaimed as the most important work of their research. Many present-day categorizations of ASL linguistics got their beginnings at Salk Institute; there were only two other linguistic laboratories at the time, including one at Northeastern University in Boston.

What, Exactly, Is ASL?

At the heart of every community is a language. As explained by Baker and Cokely,[20] a language embodies the thoughts and experiences of its users. Inspired by the work of Stokoe and the expanding research, Baker and Cokely, both hearing sign language teachers, incorporated ASL structure in their teaching materials instead of stressing only sign language vocabulary. They enlisted the help of 15 of the nation's leading sign language researchers and teachers; of the 15, eight were native signers. The material then became two teachers' resource books, one containing grammar and culture for ASL teachers and the second one containing curriculum, methods and evaluation. The books, published in 1980, were accompanied by a set of three student textbooks. Today, the books are often referred to as the "green books."

Baker and Padden[21] and Baker and Cokely[22] wrote that ASL was a visual-gestural language created by Deaf people in America and in part of Canada.

What is meant by visual?

1. Since American Sign Language uses body movements instead of sound, listeners use their eyes instead of their ears to understand what is being said.
2. Because all linguistic information must be received through the eyes, the language is carefully structured to fit the needs and capabilities of the eyes.

What is meant by gestural?

1. The units of ASL are composed of specific movements and shapes of the hands and arms, eyes, face, head and body posture.
2. These movements or gestures serve as the words and intonation of the language.

Other points they made were that like spoken English, ASL possesses its own phonology, morphology and syntax, and that ASL is not:

- An aural/oral language.
- A universal language.
- A written language.
- All iconic (picture-like).
- Equaling the grammar and structure of spoken English.

The viewpoint that ASL lacks grammar or is "broken English" usually stems from attempted translations using English words in ASL order. This is based on the assumption that ASL must be structured exactly like English.

An English sentence might read like this: Have you been to San Francisco? The sentence, expressed in ASL, would be TOUCH FINISH SAN FRAN-CISCO YOU?, with various grammatical markers that cannot be recorded in writing. This creates the incorrect assumption that ASL is broken English. Once again, ASL has its own vocabulary, grammar, and structure unrelated to English.[23] Also, ASL does not have a written language, nor is it a code for English. Therefore it cannot be translated word-for-word in English.

How ASL Builds Signs: Selected Studies on ASL Phonology

The subsequent sections will introduce interesting research findings on ASL linguistics. As you read, consider how linguists have dissected ASL into components and identified the language's phonology, morphology, and syntax. This chapter does not intend to be a treatise but is simply a presentation on ASL's many facets and its role as Deaf people's versatile, visual language.

Comparing, grouping, and classifying signs according to what parts they have in common and what parts they do not is *not* simply a convenience for organizing dictionaries. Like words, signs must be categorized into parts in order to perceive their meanings.[24]

At the beginning of his study, Stokoe proposed what are now commonly known as three independent parts of a sign: (a) handshape, (b) location, and (c) movement. These three parts of a sign are called parameters. He eventually created a system with 19 different basic symbols for handshapes, 12 different basic symbols for locations, and 24 different basic symbols for types of movements.[25]

Approximately ten years later, at least three investigators[26] agreed that the description of hand orientation was necessary to distinguish signs such as SHORT and TRAIN. Thus, palm orientation became the fourth parameter.

Examples of these parameters include:

- Handshape (CHURCH, DUTY) Represent different handshape, but similar in other parameters.
- Location (STAY, SAME) represent different locations, but similar in other parameters.
- Movement (ZERO, PERCENT) represent different movement, but similar in other parameters.
- Orientation (LECTURE, WILL) represent different palm orientation, but similar in other parameters.

Later on, non-manual signals, or facial behaviors, were adopted as the fifth parameter. Researchers reasoned that facial expressions are an important component of any discourse.[27]

In everyday conversations among Deaf signers, one can observe that all five parameters, especially non-manual signals, dominate particularly among native signers or those who have signed long enough to acquire the nuances of ASL.

How ASL Changes Meanings: Selected Studies on ASL Morphology

Linguists defined morphology as a study of word formation, of how words are formed to build new words or signs. Morphemes are found in areas of noun-verb pairs, compounds, contractions, classifiers, and inflectional processes. Deaf people have used and appreciated ASL for years, but many might not realize that there are basically similar patterns in some signs, both at the phonological level and at the morphology level. An example of morpheme is a noun-verb pair; the sign for FLY and PLANE are similar since they possess the same parameters. However, since FLY is a verb and PLANE is a noun, they have different characteristics.

In another instance, morphemes, in both spoken English and ASL, are combined to create a new word, or compounds. The process of compounding is often a very useful and productive means of enlarging a language's vocabulary. Some examples of spoken English compounds include icebox, spaceship, microwave, greenhouse, and breakfast.

ASL compounds are created from two separate signs, which then work together like one sign. An earlier cited example is the sign for HOME, which emerged from SLEEP and EAT. Like assimilation in spoken English, when a compound is widely used for a long time, the form changes, and the two words become one. In ASL assimilation, two signs begin to look more like each other in the process and become one sign.

How ASL Arranges Sign Order: Selected Studies on Syntax

Sentence types in *spoken* English are shown mostly through inflections in voice. Sentence types in *written* English are revealed through punctuation such as question marks or exclamation marks. In ASL, linguists have identified facial and body behavior that determine sentence types. It was not until the early 1980s that Scott Liddell[28] provided the earliest discussion on ASL syntax.

Seven basic sentence types in ASL have been identified by Baker and Cokely,[29] and Valli, Lucas and Mulrooney[30]:

- Declarative sentences (most basic sentence in ASL; do not seem to be marked by one particular non-manual signal like other sentence types)
- Three types of questions:
    - YES-NO are questions that normally require a yes or no answer. The question being asked by the inquirer is usually accompanied by nonmanual signals, such as a forward tilt of the head and body, raised eyebrows, and widened eyes.
    - WH-word question (asking a question starting with WHAT, WHEN, WHERE, WHY, WHO or even HOW and HOW MANY; the interrogative signs can occur either at the beginning of the sentence or at the end)
    - Rhetorical question (abstract question, or question not requiring an answer; a way to draw attention to the information supplied; the interrogative signs include WHY, WHAT, WHO and HOW)
- Conditionals (indicates an action will be taken pending another action)
- Negation/Assertion (negation indicates something is not true or did not happen; assertion emphasizes that something is true, did happen, or will happen)
- Commands (give an order to do something, emphasizing the action word [verb] by making the sign faster and sharper)
- Topicalization (indicates what topic to discuss, then to make a statement, or question about the topic; often known as topic-comment)
- Relative clauses (identify a specific person or thing to be discussed)

As mentioned earlier, non-manual signals, rather than signs themselves, often determine the sentence types used in ASL. The signs of a sentence may be identical in production, but it is the non-manuals that create the different meanings.

In summary, try to observe how each sentence in the following three different sentence types is made with appropriate facial expression and head behavior.

Questions	Commands	Declarative Statements
Brows squint or raise, forward tilting of the head	Forward tilting of the head, frown; strong signs	Brows relax; nodding of head
YOU GO?	YOU GO!	YOU GO
DOG FIND?	DOG FIND!	DOG FIND
LETTER WRITE?	LETTER WRITE!	LETTER WRITE

A Recipe for ASL

½ cup refined American signs;
¼ cup natural gestures;
¼ cup of American manual alphabet;
1 cup facial expressions;

Mix all ingredients gracefully in the Deaf Community, then...

Sprinkle with a handful of care;
Add a dash of visual love;
Brush with bodily energy;
Pour in DEAF Culture;

Add DEAF pride to suit your taste.
Serve as a communication feast
for all to enjoy!—*Gil Eastman*[31]

In Retrospect

Much has happened since the early days of pioneering linguistic research on "sign language." It is evident from studies, and people's experiences, that ASL is a beautiful and unique language in its own right. It seems almost contradictory that research into ASL was originated by "an English professor who could not sign his way out of a wet paper bag," as Lou Fant[32] said. However, in fairness, Stokoe did have a passable command of ASL, and his revolutionary discovery about sign language, along with unmatchable contributions to language study in ASL, was valuable. Mervin Garretson perhaps succinctly expresses it best[33]:

> To know, once and for all, that
> our "primitive" and "ideographic gestures" are really
> a formal language on par with all other languages
> of the world is a step toward pride and liberation.

SIX

Expansion of Visual Languages

Historical Influences on Some ASL Signs

A unique characteristic of any language is that it changes over time, and this change is continual. This is true for ASL, which experiences changes constantly. In the late 1800s, many signs were made on the waist or lower chest; those signs have, through time, moved higher and are now predominantly produced in the upper chest or neck regions. An example is the sign for WILL. As shown below, the older version started at the waist; currently, the movement starts at the head.

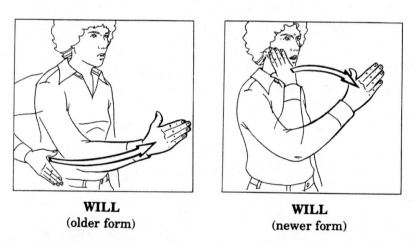

WILL
(older form)

WILL
(newer form)

WILL (older and newer forms) © 1980 Dennis Cokely and Charlotte Baker-Shenk. Reprinted with permission.

Some of the older signs were more picturesque in bodily actions (and perhaps more gestural to show action). Two other examples of how signs have become more compact include GUIDE and SUPPORT.

116

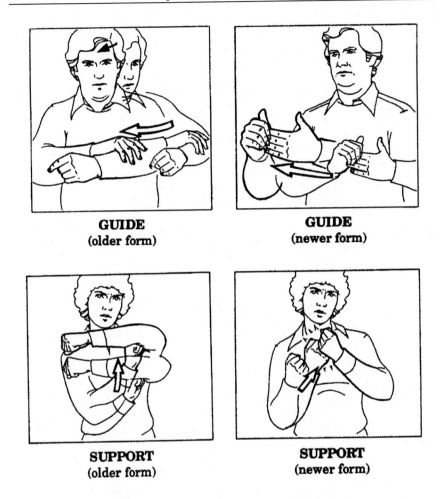

GUIDE, SUPPORT (older and newer forms) © 1980 Dennis Cokely and Charlotte Baker-Shenk. Reprinted with permission.

Researchers suggest that this shift occurs because of what they term high visual acuity. In conversation, signers tend to fix their gaze on the lower part of the signer's face; therefore, sign movements have evolved toward a smaller space.

Often, older signers have ways of signing that differ from younger signers. The old form and the new form may co-exist for a while, and then the old form may disappear along with those signers' passing. This process is called *historical change*. The table below shows examples of old signs that have changed over the years. Most of the changes are made with one or more parameters, usually handshape or location.

Sign	Old Form	Present Form
MEMBER	JOIN+PERSON	BENT-B handshape moving from shoulder to shoulder
RABBIT	(2h) wiggle U handshape on each side of forehead	Same handshape being made on hands in neutral space
TELEPHONE	Using both hands with one S handshape on ear and another S handshape on chin	Y handshape on cheek

Some other changes are subtle, but interesting. For instance, the sign for LAST has evolved from using the index finger to the little finger — probably to emphasize the *finality* of the matter. DEPEND has the index finger of the dominant hand pressing upon the non-dominant hand, which is in a "B" handshape. The modern version shows only the index finger of the non-dominant hand.

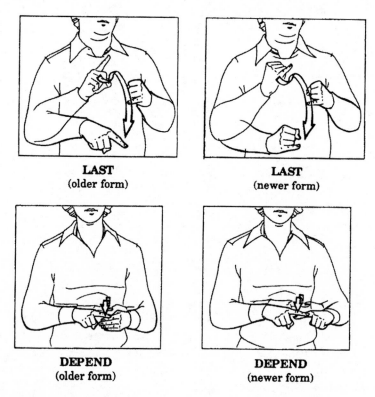

LAST
(older form)

LAST
(newer form)

DEPEND
(older form)

DEPEND
(newer form)

LAST, DEPEND (older and newer forms) © 1980 Dennis Cokely and Charlotte Baker-Shenk. Reprinted with permission.

GENERATIONAL GAPS

Often elderly signers retain old-time signs while younger signers use newer versions common among their peers. The authors recall that during their school days they would bring home signs they learned from their peers at school, only to discover that their parents did not understand the newer signs and would often scoff at the "new" signs. On the other hand, sometimes the authors brought to school some signs that they normally used with their parents at home and were put down by their peers.

Proliferation of Sign Systems

The initial identification of ASL by Stokoe and his colleagues, as described in the previous chapter, provoked a flurry of interest in sign systems among other researchers. Many of those researchers had their own descriptions of sign systems. The proliferation of sign systems that appeared mostly during the early 1970s included:

- Signed English by Terry O'Rourke, 1970
- Ameslan by Louie Fant, 1972
- Pidgin Sign English (PSE) by James Woodward, 1972
- Siglish by Louie Fant, 1972
- Ameslish by Bernard Bragg, 1973

In addition, there was, unfortunately, further proliferation of artificial sign systems adopted and used in some schools. Needless to say, with this proliferation came confusion that usually developed with emerging ideas or theories. After the movement became stable, most of the sign systems eventually faded away, except for two discrete languages on the continuum: ASL and "a manual representation of" English, as Woodward called it.[1]

Visual and Artificial Sign Systems

Like English, ASL is not a static language. The signs are not carved in stone but rather, undergo continuous changes. Signs may change over time, but let's take a look at sign systems.

Sign language is said to be mostly imported from France when Clerc came to America with Gallaudet. Since sign language was primarily used in teaching in most early schools for the deaf, a single dialect was recognized as early as 1834.[2] Sign language flourished in the late nineteenth century but went into disfavor after the infamous 1880 ban on sign language. Since sign language at that time was considered as having no grammatical or linguistic principles, the early approach was to "graft the grammar of spoken language onto sign language."[3]

ROCHESTER METHOD

All-inclusive fingerspelling was probably the first and earliest deviation from traditional sign language. It was conceived in 1878, shortly after the opening of the Western New York Institute for Deaf-Mutes (now known as the Rochester School for the Deaf). The school founder, Dr. Zenas Westervelt, not only considered a system midway between the oral and the manual approaches to communication but also believed that deaf children should be exposed to correct English. He invented what is now known as the Rochester Method, where every letter of all communication is fingerspelled with the hand on the same level with the mouth so the students lipread while reading the fingerspelling simultaneously. During the 1950s, the California School for the Deaf at Riverside used this method in teaching, and the 1970s saw short-lived attempts to adopt the Rochester Method, often known as Visible English, at the Florida, Louisiana, and Mississippi Schools for the Deaf.

Author Ronald taught at Rochester School for the Deaf during the 1959–1960 academic year. As a deaf person and professional who signed all his life, he found the experience to be fascinating and enlightening. It was straining to fingerspell every word on one hand. On top of that, it was a struggle to view the fingerspelled letters, and it was even worse if the fingerspeller spelled in a monotonous tone, so to speak, or did not make facial expressions. While in Rochester, Ronald noticed that the influence of sign language was starting to creep into the school. The "contaminated" students were starting to use hand movements when fingerspelling — for example, when the word D-O-W-N was spelled, the hand would move downward simultaneously. The Rochester Method fell out of favor during the 1980s, given that it was tedious and time-consuming to spell everything manually in addition to the difficulties of reading the spelling in restricted space.

COMBINED METHOD

As related in Chapter Two, the term "combined" was coined by Thomas Hopkins Gallaudet while he was in Europe. He was trying to combine the features of the English and French modes of instruction. In England, deaf children were instructed through the oral approach, while the French schools used sign language.

It has been mentioned that because of the influence from the 1880 Milan conference, teaching in some schools moved toward oral-based methods, while most of the schools adopted the combined method (or combined system) of instruction. Dr. Richard Brill, a former superintendent of California School for the Deaf in Riverside, referred to these schools as "combined schools."[4] Some schools allowed some manual communication in all or nearly all classes, while other schools limited the communication in classrooms to oral communication but allowed manual communication at all other times, e.g., outside of classes, in vocational classes, or in dormitories. Simultaneous speech and sign language were allowed in high school departments at some schools.

The underlying philosophy of those supporting the combined method was that the approach should fit the method to the child rather than the child to the method. As an aftereffect of the Milan 1880 resolution, deaf teachers were reassigned to teach "oral failures" in the vocational department or in high school departments. Practically no teacher in the lower and middle schools was deaf, especially because teaching speech was a job requirement.

Artificial Sign Communication Systems

With the rapidly expanding number of single classrooms for deaf pupils in "normal" school settings during the late 1960s, attempts in providing different sign systems proliferated. This was further propelled by Public Law 94-142, passed on November 29, 1975, a catalyst for the establishment of classrooms not run by the traditional schools for the deaf. Those new programs possessed no past, thus were more receptive to innovations in teaching deaf children. Administrators who were unfamiliar with traditional sign language were more open to the appeal and use of the English-based alternate sign language systems in schools. The creators of the newly developed system of signs had a similar goal, which was to help deaf children learn complete and exact English, both manually and orally. Several sign systems, with their acronyms, are described below.

Seeing Essential English (SEE I): A type of manual English was developed by a deaf teacher, David Anthony, in the 1960s when he worked in Michigan and later in California. His rationale for inventing this new system of signs, Seeing Essential English (SEE I) was that in spoken English, hearing people hear a certain word in different types of sentences. They learn that the meaning depends on how the word is used in a sentence. So, he theorized, why couldn't sign language also be like that? Anthony mandated the use of one sign for a word regardless of its meaning. For example, he used the same sign for "right," although the sentences "please turn *right* at the next corner" and "you are *right* about that" had different meanings.

He also invented many signs unfamiliar to sign language traditionalists and developed new signs for word endings, such as "-ing," using a sideway sweeping "I" handshape after a verb sign, "-ness" using a "N" handshape sweeping down the palm of the other hand, and "-ly" using the ILY handshape waving downward after an adverb sign. He also used different signs for different forms of the verb "be," such as an "A" handshape for "am," "I" for "is," and "R" for "are." Today, this sign system is no longer in widespread use, although some signs are still utilized.

Signing Exact English (SEE II): Signing Exact English (SEE II) is morphologically similar to SEE I and was developed by a deaf woman, Gerilee Gustason, Ph.D., Anthony's former co-worker. Gustason was later the chairperson of the Department of Education at Gallaudet University and coordinator of San Jose State University's teacher preparation program for teachers of deaf students. She followed some of Anthony basic rules for SEE I; however, she chose to use traditional ASL signs and created signs for pronouns and affixes. This sign system is still used in many mainstreamed school programs. Two of the "to be" signs are illustrated below:

Linguistics of Visual English (LOVE): Linguistics of Visual English (LOVE) was developed by a deaf man, Dennis Wampler. LOVE, much like SEE I, has only one sign for each printed word, with the addition of new signs for plurals and nouns. He followed some of Anthony's rules but developed signs for the first letter of the word as part of the sign. For example, the basic sign for WORK is the traditional "S" handshape; Wampler's sign for function was the "F" handshape, "O" for operation, "E" for employment, "J" for job, "P" for practicum, "R" for rehearsal, "T" for training and "V" for vacuum using similar movement for the sign WORK or PRACTICE. This sign system was short-lived.

A little known fact is that the developers of the three preceding communication systems used to work together. In 1969 in California, Anthony, Gustason (with Donna Pfetzing and Esther Zawolkow), and Wampler developed guidelines and principles for inventing new signs in an attempt to change existing ASL signs to represent English words. However, they had slight differences in thought and moved in different directions.

Pidgin Signed English (PSE): Pidgin Signed English (PSE) became commonplace in the 1970s. PSE uses the simplest form of manual English, using ASL arbitrarily in English word order. However, signs representing articles ("a," "an," "the") or word endings ("ing," "ness," or "ly") are generally not used. PSE often appears in deaf-hearing interactions. It is sometimes also used in the deaf community for the sake of clarity or full comprehension of particular words.

Signed English (SE): A hearing English professor at Gallaudet University, Harry Bornstein, invented many initialized signs and affixes. Most of the signs were of one meaning, thus SE was considered as a one-sign principle. This sign system is still used in parts of the country. Books containing classic stories, such as *Goldilocks and the Three Bears*, *Little Red Riding Hood*, and *Nursery Rhymes from Mother Goose* can be found in public libraries.

The most probable purposes for the inventions or adaptations of those artificial sign systems during the 1970s were:

- Some educators believed that by using an English-based sign system, deaf people would eventually improve their written or spoken English skills for the sake of social integration into the mainstream world.

- It would be easier for non-deaf persons to understand receptively what was signed to them because in their minds, they could transmit the signs into spoken English word order.

- ASL, especially its structure, was too difficult for some non-deaf persons to learn.

There was some support for this seemingly innovative approach to teaching deaf children, but the resistance by the majority was greater. There were some instances where deaf students from one school were not able to understand deaf students from another school because of the schools' different approaches to sign systems. As a consequence, support and use of SEE I, SEE II, LOVE and the Rochester Method faded away while ASL became adopted by a vast majority of schools and programs as the most effective for teaching and learning, utilizing a bilingual approach (ASL and English).

SIMULTANEOUS COMMUNICATION (SIMCOM)

Simultaneous Communication, as the name implies, is practiced by persons who use spoken words while signing at the same time. One of its supposed advantages is that the receiver can hear or read lips when the sign is not understood. On the other hand, the problems — which far outweigh the advantages — are that the speaker (a) ends up speaking and stops signing, (b) skips some signs during a discourse, (c) produces sloppy fingerspelling, and/or (d) signs in an unclear fashion while speaking simultaneously.

Although some deaf and hard of hearing persons continue to try and use SimCom, many believe it is not possible or appropriate to try and articulate two languages at the same time. Additional reasons for the resistance to SimCom are that SimCom speakers typically use the grammar and structure of the spoken language and use inappropriate sign parameters (handshape, movement, palm orientation, and location).

TOTAL COMMUNICATION

Total Communication was originally referred to as Total Approach and has its beginning in a day school program in Anaheim. The reasoning behind the approach was that the child had the right to multiple educational approaches in addition to speech and sign language. Originally, the concept was especially prevalent in school settings where both deaf and hearing children attended. It had its formal start in the fall of 1968 with six classes serving 34 deaf children aged from three to 12 years in Santa Ana's James Madison Elementary, which served an enrollment of 800 hearing children. Roy Holcomb, Ph.D., was the supervisor of the program, and in 1969 he changed the term to "Total Communication."

The "Father of Total Communication," as Holcomb was known, began to publicize the system. He implemented Total Communication at Delaware's Sterck School, a similar program, in 1972 when he became its superintendent. Maryland School for the Deaf was the first residential school to offer "the full spectrum of language modes: child-devised gestures, formal sign language, speech, speechreading, fingerspelling, reading, and writing."[5] In 1976 members of the Conference of Executives of American Schools for the Deaf approved an official definition that read: "Total Communication is a philosophy requiring the incorporation of appropriate aural, manual, and oral modes of communication in order to insure effective communication with and among hearing impaired persons."

The acceptance of Total Communication, along with the appearance of the artificial sign systems described earlier, swung the pendulum back toward the use of sign language in schools. Despite all the artificial variations of sign language, the efforts to discourage some oral and cochlear-implanted children from signing, and genetic engineering's attempts to eliminate deafness, ASL is increasingly taught to hearing children in public schools at all levels. Infants and toddlers are learning sign language, also; in fact, research has showed that babies — hearing and deaf— experience better language acquisition when they learn sign language first. It is odd that hearing people are encouraged to learn sign language while deaf people may not be.

The separation of deaf children from deaf environments and culture is considered by many as communication abuse. Similarly, if it is inhumane to prohibit Spanish-speaking children from using Spanish to learn English as a second language, why is it not also inhumane to prohibit deaf children from using ASL to learn English?[6]

CURRENT LEARNING OPPORTUNITIES

Currently, deaf children have access to various types of educational settings: private schools, religious schools, mainstreaming programs, federally and state-supported residential schools, day schools, and charter schools. In fact, children nowadays have a wide choice of educational programs that they are eligible to attend. For example, children residing in metropolitan areas can opt for self-contained programs, interpreted programs or mainstreamed programs in their hometowns, or attend a nearby residential school. Some are bussed daily to residential schools. Some residential students even fly between school and home on weekends, e.g., between Tennessee School for the Deaf in Knoxville and home in Memphis on the west end of the state. Some younger deaf children attend elementary schools in their localities and then enroll at a residential school where they can have the advantage of mixing with their own peers — especially in sports and school activities. One of the most positive points about the increased number of school programs serving deaf children is that the awareness and usage of sign language, and Deaf culture and Deaf history, are more widespread and accepted.

Since 1975, with the introduction of innovative approaches in instruction, more and more Deaf teachers have been found to teach at public elementary and primary school levels,[7] where, in many cases, they are paired with a hearing colleague.

With the federal passage of the 1965 Bilingual Act about spoken languages, some schools for deaf children adopted the concept of a bilingual approach as the basis for instruction. This approach emphasizes using the deaf children's natural language, which is ASL, to learn English as a second language. This concept is based on the work of a renowned bilingual researcher, Jim Cummins, Ph.D., who has received extensive support for his theory that skills in one language can transfer to a second language.[8] The authors advise that:

- The key to successful bilingual education is that both languages are respected and nurtured equally, and that
- Deaf bilinguals value the significance of both ASL and written English.

Another approach used in the classroom that should be noted is Cued Speech. Introduced by Orin Cornett, Ph.D., it is a visual communication system in the sense that the use of "cues" enhances the understanding of speech. Cues are provided through eight handshapes at four locations near the mouth to distinguish vowel phonemes. A handshape and a location together cue a syllable. Deaf children, who never possess an understanding of speech through aural means, are helped by the cues. Cued speech provides visual comprehension of the speech. In rebuttal to some claims, cued speech is not considered "sign language," nor should it be considered equivalent to spoken language, but rather, it is a tool that gives support to read and pronounce the speech sounds. Both the speaker and the receiver need to know the cues to transmit the words.

The term "cued language" has become more used during the last decade.

In describing cued language, Earl Fleetwood and Melanie Metzger advised that cued speech and cued language were not interchangeable.[9] They further explained that "...it's true that cueing is not a language — in the same way that speaking, writing and signing aren't languages. They are all ways to express a language."[10] In other words, cued speech presents cues; cued language presents language utilizing linguistic principles.

Transitions in Signs

INITIALIZATION OF SIGNS

During the 1970s, mostly through the influence of Signed English, the trend was to initialize signs by using the fingerspelled letter while signing a word. For instance, the standard index finger handshape away from the mouth was signed to represent the verb "to be." With synthetic sign systems used in the schools, the handshape for IS became an "I" hand-shape, WAS the "W-S" handshapes, and ARE, an "R" handshape, all originating at the mouth.

Another common tendency was to use the handshape "B" to represent BUS, "C" for CAR, "T" for TRUCK, "V" for VAN, so on. Some signs have faded into oblivion, but others remain to this day. One classic example that is still glossed (or signed) nowadays is the original single sign ("C" handshape) for CLASS that used to represent ASSOCIATION, FAMILY, GROUP, ORGANIZATION, and TEAM. Currently the CLASS gloss remains the same, but the other terms are glossed with the handshape representing the initial letter. For example, the letter G, with similar movement for CLASS, is glossed to represent GROUP. Likewise, the "F" handshape, with similar movement, is glossed to represent FAMILY.

ARE
R just below lips moves forward

IS
I on chin moves straight forward

IS, ARE © 1993 Modern Signs Press, Inc.

Variations in Signing

Variation in language refers to people who have different ways of saying the same thing. The earliest studies of variations in signing focused on regional variation. People in one geographic area often use a sign differently from people in another geographic area, even though they all are using ASL. This is akin to hearing people speaking English differently in various parts of the country. For example, people in one region may say *sofa*, while others say *couch*, and yet others *davenport*. The same type of variation exists in ASL.

Many graduates of what is now the American School for the Deaf eventually moved to other states and founded schools for deaf students in their areas. For a long time these schools were isolated from each other. The signs learned at the American School for the Deaf were brought to those other locations but likely changed due to new signs created within these schools by the students, administration, or alumni. Additionally, regional signs also often stem from ways of life in different areas.

Since Deaf people are more mobile than before and frequently travel over state lines or communicate via videophone, it is safe to say that regional signs are not as foreign to people from other regions; some signs have become more uniform. Moreover, there is an increased number of competitions among schools for Deaf students, such as sports, organizations, and academic bowls that provide participants opportunities to interact with peers across state lines.

Other kinds of variations in ASL may include gender variation and ethnic variation. Regional signs often originate at residential schools where they may be developed and later used by alumni.

HALLOWEEN
(Louisiana)

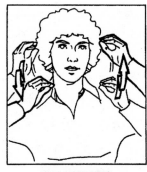

HALLOWEEN
(Virginia)

HALLOWEEN
(more conventional)

HALLOWEEN (three variants) © 1980 Dennis Cokely and Charlotte Baker-Shenk. Reprinted with permission.

BIRTHDAY (four variants) © 1980 Dennis Cokely and Charlotte Baker-Shenk.
Reprinted with permission.

A limited study was conducted by Byron Bridges[11] for his sociolinguistics class. He interviewed several native male ASL signers (a female colleague interviewed female subjects) to evaluate their responses toward 13 sex-oriented pictures. He found out that the males had a tendency to sign the adjectives and used more classifiers than the females. They also took more time to describe the pictures.

The study indicated the common belief that there are variations in signs among deaf male and female signers. However, the topic still needs to be researched. Another example of variation is the sign for the word TERRIFIC, pictured at the top of the following page.

Yet another factor for variation is race/ethnicity. Again, differences

TERRIFIC
(Gallaudet females)

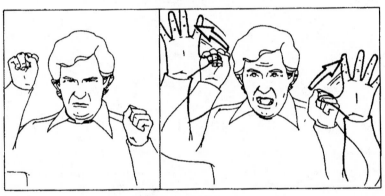

TERRIFIC
(Gallaudet males)

TERRIFIC (male and female variants) © 1980 Dennis Cokely and Charlotte Baker-Shenk. Reprinted with permission.

depend on where one lives. Black Southern signers and white signers have some different signs. For example, black Southern signers express different signs for YOUNG and PREGNANT from white signers.

Although research is still emerging in this area, there seem to be quite a few variations among black signers; this may stem from isolation and lack of contact between black and white deaf communities as a result of segregated education.

The illustrations may represent examples of the observations that "...African American signers use the same lexical and syntactic structures as white signers, their signing may be said to look black or possess some characteristic Blackness."[12]

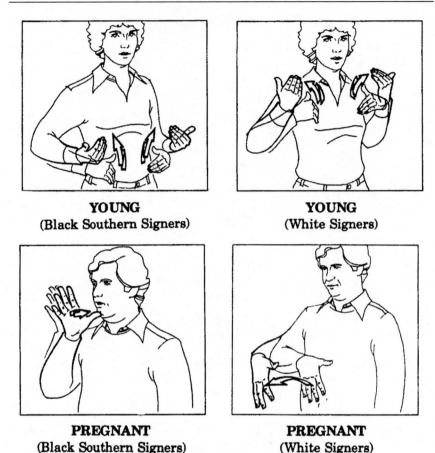

YOUNG
(Black Southern Signers)

YOUNG
(White Signers)

PREGNANT
(Black Southern Signers)

PREGNANT
(White Signers)

YOUNG, PREGNANT © 1980 Dennis Cokely and Charlotte Baker-Shenk. Reprinted with permission.

TECHNICALLY MOTIVATED SIGNS

Another factor contributing to the emergence of new signs is technological developments. Whenever new technological devices are on the market, the initial action is to spell out the device's name, but there usually is an instantaneous appearance of different signs. Eventually unpopular signs are forgotten or phased out, and the most liked ones survive. Currently recent signs include cell phone, cochlear implant, videophone, microwave oven, and pager.

Interestingly, among the deaf and the non-deaf, there are different names for a similar item, such as iPhone or HTC Evo. Because the non-deaf use the device mostly to talk, they call it cell phone. Deaf people, who use these devices mostly as text messengers, call them pagers.

History of Fingerspelling

Fingerspelling (sometimes known as dactylology) is the representation of the letters of a writing system, and sometimes of numeral systems, using only the hands. Fingerspelling is also known as the manual alphabet, finger alphabet or hand alphabet.

According to research by Frenchman J. Barrois in 1850, the body and hands were used to represent alphabets in Greek, Roman, Egyptian and Assyrian antiquity. The Benedictine monk Bede, in the eighth century, is credited as having recorded the earliest known manual alphabet. Manual alphabets were also learned for various reasons, including silence (monks from at least the time of Bede), secrecy (communications between two persons or possibly spies), and literacy (as a requirement for legal recognition as an heir). The first book on deaf education, published in 1620 in Madrid, included a detailed account of using a manual alphabet to teach deaf students to read and speak.[13]

Charles de La Fin published a book in 1692, describing a unique alphabetic system where pointing to a body part represented the first letter of the part (e.g., Brow=B) and vowels were located on the fingertips, as still used today in British Sign Language.

MODERN MANUAL ALPHABET

Fingerspelling is a vital part of ASL; however, it has been stated that fingerspelling is not a substitute for signs.[14] Fingerspelling makes up about 8.7 percent of casual signing in ASL.[15] Names of persons, things, and places are usually fingerspelled, unless they have name signs. Some learn fingerspelling quickly, and others take a longer time. Proficiency in expressive skills (spelling out) is much more attainable than receptive skills (reading fingerspelling). The authors have met many individuals who can sign and fingerspell proficiently but are weak in "finger-reading."

As mentioned previously, ASL is not a static language; signs evolve over time. The same is true of fingerspelling, although to a somewhat limited extent. The popular trend, and now becoming a staple, is the double "Z" handshape as in P-I-Z-Z-A and B-U-Z-Z. Instead of spelling out the letter Z twice with the "Z" handshape, the trend is to spell out "Z-Z" once with two fingers (index and middle fingers). Another handshape was attempted years ago, as recalled by Toivo Lindholm[16] in his *Humor Among the Deaf* article. He wrote of the double "R-R," spelling "R" using four fingers — crossed index and middle fingers and crossed ring and little fingers — for words such as H-U-R-R-Y, L-A-R-R-Y, and W-O-R-R-Y. This hasn't met with much success, given how much effort it takes to create the double R handshape.

Last, but not least, many deaf adults are unhappy about the unique use of the handshape "E" that some of the younger generation and ASL interpreters are currently using. Instead of clenching the hand with tip of fingers touching the thumb, to form a tight "E," the fingers are separate from the thumb to give an appearance of loose "E" or almost a "C."

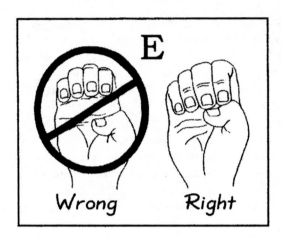

"E" not "C." Reprinted with permission of Ernie Hahn, *New Horizons*.

The concern has been mentioned in at least two national magazines. Robert Sanderson, a former president of the National Association, issued a call to "cease and desist" the sloppy handshape with the following quotation[17]:

> Our beloved, beautiful expressive and specific manual alphabet does not deserve to be prostituted and abused by anyone.

More recently, the lament was repeated by editor Ernie Hahn as his "alphabet pet peeve" in Deaf Seniors of America's newsletter *New Horizons*. His editorial[18] urged action to correct the "newfangled hand sign" and bring back the old "E" sign. The authors of this book wholeheartedly agree.

Fingerspelling is also highly varied among nations in the world. Anthropologist Simon Carmel, Ph.D., has printed a collection of approximately 50 alphabet cards from all over the world.[19] Since France historically contributed hugely to the education and lives of Deaf people in America, a manual alphabet of both French and American handshapes was created by Frenchwoman Fanny (Yeh) Corderoy du Tiers, formerly of Taiwan and the United States. The illustration on the following page shows eleven handshapes that are different between the French and American manual alphabets.[20]

Sharing Our Visual Language

INCREASING DEMAND FOR ASL

There are an estimated half a million to one million people in the American Deaf-World, although an untold number of individuals have taken sign language classes at the elementary, secondary and postsecondary levels. Many

Manual Alphabet (American)
Alphabet en Dactylologie (français)

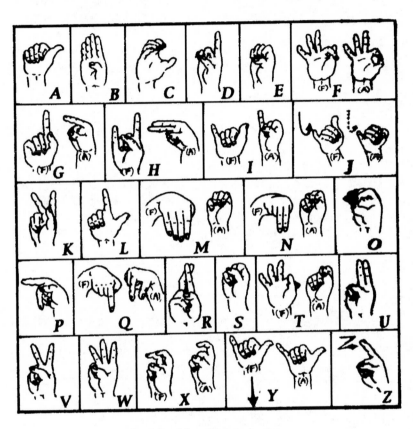

Designed by: /Dessinée par:
Fanny (Yeh) Corderoy du Tiers (deaf/sourde)
Paris, FRANCE - ©1996

American-French Manual Alphabet © 1996 Fanny (Yeh) Corderoy du Tiers.

have gone on to become sign language interpreters or to work within fields serving deaf people. ASL users also include parents of deaf children, hearing children of deaf parents—who are commonly known as Children of Deaf Adults, or CODAs—relatives of deaf people, and adults who are late deafened and are learning sign language. In fact, the growing popularity of ASL has made it one of the most widely used languages in America.[21] In 2010, *USA Today* published an article stating that ASL is the fourth most commonly used language in the United States after Spanish, French and German.[22]

As of 2007, 42 states had officially recognized ASL as a language, and ASL had become federally recognized as a foreign language. Many colleges and universities have allowed ASL to fulfill requirements for foreign language.[23]

Enrollment in ASL courses increased by 432 percent between 1998 and 2002. Spanish is far ahead with enrollment of almost 750,000 students, followed by French with 202,000, German with 91,000, Italian with 64,000, and ASL with 61,000 students, according to a 2002 survey.[24] Community colleges account for 64 percent of total ASL enrollment.

Recent information indicates that ASL continues to show greater gains. The 2006 survey[25] shows ASL moving up from fifth to fourth place in enrollment, with an increase of 30 percent from 2002 to an enrollment of 79,000 students in 2006. Spanish, French and German had smaller enrollment increases, between 2 and 10 percent during that time span, but remain in the top three. The latest survey shows a total enrollment of 91,763 students enrolled in ASL courses in 2009, an increase of 16.4 percent over 2006.[26]

Signing Hearing Infants and Children

Just as crawling encourages children to walk, signing gives them a jump-start on speech. For years, sign language has been used to communicate primarily with deaf children. Since ASL is now more acceptable, there have been increased efforts to teach sign language to hearing infants.

One of the pioneers in the field is Joseph Garcia, Ed.D.[27] Coming from a non-deaf family, he studied ASL in 1975 and became a certified interpreter. During his involvement with the Deaf community, he observed that hearing children of deaf parents started communicating with sign language at an earlier age than hearing children did with spoken language. The observation led to his choice of subject for his graduate thesis and, later, his professional career.

Additional research studies about babies have indicated that they use hand gestures before they talk, by pointing or reaching. Thus, it is reasonable that pre-verbal babies are capable of using their hands to speak. Parents have reported that instead of screams to express their needs or wants, their children use hands. The children also tend to enjoy closer bonds with their parents and learn to develop larger vocabularies early on.

The main boost from this early signing is to make the children's lives uncomplicated and less stressful. Parents do not have to be fluent in sign language to start with. Many basic signs are "iconic," meaning the signs look like the things they represent. A few examples of iconic signs:

• BALL, BOOK, LOVE, FOOD, DRINK.

Sign language is very useful not only for Deaf children but for other children as well. Hearing toddlers usually drop signing as they learn to speak proficiently. This debunks the myth that sign language interferes with the development of speech.[28]

The increased acceptance of sign language has influence on the concept of infants learning sign language. The 2004 comedy *Meet the Fockers*, starring Robert De Niro, Barbra Streisand and Dustin Hoffman, demonstrated the natural interaction between the adults and the toddler in sign language.

CHILDREN OF DEAF ADULTS (CODA)

Ever since the beginning of deaf American history, many deaf adults have married other deaf adults. Yet, a great majority of children born to deaf parents have normal hearing. Those children typically grow up with two languages (signed and spoken) and two cultures (deaf and non-deaf). In 1983, CODA was established as a national organization by Millie Brother, herself a CODA, for the purpose of providing advocacy efforts and resources for its members.

Members often share similar backgrounds, such as experiencing identity confusion. They might be unsure of whether they are deaf or hearing, and they usually acquire signing skills before speaking skills. CODAs often have taken on the role of interpreter/translator since childhood, often unintentionally. Fortunately, it is believed that, with increased awareness of deaf people and improved access to services — especially relay services — the situation has changed for the better.

In adulthood, hearing offspring of deaf parents usually learn to understand and embrace their cultural differences. Many of them continue being close to the Deaf community. In 1996, CODA established an annual celebration of MOTHER, FATHER DEAF Day on the last Sunday in April to honor their deaf parents and to recognize the gifts of culture and language they received.

SIGN LANGUAGE INTERPRETERS

Once upon a time, deaf people had to depend on hearing people to make phone calls or to transcribe messages on the phone. Both authors, as well as their deaf parents and many other deaf people, used to depend on their neighbors for phone calls. The neighbors would relay messages via paper and pencil, or in-person communication; many would receive calls for the deaf person at their phones and then stop by the deaf person's house to share the message. Needless to say, the messages could be sometimes personal or embarrassing. As mentioned earlier, Alexander Graham Bell's invention was not a boon but rather a disability to deaf people, since the telephone became the main communication vehicle for making appointments, as well as other necessities of everyday life.

In many workplaces, deaf people were stuck without interpreters — even to this day, especially in smaller firms — and had to be content with reading notes received from colleagues. Many deaf or hard of hearing employees in government or large firms were prevented from participating in meetings or seminars. Many were forced to be satisfied with summarized, often superficial, notes, even if the meetings dragged on for 30 minutes or an hour. Deaf people often missed the detailed interactions among colleagues and were unable to participate in or to contribute to making decisions that might influence their roles in the workplace.

In education, deaf people had to rely on written class notes or reading textbooks to keep up. Author Ronald survived a master's degree program at University of Maryland during the mid–1960s without an interpreter. He received B's in all his courses, except one, because — as one professor explained — the author did not participate in class discussions. He received an A in the one course that required a seminar paper. At that time interpreting was mostly voluntary and not yet considered a profession.

When the field of interpreting became professionalized with the establishment of the Registry of Interpreters for the Deaf in 1964, it was the beginning of an unprecedented range of opportunities for deaf persons who benefited from the ease of communication with hearing individuals. In 1973, RID began a national interpreter certification program. That same year, Congress strengthened the interpreting program when it passed the Rehabilitation Act of 1973 in which Section 504 mandates the provision of interpreters for deaf people in education and for professionals affiliated with agencies receiving federal funding.

Students attending mainstreamed schools or colleges/universities now can get full access to information, thanks to interpreters and other support services. The Americans with Disabilities Act (ADA) of 1992 mandates that private companies with 25 or more employees receiving federal funds are required to provide "reasonable accommodations" to deaf applicants or employees.

Sign language interpreters usually work either as freelancers or for an interpreting agency or social agency. It is interesting to note that some deaf entrepreneurs have established interpreting agencies. David Birnbaum and Moon and Eric Feris are among the individuals who have successfully ventured into the interpreting field. Birnbaum founded Birnbaum Interpreting Services (BIS) in Maryland in 1995. Prior to this, he owned a thriving courier service in the Washington metropolitan area. While making a delivery, one of his clients suggested that he establish an interpreting service as an opportunity to give back to the deaf community. Eventually, BIS was recognized by *Forbes* magazine as one of the top 500 small business successes in the country.

Western Interpreting Network (WIN) is the only deaf-owned agency in California. Established by Moon and Eric Feris, the agency has provided interpreting services throughout Southern California and beyond since 2004. The agency also provides services such as real-time captioning, dual and trilingual foreign language interpreting, and document translations.

PHONE INTERPRETING

Since the mid–2000s, video relay services (VRS) have created a demand for more interpreters. Unlike on-site interpreting, VRS interpreters generally work from a cubicle containing a video camera and a high-speed Internet connection. VRS interpreters translate calls between deaf and hearing people. Some interpreters prefer this kind of work as they do not need to travel to work and the income is more stable than freelancing.

International Signs

Anthropologist Margaret Mead mentioned that sign language was a true universal language. Moreover, it was easy to learn and could be used by anyone for communication all over the globe. This has not happened and will not happen until pigs fly. There are too many variations in sign language systems, even within some nations.

In the Ethnologue database (www.ethnologue.com), librarian Thomas R. Harrington[29] of Gallaudet University has identified 271 sign languages, dialects, and other sign systems from countries around the world. Clearly, like spoken language, various sign systems are not readily understandable when a person visits a foreign country. Even in some countries, there is more than one sign language system, usually due to local influences and cultures.

The following illustrations present some examples of different signs.

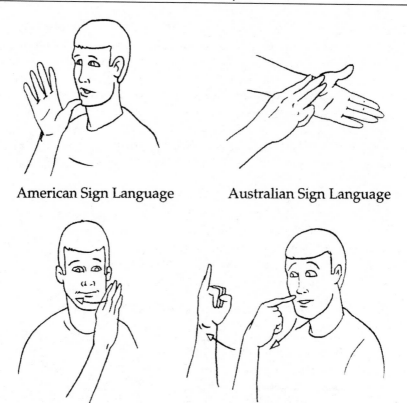

American Sign Language   Australian Sign Language

Spanish Sign Language   Japanese Sign Language

MOTHER in American, Australian, Spanish, and Japanese Sign Language © 1992–2011, MSM Productions, Ltd. Reprinted from *Hearing People Only*, 3d ed. with permission. For more information: www.hpobook.com.

Gestuno

Numerous international organizations of Deaf people, such as the World Federation of the Deaf (WFD) and Deaflympics, conduct their conferences in Gestuno. Briefly, Gestuno is[30]:

- An Italian acronym meaning "one system of gestures."
- A collection of approximately 1,500 signs and gestures, many of which share universal qualities.
- A visual-gestural aid to international sign communication.

Willard Madsen points out that Gestuno is not a language and should not be considered an international sign language. Furthermore, Gestuno is not a collection of signs or gestures intended to replace any national sign language dictionary.

Gestuno had its beginnings in 1951 at the WFD conference, when Gestuno was initially discussed as a way to communicate among participants. WFD's official written languages are English and French, but there was a need to adopt effective means to transact business, especially during general assemblies at international conferences. In 1973, a WFD commission was formed to create a system of international gestures. The outcome was the publication of *Gestuno: International Sign Language of the Deaf: The Revised and Enlarged Book of Signs Agreed and Adopted by the Unification of Signs Commission of the World Federation of the Deaf.*

Gestuno has continued being used at international conferences, but in other situations, Gestuno is not widely used. Even so, American travelers visiting other countries of the world may use Gestuno to facilitate communication with deaf natives. Following are some examples of Gestuno:

Sign	*ASL*	*Gestuno*
YESTERDAY	Y handshape moving backward by cheek	Index finger moving backward by cheek
APPROVE	"S" handshape stamping on opposite palm	"3" handshape stamping on opposite palm
UNDERSTAND?	"11" handshape on forehead	Think Grasp?
YES	"S" handshape moving upward and downward	YELLOW as in ASL
INTERPRET	(2h) "F" moving clockwise	COOK as in ASL

When attending international conferences for deaf people, watching several interpreters at one time always fascinates the authors. For example, if an American signs a presentation, there may be sign language interpreters for Gestuno (international sign language), Chinese, Japanese, and other sign languages. There are also voice interpreters, so as many as ten interpreters may translate a single presentation at those events.

In Closing

The attempt here has been to summarize the development of signed language from early sign language to the current status as linguistically based ASL. It is interesting to note the parallels among signs and sign language, cued speech and cued language, and English words and English language, whether they are in the form of speech, signs, or writing. Again, ASL — like

English — has evolved over the years, with certain signs being phased out in favor of others, based on usage. There are no good or bad signs, but their fate is determined, appropriately, by those who use them.

ASL serves so many vital roles in the Deaf-World, as a symbol of identity, medium of interaction, source of values, customs and information. It is understandable, then, why deaf people — much like the members of other language minorities — are so ferociously attached to their language and have fought valiantly to preserve it throughout their history.[31]

ASL remains constantly in a state of flux, as made evident by the evolution of signs. With continuous flexibility, ASL will continue to thrive.

SEVEN

Emergence of Colorful Communication

Folklore Through Signs, Words, and Art

We now embark into the facets of the deaf community. We will learn what makes Deaf people tick and how they compensate using a unique fifth sense as described in the next paragraph. Most of the mysteries are revealed through several forms of folklore, some partially real; however, most have been constructed in cultural humor.

Mainstream American culture teaches that "normal" people are born with five senses: hearing, sight, smell, taste, and touch. Of course, since Deaf people can't hear, this causes many people to view Deaf people as deficient and deprived. Nothing could be further from the truth — we have always had five senses: sight, smell, taste, touch, and a sense of humor.[1]

Traditional literature can be enjoyed through two forms of expression: written and oral. Although both forms are well received by many scholars in the non-deaf world, the oral form of literature is unfortunately considered by many to be inferior to written literature. The oral form of literature loses a great deal when transcribed. Furthermore, anyone outside of the culture tends to have a great deal of difficulty in understanding the full meaning, complexity and significance of the tale, because understanding the story means also understanding the complexity of the culture itself.

Inasmuch as Deaf culture is preserved through both written and oral (excuse the pun) forms, the oral (or signed) language as described previously is also lost in translation and can be difficult to comprehend by outsiders. That may explain why Deaf culture has been stigmatized by the "literate" culture — because it lacks a written language.[2]

Characteristics of Deaf culture are passed on from one person to another as well as from one generation to another — thus, after a while, those characteristics have blended into what is considered Deaf folklore. Deaf folklore is important to the deaf community because it helps develop one's pride in his or her Deaf identity and Deaf culture. Folklore, in its various forms, naturally helps hearing people understand how Deaf people think and perceive the world.[3]

Folklore illustrates how Deaf people have created legends, Deaf jokes and riddles, signlore (signed puns, handshape and number stories), ASL poetry and personal experience narratives. Rhythmic performances, such as ritual clapping, are also staples in Deaf culture. Folklore is predominantly carried down through schools, families, and gatherings, such as clubs, sports, camps, and reunions. Unfortunately, similar to oral transcription, the sign language versions of many works by Deaf people are either forgotten or hidden. At present, with the availability of user-friendly home videos for the general public, conscious efforts have been made to record folklore and jokes for posterity.

Deaf Storytelling Genre

Storytelling in ASL can be described as "...a combination of gestures, mime, signs, and facial expressions. ASL storytelling is like painting a visual picture of the tale. It also provides a structure for Deaf people's perspectives: without air, our cells die; without ASL storytelling, our (Deaf) selves die."[4]

ASL storytelling is believed to have emerged historically at residential schools for deaf students. It likely started with mimicking idiosyncratic mannerisms of hearing teachers or dorm staff, or elaborated retelling of horror, western, romantic or war movies. Because films were not captioned back in the old days, the storyteller often became skilled at fabricating dialogues that led many to be very creative and often correct in guessing what was being said in movies.

DEAF EXPERIENCE STORIES

Deaf experience stories may be about life experiences, usually about deaf people succeeding or outsmarting hearing people. The stories, fictional or non-fictional, may also present a perspective, a wish, or an idea unique to Deaf people. They might also use personal experiences that reveal the hearing community's ridicule.

The following stories are examples of common occurrences.

DEAF EXPERIENCE STORY ONE

A young graduate of Gallaudet University happened to drive through Houston, Texas, one summer. He wanted to look up a girl from college, whom he admired. He stopped at her house and noticed a woman ironing clothes in the hallway beyond the screen door. He knocked on the door, and she came to the door. The young guy gestured that he was Deaf, took out his pad and pencil, and wrote, asking about his lady friend. The woman said her daughter was at her summer job and would not be able to come home until the evening. The young guy already had a previous engagement for that evening, told the woman that he had to leave, and asked her to pass along his hello to her daughter.

Two weeks later, the young guy learned through his lady friend that her mother was Deaf. What happened was that the young guy assumed that the woman, who had come to the door when he knocked, was hearing. The woman did not respond to the knocking; she approached the door because she saw a human figure through the screen. This true story happened in 1959 to author Ronald. The young lady he was hoping to visit is now his wife, author Melvia.

DEAF EXPERIENCE STORY TWO

A hearing man was fascinated with a deaf woman who was sitting in a bar. He decided to strike up a conversation with her by writing notes on a piece of paper. To his delight, she was friendly enough to write back. They wrote back and forth for some time. Another man jumped into the conversation and began to write, too. All three, with the woman in the middle, continued their conversation by writing. After a while, the deaf woman realized she was late for a commitment and told her new friends that she needed to leave. The two men waved good-bye to her and then resumed writing with each other, without realizing that neither one of them was deaf. A similar situation actually happened to Byron B. Burnes, affectionately known as BBB, who was a long-time teacher at California School for the Deaf in Berkeley and president of the National Association for 18 years. He was the person in the middle. After enjoying his two beers, he left the bar but then looked back to see the two men writing to each other.[5]

FICTIONAL ORIGINAL STORIES

This original story is based on a historical anecdote and contains fictional adaptations illustrating how Deaf people have contributed to epoch-making episodes of United States history. It is well documented that renowned Philadelphian Benjamin Franklin discovered electricity with his kite-flying equipment. But few people know how this really happened. Franklin's deaf printer had gone home early one evening and was already in bed when Franklin realized he just had to see his printer. Unfortunately, the printer lived on the third floor, and the front door was locked. How could poor Franklin get to the sleeping printer?

The quick-thinking Franklin got the idea of flying his young nephew's kite near the window, hoping to get the printer's attention. (But his printer was asleep, so we assume that Franklin added a candle to the kite tail.) After the kite flew repeatedly back and forth past the window, the deaf printer awoke, stuck his head out the window, and saw Franklin on the ground three floors below. Franklin indicated that they needed to talk and asked if he could come up. Rather than toss Franklin the key to unlock the door downstairs and perhaps lose it in the grass (he was too lazy to go downstairs), the printer tied it to the kite string. It was shortly afterward that lightning struck and Franklin became the discoverer of electricity — thanks to the deaf printer![6]

CREATIVE STORIES

Creative stories are another favorite pastime of deaf children. Similar to American folklore about individuals such as Paul Bunyan or Pecos Bell, many creative stories in the past were generated in dormitories at residential schools. They usually were adaptations of movies, especially the war movies during World War II, embellished with the beauty of signs accompanied by facial and body movements.

Such stories continue to be created, albeit with different approaches. They are more likely to be created in the classroom, often by the teacher's encouragement. The stories are created by using a particular rule, such as stories being told in alphabetical order, numerical order, or using a particular handshape. One example is using only the index finger (an "1" handshape) with both hands. The story might be told like this:

Friends, one hearing (and) one deaf walk (from) opposite, meet, sign for hours. (Then) friends walk (away in) opposite (directions).

The words in parentheses are not signed. ABC, number and handshape stories are best appreciated by watching a person signing the stories. Usually the signs are accompanied with gestures or facial expressions; it is not always possible to have suitable translations on paper.

DEAF LAUGHS

Loss of hearing has nothing to do with loss of humor. Deaf people might laugh at the world or at their own world. Ben Bahan[7] advises that deaf humor is often so deeply embedded in culture that individuals unfamiliar with deaf culture are likely to find some things not funny if presented in translation through interpretation or print.

M.J. Bienvenu[8] explains that humor is one way that people share their perceptions of the world, express different levels of intimacy, and find comfort in knowing that others share their beliefs. In reflecting the values, norms, and belief systems of the American Deaf culture, she classifies deaf laughs into four categories: visual; can't hear; linguistic, and response to oppression.

Visual: Again, deaf people perceive most things through their eyes, acquiring language visually. Deaf people also acquire world knowledge visually. It should come as no surprise, then, that deaf humor has a strong visual base. Deaf people find many visual things humorous that aurally dependent people may not. The culture is reinforced through the shared experience of how deaf people, as a group, see the world and translate it into humor.

Can't Hear: Being deaf is much more than the inability to hear. It is a complete culture, where one's decibel loss is far less important than one's allegiance to the deaf community. Yet, a significant amount of deaf folklore contains jokes and stories that deal with the inability to hear.

There are many stories that illustrate the convenience of being deaf. The following popular tale shows how Deaf people can solve a problem creatively and humorously: A deaf couple arrives at a motel for their honeymoon. After unpacking, the nervous husband goes out to get a drink. When he returns to the motel, he realizes that he has forgotten their room number. It is dark outside and all the rooms look identical. He walks to his car and leans on the horn. He then waits for the lights to come on in the rooms of the waking hearing guests. All the rooms are lit up except his, where his deaf wife is waiting for him.[9]

Linguistic: Much of linguistic humor is lexically based, and the punch lines in many ASL jokes are related to the word productions. A huge giant (think King Kong) is stalking a small village of wee people, who scatter through the streets trying to escape the ugly creature. The giant notices one particularly beautiful blonde woman scampering down the cobblestoned street. He stretches out his clumsy arm and sweeps her up, then stares in wonder at the slight, shivering figure in his palm. "You are so beautiful," he exclaims. The young woman looks up in fear. "I would never hurt you," he signs, "I love you! We should get married." When producing the sign MARRY, he inadvertently crushes her to death. Heartbroken, the giant laments, "Oralism is better, after all."[10]

Response to Oppression: On the other hand, in response to oppression, deaf people who experience oppression fight back through humor by showing hearing people being outsmarted by Deaf people. Often this category, sometimes called "zap" stories, features deaf people getting even. The example that is a pet peeve to many of the deaf people is "Can you read my lips?" A common, funny response is "Can you read my signs?"

The following true story provides another example of a clever response to oppression. In a restaurant, a group of deaf people was chatting away when a group of non-deaf people at the next table began to rudely mimic their signs. One of the deaf women decided she had enough. She walked to a public telephone booth, inserted a coin in the telephone. Making sure that the hearing group was observing her, she signed a complete conversation into the handset, including pauses for the person on the other end to respond. When the deaf group left the restaurant, they were amused to see the hearing people run over to inspect the phone.[11]

Deaf people love this one, because they have the last laugh. These tales are rich with justice, and always the offender is put in her/his place.

When we analyze minority cultures, we find that they all incorporate examples of battling oppression into their humor. It is a common response to the frustration of our everyday lives, for in humor, the storyteller determines who will "win." Here is a story that occurs on a train.

A Russian, a Cuban, and a Deaf person are on a train. The Russian is drinking from a bottle of vodka. She drinks about half a bottle and then throws the bottle out the window. The Deaf person looks at her, surprised, and asks, "Why did you throw out a bottle that was only half-empty?" The Russian replies, "Oh, in my country we have plenty of vodka!" Meanwhile, the Cuban is smoking a rich, aromatic cigar. He smokes about half the cigar and then throws it out the window. The Deaf person is again surprised, and asks, "Why did you throw out the cigar?" He replies, "Oh, in Cuba we have plenty of cigars!" The Deaf person nods with interest. A little while later a hearing person walks down the aisle. The Deaf person picks him up and tosses him out the window. The Russian and Cuban look up in amazement. The Deaf person shrugs, "Oh, we have plenty of hearing people in the world."[12]

JOKES/HUMOR

Like any people outside of Deaf culture, for the fun of it, Deaf people make fun of themselves or of others. The following jokes are informally categorized into ASL, Deaf Culture, Deaf-Blind, Hard of Hearing, and Lipreading Crisis.

The late Stephen Ryan had an outstanding sense of humor. In his stand-up comedy act, he often presented fun, imaginative scenarios, such as "The White House with a Deaf President will be with flashing lights all over there," or "There will be a Registry of Interpreting for the Hearing (RIH)— Deaf Interpreters for Hearies."

ASL: Dr. Lynn Jacobowitz, who was Ryan's mentor, also possesses a collection of original humorous thoughts, especially on the subject of ASL. Among them are such gems as: "I predict that in the future, the business of plastic surgery will end. WHY??? More and more people will attend ASL classes and use facial expressions to keep them looking young. It is much cheaper and fun!!!" Another one is: "In the year of 2093 ... cochlear implants will be on hands (instead of the ears) to sign better."

Deaf Culture: Two Deaf men are signing to each other. The first man asks, "What did your wife say when you got home late last night?" The second man replies, "She swore a blue streak." And the first man asks, "What did you do then?" The second man replies, "I turned out the light."[13]

Hard of Hearing: Hard of hearing people also enjoy humor about there being misunderstandings.[14]

- There's a good reason why I've never made much of my life: Every time opportunity knocked, I was in the shower with my hearing aid on the sink.

- A man who is hard of hearing tells an acquaintance he's been married to the same woman for 55 years. The acquaintance asks if he has to put up with a lot of nagging. The hard of hearing man says, "What?"

- A woman who was hard of hearing ordered a Danish pastry at a coffee counter. "Would you like me to heat (mouth movement resembling "eat") it for you?" the attendant politely asked. He was startled by the glare the customer gave him as she backed away and said, "What makes you think I'm not capable of eating it myself?"

Lipreading Crisis: A 92-year-old man went to a doctor to get a

Can you read my lips? © 1994 DawnSign-Press. Illustration by Frank Paul, reproduced with permission from *Deaf Culture, Our Way.*

physical. A few days later the doctor saw him walking down the street with a gorgeous young lady on his arm.

A couple of days later the doctor talked to the man and said, "You're really doing great, aren't you?"

The man replied, "Just doing what you said, doctor, 'Get a hot momma and be careful.'"

The doctor said, "I didn't say that. I said you got a heart murmur. Be careful."

And there are even cartoons on lipreading endeavors. A mustached person, e.g., the policeman in the illustration, often wonders why a deaf person cannot lipread him. In the old days it was common to find mustached and bearded teachers in oral classrooms, creating additional learning barriers for deaf students. The accompanying illustration is a modern version, and unfortunately it occurs just as often these days.

TRADITIONAL JOKES

Some traditional deaf jokes take advantage of the theme of deafness to solve a problem. Several samples follow:

The Lumberjack and the "Stubborn" Tree: A lumberjack chopped down a tree, hollering "Timber," but the tree did not fall down. The lumberjack decided to try fingerspelling T-I-M-B-E-R, and the tree, which was deaf, fell down.

Other versions include:

- After putting a hearing aid on the tree, the man climbed down and yelled "TIMBER." The tree fell down. (see illustration below)
- After teaching lipreading to the tree, he climbed down and mouthed the word, "TIMBER." The tree fell down.
- After teaching the tree how to read, he climbed down and showed a printed word, "TIMBER." The tree fell down.
- When the deaf tree did not fall down after the letters T-I-M-B-E-R were spelled, the lumberjack tried again by fingerspelling and pressing each letter against the bark. The tree fell down because it was deaf-blind.

Birds on a Telephone Line: A child asked his father why the birds on a telephone line were kind of jumpy while other birds on a different line were sitting quietly. After a moment of thinking, his father replied that that particular line was a TTY line, causing the birds to jump with every press of a key.

Cartoon Deafactory©

Hearing aid tree © 1994 Heriberto Quinones.

FAMILY ANTHOLOGY OF HUMOR

The late Roy Holcomb's contributions to deaf humor through prose and art are well known. His humorous output always brought a chuckle to his readers. His family did not realize that he was deaf until he was nine years old. After graduating from Texas School for the Deaf, he went to Gallaudet University and eventually earned several master's degrees from other universities during a time that interpreters were not provided. As one of the few early Deaf school administrators, he was also known for popularizing the "Total Communication" philosophy, described earlier. Tom and his wife Marjoriebell raised two Deaf sons, Samuel and Thomas. Samuel is currently a lecturer in American Sign Language and Interpreting Education at NTID, and Thomas a professor of Deaf Studies at Ohlone College in Fremont, California. The three men collaborated to publish *Deaf Culture Our Way*,[15] a collection of anecdotes from the deaf community. The book is the third revision of the original *Hazards of Deafness*[16] and second version titled *Silence Is Golden, Sometimes*, both of which Roy put out. Some of the amusing snippets are:

- You put silver or dishes away and make enough noise to compare with the battle of Gettysburg.
- Burglars come near your house during the night, and your dog nearly barks its head off trying to warn you, but you sleep through everything as if the entire U.S. Army guarded your place.
- After observing a deaf person in a public place, a hearing man decided to approach him and find out if deaf people are literate. He wrote, "Can you read?" and handed the note to the deaf person. Disgusted with this kind of ignorance, the deaf person wrote back, "No. Can you write?"

Another book, *For Hearing People Only,*[17] compares the enjoyment of jokes between hearing people and deaf people. The book explains that to learn English word play, hearing people need to have some degree of everyday immersion in English to understand jokes and puns that involve homonyms (sound-alike words). Often, Deaf people do not follow the hearing humor. Conversely, non-deaf people often do not comprehend Deaf humor since Deaf humor is visually based. Deaf humors involve mime, gesture, cinematic effects (like zooming, close-ups, fast and slow motion), and a lot of spontaneous sign-play. As for translating homonyms-based English puns and phonetic wordplay into sign or fingerspelling, it does not work at all. It is as true the other way around.

DEAF RIDDLES

Deaf people even create riddles about themselves. One such riddle was reprinted in *Deaf Digest*[18]:

Q. People of their own ethnic groups tend to eat their own ethnic food. What do deaf people eat?

A. Finger food.

INTERPRETER JOKES

Interpreters have played important roles in the lives of Deaf people. They facilitate the spoken and signed intercourses between Deaf people and hearing counterparts. Deaf people love and need interpreters, especially when interacting with hearing persons. Fortunately (or unfortunately) some interactions may have unintentional or undesired results, for a variety of reasons. However, it is sometimes entertaining to create jokes about interpreters, since they are part of the deaf community, jokes such as this one:

A hearing man robs a bank and decides to bury the loot in his back yard. His next-door neighbor who is deaf sees him burying the money and that night digs it up and hides it in a tree in his back yard. The next day the hearing man goes out back and finds that his money is gone. He decides to hire an interpreter to get his money back from the deaf man. The interpreter and the hearing man go up to the door of the deaf man, and the hearing man demands the money back. The deaf man signs that he doesn't know what the hearing man is talking about. The hearing man says that if the deaf man does not tell him, he will kill the deaf man. The deaf man decides to tell him where the money is. The interpreter then tells the hearing man to go ahead and shoot the deaf man because the deaf man will never tell.

CARTOONS

Many deaf and hard of hearing illustrators have created remarkable works that entertain or humor readers. Many have been collected from magazines, books, or e-mail for years. In the following pages, you will find some of the many cartoons. They are broken into five broad themes: Communication, Lipreading, ASL, Interpreter, and Technology.

Communication: Expression of humor in sign language. Often deaf persons are caught in situations where they are not able to communicate with their hands. The illustration by Matt Daigle shows the guy with his back to the door trying to communicate his painful predicament via blinking eyes to his helper.

"Tied-up hands" produce exasperation and awkwardness for signing deaf people. For instance, at receptions deaf people have found it frustrating to communicate while holding a drink in one hand and a plate of finger food in another (unless they decide to quietly listen). The person might try to gesture or make "gross" signs without spilling the drink or dropping the food. Having a

WHEN DEAF HANDS ARE OCCUPIED, THE BLINKING CODE IS USED AS BACK-UP COMMUNICATION

Blinking codes © 2010 Matt Daigle, *Adventures in Deaf Culture.*

free hand helps the person to sign, spell, or write (or communicate without restraint).

Lipreading: Some inopportune misunderstandings occur in real life. As artist Ruth Peterson recounts the incident about her friend, the story started with "Once upon a time Lois Burr left the military office she works for ... early in the day thinking that her boss had told her she was discharged that afternoon. The next day to her embarrassment she found out that he really said, 'You are in charge this afternoon.'"

Lipreading can be misunderstood. Courtesy Ruth Peterson.

ASL: Learning sign language without trying. Often a clueless hearing person expresses to a deaf person, or one familiar with sign language, a desire to learn sign language — probably promoted by a sudden interest in an attractive social contact — so he can hold conversations with a deaf individual. As we know, learning sign language is similar to learning a foreign language — it takes effort, time, and dedication, and it requires continuous use (application) before the clueless could become proficient. Thanking

"That tanning lotion is _good_! It will help you sign in ASL better.

Tanning lotion to improve ASL © Shawn Richardson.

artist Shawn Richardson for the humorous thought, the authors give the product a rating of zero.

Interpreter: Looks like the authors are making fun of the interpreters again. These illustrations can be perceived as "occupational hazards." When signing slipshod, a number of adverse things can happen without warning. Eyeglasses are in the way of the fingers, and they can fly and land with a thud, attracting attention of everybody in the room.

This one distracts the attention not of the audience but of the consumer, who might be elated by the attention of the winking interpreter. Anybody who uses contact lenses knows it could be agonizing to have a loose piece of glass or plastic wandering randomly around the eyeball.

A Bad Interpreter Day © Maureen Klusza.

The winking interpreter © Maureen Klusza.

Technology: Creative ways to use modern technologies. Whenever new devices come on the market, there is usually some creativity in deciding how the new-fangled devices can enhance the everyday lives of deaf people. Multitasking is an attractive option in our busy lives. When the TTY was first available, artist Richardson connected the daily routine of the bathroom with a TTY device, to perform the tasks simultaneously. Now that face-to-face contact provided by webcams and videophones has replaced the analog characters or typed documents, an updated product replacing the keyboard might not sell.

©1995 SHAWN RICHARDSON

"Here is our newest model called Toiletty 7000. What do you think of the combination of TTY and toilet?"

TTY toilet © Shawn Richardson.

Current communication technology can be instantaneous. With computers, via e-mail, the Internet, or texting, breaking news is spread all over the world instantly. While you go on a picnic, you might wonder how the ants invite themselves to your food. Underground is a tribe of deaf ants, and the illustration shows how the deaf ants can compensate by having visual alerts throughout their colony. This is an example of artist Heriberto Quinones' imagination.

Picnic Alert © 1992 Heriberto Quinones.

ASL/English Genre

WRITTEN POETRY

Over the years, Deaf people have enjoyed expressing themselves or thoughts about life by writing poems. The earliest known collection of over 500 poems written by deaf individuals, *Silent Muse Anthology,* was printed in the early 1960s. Written poems and their styles and rules are usually taught as part of literature in schools and through college courses. Poems by deaf poets are usually written from the poets' experiences as deaf people.

SIGNED ASL POETRY

Prior to the 1970s, there were no known published records about ASL poets or poetry. Probably as a result of the appreciation created through the studies in ASL linguistics during the 1960s, deaf people started to create what we called visual (ASL) poetry or signed poetry. As Patrick Graybill[21] describes it, "In English poetry we play with words; in ASL poetry, we play with signs." Visual poetry is best understood when it is signed or seen in motion. Consequentially, much like ABC, number and handshape stories, ASL poetry is difficult, if not impossible, to be recorded in writing.

The late Clayton Valli, born deaf in New Hampshire, is considered the first person to have analyzed ASL's poetic devices. In his 1983 research into the technical nature of English poetry, he made analogies with poetic devices in English poetry, such as rhyme. He recognized that there are many features in ASL that create "rhyme," such as the sign's direction or quality of movement, handshape, location of signs and orientation of the hands. The signer's facial expression and other non-manual signals are also involved.[22]

The videotape *ASL Poetry: Selected Works of Clayton Valli* contains an outstanding collage of various ASL poems. The tape presents enhanced pictures of what the visual poem is like and guides viewers through the hidden meanings in the poems. Like written poetry, it is not always easy to comprehend ASL poetry right away. In fact, it may take repeated viewing before full comprehension of the poem's meaning is realized. A set of three one-hour videotapes, called *Poetry in Motion*, presents additional insight into the American Deaf community through poetry as articulated by Patrick Graybill, Debbie Rennie, and Clayton Valli, all well-known deaf poets.

Deaf-Related Art Genre

In order to stress the difference between art *by* and *about* deaf people, a group of eight deaf artists gathered for a four-day "What is Deaf Art?" workshop prior to the 1989 international Deaf Way arts festival held at Gallaudet University. Betty Miller, a painter, and Paul Johnston, a sculptor, facilitated the workshop. The other seven participants were art historian Deborah Sonnenstrahl, painter Chuck Baird, sculptor Guy Wonder, painter Alex Wilhite, fiber artist Sandi Vasnick, fiber artist Nancy Creighton, and video artist Lai-Yok Ho.

At this historical gathering, the Deaf artists decided to distinguish themselves from Deaf artists who produce art in any form for general audiences. They created the *De'VIA Manifesto*, with the word De'VIA standing for Deaf View/Image Art. This manifesto was specifically written to cover the traditional fields of visual fine arts (painting, sculpture, drawing, photography, and printmaking) as well as alternative media when used as fine arts, such as fiber arts, ceramics, neon, and collage. The guiding principle is that De'VIA represents:

> ... Deaf artists and [their] perceptions [as] based on their Deaf experiences. It uses formal art elements with the intention of expressing innate cultural or physical Deaf experience. These experiences may include Deaf metaphors, Deaf perspectives, and Deaf insight in relationship with the environment (both the natural world and Deaf cultural environment), spiritual and everyday life.[23]

In representing their symbolisms of Deaf culture, artists may exaggerate facial features such as eyes, mouth, ears, and hands, although this isn't always the case. Since the emphasis in De'VIA art is to symbolize the Deaf experience, the artists themselves do not need to be deaf. Some of them might be hearing children of Deaf parents who grow up in a deaf environment.

Conversely, the works of some Deaf artists, such as Brewster, Carlin, and Tilden, whose works are mentioned in Chapter Nine, are not considered De'VIA.

The following highlights some artists whose work has appeared in various deaf-related publications or exhibits. Many of their works relate to deafness, whether the work is funny, satirical, or serious.

MATT DAIGLE (B. 1970)

As described on his website, "Matt Daigle is profoundly deaf but has ears to wear." He earned a bachelor's degree in advertising and graphic design from Rochester Institute of Technology and has worked for more than 13 years as a full-time graphic designer. At the time of this writing, he is a stay-at-home father while being a freelance graphic designer and cartoonist.

At his website, Daigle expresses a desire to expose people to the unique culture of the Deaf world and stresses that his cartoons are not to be laughed at but rather are to show the humor

Breastfeeding icon (public domain) designed by Matt Daigle.

when deaf and non-deaf people meet. His subjects vary from technology that is used by Deaf people to interpreters to hearing-ear dogs. He also produces cartoons for non-deaf audiences.

Examples: *Blinking Codes* (Chapter Seven), *Smoke Signals* (Chapter Eight)

In 2007, his logo for a breastfeeding symbol contest was selected from among 500 entries and has now become an international icon. The symbol is used to mark breastfeeding-friendly facilities in public places such as airports, restaurants and businesses.

Maureen Klusza (b. 1970)

Creator of a popular comic strip, "The Deaf Side," Maureen Klusza shares a view of the world through Deaf eyes. She had her beginnings in drawing cartoons for her teachers in elementary and high school. She graduated with a bachelor's degree in illustration from Rochester Institute of Technology. At present she teaches art and drama at California School for the Deaf, Fremont. She has been the school's yearbook advisor for ten years. She also publishes illustrations for beginning readers, using a bilingual approach to help them learn and appreciate ASL and English at young ages.

Examples: *A Bad Interpreter Day*, *The Winking Interpreter* (Chapter Seven)

Betty Miller (b. 1934)

One of the founders and considered the mother of the De'VIA movement, Betty Miller, Ed.D., is known for her art depicting experiences of many deaf persons who encounter discrimination and disappointments in the hearing world. Miller was probably the first artist to expose the deep-seated resentment of deaf adults who were bombarded with emphasis on hearing, speech and lip-reading. She has produced many paintings and multimedia creations in which she presented

> ... both the suppression and the beauty of Deaf Culture and American Sign Language as I see it, in the past, and in the present. I hope this work, and the understanding that may arise from this visual expression, will help bridge the gap between the Deaf world, and the hearing world.[24]

A lifelong artist who was influenced by her deaf artist father, Miller earned a doctorate in art education from Pennsylvania State University in 1976. She taught at Gallaudet University for 18 years before leaving to co-found Spectrum, Focus on Deaf Artists, in Austin, Texas. Her works on the theme of "The Deaf Experience" have been shown in several cities. She authored and illustrated the highly admired book, *Deaf and Sober: Journeys through Recovery.* She currently resides in Philadelphia, and her latest works include several commissions in neon artwork.

RUTH PETERSON (B. 1926)

Although born hard of hearing to hearing parents in Brooklyn, Ruth Peterson became fully deaf in 1983, when she was in her fifties. She spent the last nine years of her schooling at Rochester School for the Deaf (RSD) and earned a certificate in art from Rochester Institute of Technology. She taught at RSD for four years until her marriage to Donald Peterson in 1954.

The couple moved to Washington, D.C., where Donald taught chemistry at Gallaudet University. Peterson eventually obtained her bachelor's degree from Gallaudet in 1972. She did freelance art work and taught art at both Gallaudet University and Model Secondary School for the Deaf and taught sign language to high school students and professionals.

Peterson demonstrates her humor, creativity, thoughtfulness and wisdom in her works, which include oil paintings but are mostly pen and ink renderings. She illustrated several books and booklets and created ink sketches of buildings on the Gallaudet campus. Her illustrations appeared on a regular basis in several publications, such as the now defunct *DeeCeeEyes,* and the *Mustard Seed,* a monthly Christ Lutheran church newsletter — where she also contributed a full page of short stories, jokes, and anecdotes, mostly about the deaf world.

Examples: *ILY Handshape* (Chapter Four), *Lois Misunderstanding* (Chapter Seven)

HERIBERTO QUINONES (B. 1965)

Creator of "The Cartoon Factory," Herbie Quinones attended Rochester School for the Deaf and graduated from Florida School for the Deaf and Blind. Born deaf, he started to draw at the age of eight and realized that he was able to sketch houses and almost everything except human figures. He attended National Technical Institute for the Deaf and Florida Community College at Jacksonville.

Quinones started The Cartoon Factory because "...I liked to compete with *Far Side* but it is deaf cartoons. I have a reason to start it ... to let the deaf world have opportunities to have comic strips like Farside."[25] He resides in Florida.

Examples: *Hazards of Deaf Culture* (Chapter Four), *Hearing Aid Tree, Picnic Alert* (Chapter Seven)

SHAWN RICHARDSON (B. 1969)

An African-American native of Tucson, Arizona, Shawn Richardson lost his hearing at the age of one due to spinal meningitis. When he was young, his hearing parents moved to Baltimore. He entered Maryland School for the Deaf at the age of eleven and excelled in athletics and art. After graduating from National Technical Institute for the Deaf with an associate's degree in applied arts, Richardson moved to Washington, D.C., where he works with the National Trust for Historic Preservation.

His cartoons have appeared in several deaf publications. He usually features black characters in his cartoons, but his drawings illustrate his real-life experiences and those of his friends rather than racial issues.

Examples: *Tanning Lotion*, *TTY/Toilet* (Chapter Seven)

ANN SILVER (B. 1949)

Born to a hearing family in Seattle, Ann Silver attended public schools without interpreters. She is fond of saying that her childhood education "was 90 percent guesswork, 10 percent art."[26] She majored in commercial art at Gallaudet University and received her master's degree in deaf rehabilitation from New York University in 1977. She, along with Betty Miller, was a founding member of the Deaf Art Movement in Washington, D.C., during the 1960s and 1970s.

During her early professional career, Silver was affiliated with major publishing firms in Manhattan and with the Museum of Modern Art and Metropolitan Museum of Art in New York. Her products included poster art, graphics, drawings, logos, greeting cards and book jackets. Some of her works were exhibited across the country and in Stockholm and Tokyo.

Saying that she considers Deaf art as her soul, her heart, and her conscience, Silver's work often demonstrates protest art, political satire, victim art, or graphic art, with emphasis on Deaf experience. She now resides in Seattle, Washington.

Examples: *A Century of Difference*, *Deaf Identity Crayons* (Chapter Four)

Deaf Contributions to Performing Arts

DEAF STAGE PERFORMERS GENRE

Historically, since the early twentieth century, acting by deaf people took place in residential schools, usually during free time in the dormitories. Most schools offered a literary society, which usually met twice per month, most likely on Saturday evenings. It should be recalled that the students did not go home during the weekends back then. Membership was usually limited to advanced or high school students. The participants were encouraged to create their own scripts for declamation, poetry, storytelling, one-act plays, or to relate from existing sources of literature. Upon leaving schools, many continued to perform at deaf clubs. After all, performing was their foremost entertainment, at least until the availability of captioned movie films in the 1960s.

In the 1950s, dramatics began to make an appearance in schools. Stage productions were usually held once a year and involved more students through auditions and backstage tasks. The literary societies began to disappear during that time and became practically non-existent in the 1960s when students began going home every weekend.

The growth and evolution of drama in the schools can be traced to the popular stage offerings at Gallaudet University, which offerings started in 1882 with productions by the all-male Saturday Night Club. Later, stage plays were produced by the Dramatics Club and by fraternities and sororities. Graduates from Gallaudet who taught at schools for the deaf would persuade schools to form dramatics as a form of expression. It was not until at least sixty years later that Gallaudet University launched its first formal drama classes in the late 1950s. That was when Gilbert Eastman, a graduate of American School for the Deaf and a 1957 graduate of Gallaudet, became the first full-time professor and director of dramatics at the college.

Like Gallaudet University, the National Technical Institute for the Deaf now has a theater department thanks to its faculty, Robert Panara, a graduate of the American School for the Deaf, and Patrick Graybill, from the Kansas School of the Deaf, both graduates of Gallaudet College.

NATIONAL THEATRE OF THE DEAF

In 1967, with director David Hays and 17 founding members, including Bernard Bragg and Gilbert Eastman, the National Theater of the Deaf (NTD) was founded with funding from the Department of Health, Education and Welfare. Based in Waterford, Connecticut, NTD was the first to assemble a cast of professional deaf actors and actresses. NTD's primary focus was to bring hearing roles to a play using deaf actors with hearing actors/readers on stage, thus eliminating the need for sign-to-voice translators on the first row of seats as was traditionally done that time. The plays were designed to attract hearing playgoers, although both deaf and hearing audiences could enjoy the play equally. This unique approach helped the hearing audience to become aware of the power and beauty of signed language and Deaf culture.

Since its first performance in 1967 before an audience of six, NTD has performed all over the world. According to its website, in the past 40 years the company has made close to 80 national tours and visited all 50 states. The troupe has also made 30 international tours and a total of over seven thousand performances. Currently the company is self-supporting.

Bragg, who served NTD as an actor, director, and playwright, recalled that during the group's European debut in 1969, there were only two professional deaf theatre companies in existence — NTD, and the Moscow Theatre of Mimicry and Gesture, which was started four years earlier. Thanks to NTD, professional deaf theater has flourished in many other countries (Great Britain, Sweden, Australia, France, Spain, Finland, Italy, Germany, Hong Kong, Japan, and China) as well as through some theatres in the United States, such as California's DEAF Media and Deaf West theatres; Portland, Oregon's The Northwest Theatre of the Deaf; Cleveland, Ohio's Fairmount Theatre of the Deaf; New York City's New York Deaf Theatre, the Onyx Theatre, and several small theater groups and one-man shows.[27]

Deaf West Theatre (DWT), based in North Hollywood, California, was founded in 1991 as the first professional resident sign language theater in the western half of the United States. The 90-seat theater contains a state-of-the-art sound system, sub-woofers under raked seating, an infrared headphone system, and captioning capabilities. With Ed Waterstreet as the founder and artistic director, DWT produces plays in ASL with simultaneous translations in spoken English. In 2003, DWT's award-winning production of Mark Twain's *Big River: The Adventures of Huckleberry Finn* traveled across the nation and overseas.

National Theatre of the Deaf has become a cottage industry for enterprising deaf performers. Several groups and individuals have emerged, such as:

Rathskellar. Founded in 1998 by Jonathan Kovacs, who is deaf, Rathskellar has appeared on stages all over the world. The name Rathskellar was drawn from the students' popular gathering and watering hole at Gallaudet University, where the troupe was founded. The troupe, usually a cast of four, has performed in front of over fifty thousand viewers of all ages, expressing the beauty of sign language in combination with dance and music, accompanied with amplified sound effects. The entertaining performances also include ASL poetry, A to Z mime, handshape stories, and storytelling in their repertoire.

Invisible Hands, Inc. *Invisible Hands, Inc.*, a non-profit organization, promotes deaf awareness through art and sponsors two dance troupes, Wild Zappers and the National Deaf Dance Theater. The director of Invisible Hands is Fred Beam, who founded Wild Zappers in 1989 along with two other African-Americans, Irvine Stewart and Warren "Wawa" Snipe. The company was started so they could dance together on a regular basis. The all-male company combines jazz, funk and hip-hop dance styles, ASL and popular music in its programs that strive to promote cultural awareness within both the deaf and hearing communities. Wild Zappers and the National Deaf Dance Theatre have danced in venues such as Kennedy Center and Apollo Theater in New York and throughout the world in locales that include China, Japan, Australia, Jamaica, and Guyana.

CJ Jones. CJ Jones was six years old when he had his first acting performance as one of the children on the *Captain Kangaroo* television series. Although he came from a deaf family — his father was a deaf Golden Gloves boxer — CJ lost his hearing to spinal meningitis at the age of seven. He attended Missouri School for the Deaf and National Technical Institute for the Deaf. In college, he won the award for best comedy actor. After traveling with the NTD in the 1970s, he ventured into a one-man show and has performed for at least 30 years. Although experiencing what CJ as calls the "double whammy" of being an actor who is both deaf and black, he is also known as a motivational speaker and is the chief executive officer of Hands Across Communication to produce events for international deaf artists. He has appeared on *Sesame Street, Frasier* and several other television shows, and in several films such as *The Ride* and *See What I'm Saying.*

John Maucere. Since 1996, John Maucere, whose versatile talents include the roles of an actor, a comedian and a talk show host, has given one-man shows all over the nation. Well known for his dead-on imitation of Jay Leno, Maucere has the ability to entertain audiences with humor about a variety of subjects, especially related to the cultural differences between deaf people and hearing people, and humorous deaf experiences. The *John "Leno" Maucere Show* is part of Deafywood, which is owned and operated by Maucere. Deafywood also produces the SuperDeafy character in which the deaf superhero is always conveniently available to rescue victims from various perils. The SuperDeafy character is the first deaf superhero doll made and sold to the public.

HOLLYWOOD THEN AND NOW

During the silent movie era of the 1920s, Hollywood usually did not cast real-life deaf people in motion pictures. However, a deaf actor, Granville Redmond, had a guest role in several films with Charlie Chaplin, e.g., *A Dog's Life* in 1918. Other than that, no true experiences of deaf people were reflected. Often images of deaf characters — acted out by hearing actors — gave off gross misperceptions of true deaf people. It might be recalled that at that time, Hollywood portrayed black characters by rubbing the faces of white actors with black shoe substances; this mistaken portrayal was similar for deaf characters. The artificial deaf characters were usually seen as meek like a lamb, uneducated/feeble-minded, sad and lonely, and completely dependent upon hearing saviors. A well-known example is the movie *Johnny Belinda*, with Jane Wyman as a deaf character who was a rape victim.

Protests by the deaf community have slowly changed the images of deaf people from negative characters to positive (educated and strong-willed). Still, these misconceptions continue; hearing people continue to be hired for deaf roles even with the availability of outstanding deaf actors. Even so, some progress has been made.

The most accomplished Deaf star is Marlee Matlin, who at 21 became the youngest Academy Award winner in the Best Actress category, as well as the first deaf Oscar winner, for her performance in *Children of a Lesser God*. The other stars competing for her award were Jane Fonda, Sigourney Weaver, Sissy Spacek, and Kathleen Turner. Since then, Matlin has appeared in more than 20 movies and more than 20 television programs, including a regular role as Joey in *West Wing* and Jodi in *The L Word*. She is the author of *Deaf Child Crossing*, published by Simon & Schuster in 2002, with sequels printed in 2006 and 2007. Matlin was quoted in the *Dayton Daily News* as saying: "The real handicap of deafness doesn't lie in the ear, but in the mind."

In 2008, Matlin became the first Deaf person invited to participate in *Dancing with the Stars*, in its sixth season. Although performing in an unfamiliar audio-based musical setting, she and her partner remained in competition with eleven other couples until halfway through the season, when she was eliminated. Her autobiography, *I'll Scream Later*, made the *New York Times*' best-sellers list in 2009. She serves on the Gallaudet University Board of Trustees.

DAZZLING DEAF PERFORMERS IN FILM, TELEVISION, AND THEATRE

In addition to Matlin, during the last three decades, deaf performing artists have won awards in the United States and abroad. The most notable ones are Phyllis Frelich, who won the 1980 Tony Award for her performance as Sarah Norman in *Children of a Lesser God*, and Linda Bove, who was honored by an Italian-American women's organization in recognition of her work on television. Both toured with the NTD troupe.

Frelich has appeared in at least 15 different television series and performed in plays. She performed almost 900 times in *Children of a Lesser God* on a Broadway stage between 1980 and 1982.

Linda Bove is best known for her role as Linda the librarian in *Sesame Street.* She debuted in 1971, and in 1979 became a full-time cast member. She remained on the cast until 2003, a remarkable 32-year run. She also appeared as a deaf character in 25 episodes of the soap opera *Search for Tomorrow,* in 1973. She is currently affiliated with Deaf West Theatre, which her husband Ed Waterstreet founded.

Michelle Banks, an African American deaf woman, has acted in several television programs such as *Soul Food* and *Strong Medicine,* and in movies and plays such as *Malcolm X, Compensation* and *Big River.* Her one-woman show, *Reflections of a Black Deaf Woman,* has toured all over America. The founder and artistic director of the Onyx Theatre, the only Deaf theater of color in the United States, Banks says she chose "Onyx" because the black stone represents people of color, and the stone represents deafness. She has been awarded honors as the best director and best film and was featured in the February 1989 issue of *Essence.*

Tyrone Giordano is one of the latest up-and-coming deaf actors. At the age of 27, he appeared as a 15-year-old Huckleberry Finn in Deaf West Theatre's *Big River* and remained with the cast when the group debuted in Broadway in May 2003 and during its yearlong national tour from June 2004 through June 2005. He has also appeared in two films, *The Family Stone* and *A Lot Like Love.*

Another rising performer is Shoshanna Stern. Coming from a fourth-generation deaf family, she did some acting at the California School for the Deaf, Fremont, and at Gallaudet University before hitting the big time in television. She has performed in least ten television series, with nine episodes of *Jericho,* 11 episodes of *Weeds,* and six episodes of *Threat Matrix.* She has also performed as Sarah Norman in *Children of a Lesser God,* the same role previously played by Phyllis Frelich and Marlee Matlin.

Ever since the 1950s, when television came onto the scene, hearing actors/actresses have portrayed deaf people. Between the 1970s and 1980s, deaf actors and actresses began to appear on television programs, but they were mostly in roles as guests or cameos. In 1979 Jeffrey Bravin, a deaf child from a deaf family, had a major role in the highly memorable made-for-television movie, *And Your Name Is Jonah.* In 1985, in their leading roles in a Hallmark movie, *Love Is Never Silent,* Ed Waterstreet and Phyllis Frelich gave magnificent performances.

Television should be lauded for its recent portrayal of the real-life deaf Sue Thomas as a Federal Bureau of Investigation agent in the series *F.B.Eye.* The role was played by deaf actress Deanne Bray. The series ran for over two years on the PAX TV channel. Hopefully the television industry will continue to cast deaf actors/actresses in this millennium.

Deaf Music Genre

Music is appreciated by many Deaf and hard of hearing people. Some enjoy music tremendously while others care nothing about music in any form. Deaf and hard of hearing people not wearing assistive devices take pleasure in music by feeling vibrations, usually through conductive surfaces such as a wooden floor. Holding inflated balloons or objects such as purses also enhances the sense of rhythm from music. Watching visual rhythms and body language of the performers adds to the enjoyment.

Clapping between signs makes fine kinesthetic and visual music and is quite common in "Deaf songs." The earliest known performer of the rhythmic "one, two, one-two-three" routines was George Kannapell, a pep-squad leader during his college days at Gallaudet in the late 1920s. He can be seen "sign-singing" the following piece in an old-time film:

> Boat, Boat, BoatBoatBoat
> Drink, Drink, DrinkDrinkDrink
> Fun, Fun, FunFunFun
> Enjoy, Enjoy, EnjoyEnjoyEnjoy.[28]

The popular similar beats have evolved over the years from clapping to a multi-rhythmic approach. As an example, on frequent occasions Gallaudet University students, with the accompaniment of beats from a bass drum, sign rhythmically the university fight song, the "Bison Song." Seeing — not hearing — the song for the first time, or the umpteenth time, is always inspiring, with the vibrations from the pounding of the drum. It is always a mystery how the non-deaf audience remains sane at the end of the song.

Deaf Photographers and Filmmakers

Even long before the age of digital photography, schools for the deaf usually possessed a resident shutterbug, either Deaf or non-deaf, who recorded all the activities, took individual and group pictures, and recorded candid shots. The majority of the pictures would be memorialized in the school yearbooks. Sometimes photographs were sold to individuals for their personal albums, with the funds going toward maintaining the school darkrooms. Some schools also sponsored photo clubs as an extracurricular activity or offered vocational training in photography. With digital media nowadays, anybody with a pocket camera or cell telephone can take still or motion pictures, upload them and dispatch them via the Internet.

SELECTED DEAF PHOTOGRAPHERS

A study of the idyllic life of New England is available through the collection and glass plate negatives produced by the Allen sisters, both deaf. Frances Allen (1854–1941) and Mary Allen (1858–1941) of Deerfield, Massachusetts, are renowned for their pictures of country scenes, figures, and children, taken between 1885 and 1920. They started out as teachers but lost their hearing, so they turned to photography as a vocation. Their works were exhibited in venues such as the Third International Congress of Photography in Paris in 1900, Canadian Pictorialist Exhibit in Montreal in 1907, and the Art Institute of Chicago in 1908. They also took pictures in Great Britain and California, and these pictures are considered their best works. During their photography careers, many tourists stopped at their residence to purchase photographs from the home's front parlor. The sisters died within four days of each other. Their works, which continue to be exhibited, are published in *The Allen Sisters: Pictorial Photographers 1885–1920*, written by Suzanne L. Flynt.

The long-lost lifestyle of inhabitants of houseboats on the Tennessee River who depended on fishing as a source of income was preserved through pictures taken by Maggie Lee Sayre. She was born on a houseboat in 1920 and attended Kentucky School for the Deaf for several years with her older sister — also deaf; there they learned sign language as well as how to read and write. The older sister, Myrtle, was one of the students who received a free Brownie camera given away by Kodak on the occasion of its 50th anniversary in 1930. In 1936 Myrtle died, and Maggie inherited the box camera. Sayre continued to live in a 60-foot houseboat with her illiterate parents. She recorded the day-to-day activities of her family, relatives and friends. It was not until 1982 when she was living in a nursing home that her work in neatly organized scrapbooks containing over 250 photographs with descriptions was discovered. The collection was exhibited at the 1996 Olympic Games in Atlanta, and at the Smithsonian Folklife Festival as a part of the Tennessee exhibit. She was also profiled in the ABC television *Person of the Week* series. Her work was published in *"Deaf Maggie Lee Sayre": Photographs of a River Life* by the University Press of Mississippi in 1995.[29]

FILMMAKING BY DEAF PERSONS

The advantage of filmmaking in the early days was that the unique communication mode of Deaf people could be recorded without the need of a soundtrack. Folklore and other historical products in sign language have been kept in perpetual motion through films. George Veditz's *Preservation of the*

Sign Language, and Edward Miner Gallaudet's rendition of the classic Lorna Doone story during the early 1900s, are examples of the farsightedness the filmmakers possessed, as mentioned in Chapter Three. These films, maintained by the National Association of the Deaf, are especially significant in that they permit future generations to enjoy and critique the use of sign language at that time, and how those people used ASL. Imagine if people could hear the actual voices of George Washington and Abraham Lincoln from archival tapes, or original music by Beethoven. This is how significant the films of Veditz and Gallaudet are to Deaf people everywhere. They have become classics.

Expert filmmakers, deaf or hearing, have a slim chance to be involved with the highly competitive industry of Hollywood films. However, many deaf filmmakers possess thorough understanding of filmmaking or love filmmaking enough to be able to produce quality films for and about deaf people. One of the earliest deaf film producers was Ernest Marshall of New York City. Coming from two generations of a deaf family, Ernest was a student leader at the old New York School for the Deaf in New York City. At the time of his graduation in 1931, silent films had practically disappeared. With the purchase of a Cine-Kodak 16mm system, he produced and directed a total of seven feature films and four shorts, and acted in some of them. All of the films featured deaf actors and actresses shown in sign language — except one. *The Dream*, produced in 1961, was a satirical twist to Hollywood films, showing deaf characters portraying hearing characters. Marshall was renowned all over the city as a performer and traveled the nation to show his films. Instead of shipping the films, he always brought his films with him.[30]

The *Through Deaf Eyes* video production that premiered on PBS stations during 2007 included stories that were produced by six outstanding young Deaf filmmakers. Wayne Betts Jr., Kimby Caplan, Arthur Luhn, Adrean Mangiardi, Tracey Salaway, and Rene Visco produced vignettes that expressed their personal senses of Deaf life in America. Three of them studied at Rochester Institute of Technology, and the others came from University of Colorado, Boston University, and California State University at Northridge.

A documentary film by Ann Marie "Jade" Bryan, *9/11 Fear in Silence: The Forgotten Underdogs*, relates the infamous day of September 11, 2001, when, as she put it, "...Deaf and Hard of Hearing people ... were the FIRST citizens to become shut out from outside communication, the LAST to receive access to information, or be delivered from danger..." (capitals hers). The documentary film has been nominated for best feature documentary in the Pan African Film Festival. Ann became the first deaf African American to study at and earn a bachelor's degree from Tisch School of the Arts at New York University.

The enterprising woman established Jade Film Productions, Inc., in New York City as a commercial production company and founded Deafvision Film-works, Inc., a non-profit organization devoted to helping media artists of diverse background advance in their efforts.

ASL Films is an independent film production company founded in 2005 by Mark Wood and Mindy Moore, both Deaf. ASL Films has produced five full-length feature films. To enable audiences to fully appreciate the ASL in the films, there are no voice-overs, although some of the films have captioning. All films include Deaf cast and crew members. At the recent WORLDDEAF Cinema Festival at Gallaudet (more in Chapter Ten) the film *Gerald*, produced and directed by Wood, received the Best Narrative award. ASL Films intends to produce several more films.

DEAF MOSAIC

The *Deaf Mosaic* videotape series offers a most thorough study of the deaf community. The series, produced by the Gallaudet University Department of Film, Television, and Photography, ran from April 1985 through June 1995 and was shown nationwide on the Discovery Channel and local PBS stations. Emceed by the late Gilbert Eastman and Mary Lou Novitsky, the production covered a wide range of topics related to the deaf community, in the areas of language, culture, arts, and personalities. The series received seven Emmy Award nominations, winning three, and was awarded four CINE Golden Eagle awards. A total of 61 hours —122 half-hour shows — were produced. All episodes are available online through the Gallaudet University Video Library.

The fact is that entertainment in the form of television and Hollywood films is very influential and educational for the public, so the images of deaf characters and how they are portrayed are significant. Sign language interpreters have also appeared more often in television and movies, and even some deaf characters have made obvious the use of pad and pencil. These are important, to demonstrate that not all deaf people can lip read or speak fluently, a huge misconception among clueless hearing people.

In Closing

This chapter reminds us that Deaf people — without their sense of hearing — continue to possess all five senses, including the fifth one, a sense of humor.

Deaf people, overall, have a positive outlook on life. There are untold stories of the tribulations a deaf child undergoes during his/her youth — wondering why he/she cannot hear, if he/she should wear hearing aids or cochlear implants, if he/she should learn sign language, etc. — but eventually when an adult finds his/her place in the world where he/she can belong, he/she would become contented. Expressions as told in the chapter are articulated from such happy folks who happen to be deaf or hard of hearing.

EIGHT

Enlightenment of Independence

Enhanced Quality of Life: Technology

During the late 1800s and almost half of the 1900s, deaf people lacked instantaneous communication technology. Daily metropolitan newspapers rarely provided any news of usefulness or interest to deaf people who craved unceasing comradeship among their peers. Of course, radios were rarely found in their homes, or only served as a tabletop prettification, except in residences shared with hearing friends, spouses, children or parents.

This chapter presents historical information in areas of technology that Deaf individuals value. Technological improvements can be observed across various stages, along with how the applications of earlier technologies have developed additional uses. Deaf people were quite isolated in earlier days, but advances in audio and visual technologies have moved them closer to the mainstream of daily living with non-deaf peers.

MEDICAL PERSPECTIVES AND HEARING AIDS

In the long history of mankind, there have been — and still are to this day — numerous attempts to cure deafness. Literature has documented various barbarian efforts such as pouring "medications" in people's ears, as described in the first chapter. Those failed attempts eventually led to a greater acceptance of hearing loss in most instances, and the pendulum has swung to more humanistic approaches such as compensation or recovery of hearing loss through various devices — hearing aids, amplifiers, and cochlear implants — or simply accepting the hearing loss and focusing on other aspects of life.

The first known hearing aid manufacturing company was established in or around 1800 by Frederick C. Rein in London. F. C. Rein and Son, during its early years, manufactured non-electric hearing aids such as ear trumpets, acoustic urns, and speaking tubes for churches. In 1819, the firm made an acoustic throne for King Goa (John) of Portugal. The throne was designed

171

so that sound traveled through the heads of lions mounted on the end of the armrests, down to a resonant box in the seat, and finally via a hearing tube at the back of the throne. King Goa used the throne when he ruled from Brazil, and visitors were required to kneel before the chair and speak directly into the monstrous lions' open mouths. The earliest patents issued for hearing aids were granted in 1836 in England for a curved earpiece worn behind the ear and in 1855 in the United States for "earscoops."[1]

In the nineteenth century, attitudes toward hearing loss were extremely negative, and aids were noticeable on the wearer's body. In 1891, Dr. Grenbech wrote, "Most hearing aids are of such size and shape that they clearly draw attention to the *imperfection* [italics ours] of the wearer...."[2] Dr. Campbell, in 1882, noted that "the deaf are, as *a general rule*, very sensitive over their *infirmity*...."[3] In those days, medical professionals were considered "divine beings" — a perception that still exists to this day in many parts of the world. The stigma of using hearing devices and the public's negative reaction to those devices caused many people to attempt to conceal their hearing aids.

With the introduction of vacuum tube technology in the early 1920s, hearing aids evolved from mechanical types to electrical-based types. As a result, hearing aids became more powerful and provided greater benefits for users. Some devices were designed to look like tabletop radios and other appliances. Other aids looked like women's purses or were concealed in purses; one model from France resembled a camera.

Eventually hearing aids became smaller and, thus, were concealed more easily. Most hearing aids in the twentieth century were designed to be hidden by wearing harnesses under clothing or by using brassieres to hold the hearing aids. Sometimes batteries were in a separate pouch tied around the thigh. For men, some aids were inserted into a shirt or suit pocket. Tie clasps carried concealed microphones. For women, some hearing aids were designed as barrettes or concealed in bouffant hairdos. Yet others were pinned onto hats or scarves. "Invisible hearing aids" were promoted in magazines and newspapers, suggesting that the public would not know that the wearer was deaf. The strategy was always to mask the hearing loss as if it were a stigma to the normal population.

The development of transistors in 1952 further miniaturized hearing aids, making it possible to design and manufacture hearing aids worn in eyeglasses or behind the ears and later, inside the ears. With the aid of microprocessors, today's hearing aids can be prescribed to fit individual needs.

AUDITORY ENHANCEMENT

The earliest research on cochlear implants (CI) began in the 1950s. In 1961, Dr. William House performed the first cochlear implant in America.[4]

It wasn't until 1984 that the movement to restore hearing in infants and adults through cochlear implants started with single-channel implants.[5] Today, the procedure is widespread.

The device is a mechanical prosthesis of sorts for the inner ear. It bypasses the bones of the inner ear; the electrodes are surgically implanted directly into the cochlea where sound waves are absorbed and interpreted by the auditory nerve. The implant is secured inside the skill, and the sound and speech processor is worn externally behind the ear. The processor is held in place by a magnet connected to the implant. Implants do not restore normal hearing; rather they provide a representation of environmental sounds and may help implantees understand speech.

Some deaf and hard of hearing persons opt to have the CI surgery. However, parents considering cochlear implants for their children should be advised that implants do not cure or eliminate deafness. They are highly encouraged to research current literature and talk with deaf and hard of hearing adults on the topic before making a final decision. They should be aware of the need for post-surgery training or rehabilitation, especially for those who lose hearing early; it takes some time to identify sounds and make sense of vowels and consonants.

In the years since the surgery's approval by the U.S. Food and Drug Administration in 1984, some 120,000 people worldwide have received the implants.[6] There has been controversy about the implants among deaf and hard of hearing people. Part of the resistance is carried by opponents of the age-old "pathological viewpoint" of the medical professionals who obsess on "fixing." Another part is the fear within the Deaf community that Deaf culture and its heritage will disappear. Last, but not least, there are concerns among deaf people that parents make decisions that they may regret later on if things do not work out as they expected or if they are not provided with comprehensive, neutral information.

Like any technical devices, the implants are subject to problems or failures. Implants have been removed from individuals because incisions did not heal properly, for example. In 2004, a manufacturer recalled its product when there was a possibility of device failure due to moisture inside the implant, causing loud noises or complete loss of sound, in addition to intermittent functioning or sudden sensation of discomfort or pain. Since 2003, the Food and Drug Administration has issued three alerts about the life-threatening risk of bacterial meningitis caused by a positioner in the implants. Implant wearers are encouraged to be vaccinated to prevent meningitis.[7]

Schools and programs for deaf children have long accepted students with cochlear implants; other such children attend regular or mainstream school programs. In a *Deaf Life* article, Phil Aiello,[8] who was born deaf and has been a CI user since 2000, said, "I feel it is important for parents to recognize that the implant will not guarantee that their child will be just like his or her 'hearing' peers. The bottom line is that the child needs to be accepted as a deaf or hard of hearing individual."

Visual/Tactile Alerting Devices

Ever wonder how deaf farmers got up in the morning before milking cows or how deaf people got up on time for school or work in the olden days? How did they respond to visitors' knocks on their doors, or how did parents respond to their infants' crying, especially during the dark hours of night? Necessity is the mother of invention, and there were plenty of creative inventions back then.

Probably the most common wakening device was a household cat or dog that would jump on the bed and wake their master or mistress. Some mechanically inclined persons purchased a wind-up alarm clock, wired an electric lamp (or a socket and a bulb) to the clock, and plugged the end of the power cord into an outlet. Should a farmer forget to wind the clock, he might oversleep, to the dismay of hungry cows, horses, pigs, and hens.

Another form of alarm available today, a tactile alarm, can be used to wake up heavy sleepers. The vibrator, sometimes called a bed shaker, connected to the alarm clock, could be put under the pillow or mattress. When the alarm goes off, the pillow or mattress shakes, waking up the occupant. The heaviest sleepers, to be doubly sure, might opt for both visual and tactile alarms.

In the olden days, people tended to leave their doors unlocked during the day. Visitors would pound the front door hard enough to cause the house to shake from the vibrations. Or they would open the unlocked door slightly, grope for the light switch and flash the lights. Should there be no answer, the visitors would then walk around and wave through the windows and pound on the back door. If there still was no response, they would circle back to the front door and enter the house or leave a note on the door. Deaf people used their cars as a replacement for the telephone, which was inaccessible to them that time. None of the off-the-shelf burglar alarms, smoke detectors, and other alarming devices were designed to visually warn deaf people that time.

Communication Access

In the absence of telephones, letters were often the main means of communication among friends and relatives — after all, postage stamps cost only three cents up until the late 1950s. Usually written with fountain pen on stationery or ruled paper, the letters were an excellent vehicle for friendship and love, and to express sympathy and congratulations. Letters were even more important to deaf people who were not able to use telephones. Sharing of news through mail was usually the primary source of information to many deaf individuals who did not live in large cities. Plans for events, such as social functions or private gatherings, were also exchanged through mail.

Deaf people who happen to live with, or close to, hearing parents or siblings were usually more fortunate, but didn't always have complete control over circumstances.

Melvia's family did not have a telephone at home, so her hearing sister, Dollie, who was married and a mother herself, came to the family's house to bring her parents' messages. Dollie drove home, made the calls for her parents, and then returned with any additional messages. Such messages might be for an appointment with the parents' doctor, for example, and usually the date and time were set without input from the parents.

Ron recalls his mother going to a neighbor's home to ask the neighbor to make a call as she waited. In those days, there were more party lines than single dedicated lines, so if someone else was already on the line, the mother and the neighbor would have to wait until the line became available. Sometimes his mother had to walk back home and then trod back again later, hoping the line was available. After the authors got married in 1961, they asked their neighbors (one on one side of the house, another on the other side, or two neighbors across the street) to make calls or to receive messages. Some telephone calls were sensitive or personal, but no other choice was available. There was often trepidation that that the whole neighborhood would know the family's dirty laundry if one of the neighbors shared information. Although the TTY was in use in the mid–1960s, it was good only for TTY-to-TTY communication. Relay services were not available until much later.

ACCESS FOR DEAF-BLIND PEOPLE

Deaf-blind people are not necessarily fully blind. The federal definition of a blind person is an individual who possesses 20/200 vision as determined by a vision test. This does not necessarily mean that the person is fully blind. Thus, a deaf-blind person could be hard of hearing and have partial sight, or completely deaf and completely blind, or anywhere in between.

Data on the number of deaf-blind persons varies greatly. A study by the Department of Education estimated between 42,000 and more than 700,000, depending on how deaf-blindness was defined. The National Consortium of Deaf-Blindness conducts an annual census, and the most recent one of October 2009 shows 9,200 children identified.[9] A more reasonable number of deaf-blind persons may be between 35,000 and 40,000, as suggested by Watson.[10] Another estimate, by the National Association of Regulatory Utility Commissions, showed a total of 70,000 to 100,000 deaf-blind persons in the United States.

Regardless of the total number of deaf-blind individuals, the American Association of Blind-Deaf identified in a 2006 needs assessment and 2009 survey of SSP programs the top priority as being a need for support service providers (SSPs). The lives of many of the approximately 70,000 deaf-blind persons are facilitated by Support Service Providers, "...who act as a link between persons who are deaf-blind and their environment."[11] The SSPs' roles are:

- to provide access to the community by making transportation available (by car, bus, or other conveyance) and serving as a human guide while walking, and
- to relay visual and environmental information — visual description — that may not be heard or seen by the deaf-blind person, using the person's preferred language and communication mode.

It is stressed that an SSP provides information to the deaf-blind individual to assist in considering options, but the individual ultimately makes all decisions. It is also advised that the SSPs are not interpreters but may function like one in informal situations.

Service dogs (also known as hearing-ear dogs) also provide a form of visual alerts for their deaf-blind owners. The role of hearing dogs is similar to that of service dogs (seeing-eye dogs) for blind people, but hearing-ear dogs are trained to recognize key sounds and to alert their humans. Sounds include alarm clocks, doorbells, door knocks, telephones, sirens, smoke or carbon monoxide detectors, dropped objects, and even crying babies. Service dogs usually wear orange vests to identify themselves as working dogs.

BORROWED VOICES

As Padden and Humphries suggested, borrowing someone else's voice can be — in a sense — considered technology.[12] In that vein, "borrowing" a voice has morphed into a commercial commodity. Let's take a quick look at this evolution over the years:

- From a family member, a relative, or a friend
- From colleagues at work
- From a live interpreter
- From a relay service operator, using printed and video (TV/computer) media

- From a wireless text pager and through the Internet
- From theaters' hearing actors pairing off with Deaf actors

Now that deaf people have increased access, they have become less isolated from the general community. Deaf people can express their opinions, needs and demands to the larger communities by means of the various technologies with increased ease.

CAPTIONED MOVIES

It was indeed a dark day for deaf people when silent movies were phased out in favor of "talkies." Even so, deaf people continued to go to the movie house, looked at the moving pictures and tried to figure out the conversations or plots from the pictures that were no longer fully accessible to them. Some theatre managers were kind enough to give discounts to deaf people attending the movies. Ron's deaf parents, who were acquaintances of their hometown theatre manager, convinced the manager to allow them to attend the movies at 12 cents—which was the going children's rate in the 1940s. Ron and his sister, who were not yet teenagers, were admitted together for 12 cents, and later for 12 cents each. In the early 1950s, the standard price for children and teenagers increased to 20 cents each person.

Open-captioned movies first began in 1949 with the advent of Captioned Films for the Deaf, based in Connecticut with financial support from the Junior League of Hartford. In 1958, U.S. President Dwight Eisenhower signed the Captioned Films for the Deaf program into law. Originally, because of its service to blind people since 1931, the Library of Congress was to run the program. The newly appointed Library of Congress director shot down the idea because he thought it was not within the library's jurisdiction. The bill was reworked to have the U.S. Department of Education (then the Department of Health, Education and Welfare) run the program.[13]

Since 1958, the Captioned Films for the Deaf—now known as the Described and Captioned Media Program (DCMP)—has captioned theatrical movies and educational films for loan to schools and organizations. Later, the captions were produced on videotapes and, subsequently, on DVDs instead of 16mm films. Streaming videos are also available online.

In 1972, Malcolm Norwood, Ph.D., was appointed the first deaf chief of Captioned Films. He succeeded John Gough, Ph.D., the first director, and Gilbert Delgado, Ph.D., both hearing. Initially, the captioned films of an educational nature and general interest were loaned to schools and organizations, especially deaf clubs. The lending rules were later relaxed, so many smaller home-based organizations were set up in order to secure films for viewing. The authors were member of a potluck-style club consisting of five couples who met every month for supper, which was followed by a captioned film. The "supper club" existed for about 20 years until rental videos became readily available. The group drank and ate together and enjoyed close to 250 titles before the club was dissolved.

Back then, this medium with captions was the only source of entertainment that deaf people could fully comprehend and enjoy. Today, DCMP offers through its website a wide variety of videos and films in numerous genres including education, biographies, classic movies, history, and sports. Many of them are also captioned in Spanish.

CAPTIONED TELEVISION PROGRAMS

Many females vividly remember watching Elvis Presley swing his hips on *The Ed Sullivan Show* on television, falling head over heels in love with him. Before the era of captioned television, many also recall desperately wanting to know more about their favorite television programs, like *I Love Lucy*. Although the characters' slapstick humor was easy to follow, the dialogue was not. In mixed company, a hearing person might laugh about a funny dialogue, but a deaf person would not understand. Deaf people might break out into hysterics from visual signals that might not be so funny to hearing people. However, with increased availability of such shows in syndication being closed captioned, many are rediscovering — and finally understanding — the humorous, snappy dialogue between Lucy and Desi some 50 years after the original airings.

During his long tenure with the Captioned Films for the Deaf, Norwood had a vision of captioned television, prompted by the availability of open-captioned movies. He began to advocate his vision. In 1972, Boston's WGBH television station, with a grant from the Captioned Films for the Deaf, open-captioned 26 episodes of the PBS *French Chef* series featuring Julia Child. In January 1973, WGBH provided captioning for Nixon's inauguration address by obtaining an advance copy of his address and providing captions in synchronization with the audio.

At that time, there was no live captioning. All the captions were written in advance and were synchronized with the pictures before being broadcast. Also in 1973, WGBH obtained further federal funding to provide captions of *ABC News Tonight*. Taping the 6:30 evening feed, the captioners inserted the captions before the tape was re-broadcast on PBS at 11 P.M. By 1980, the captioned *ABC News* was available on over 142 public television stations. The first closed captioning of commercial television, *Masterpiece Theatre*, aired for deaf viewers in Boston.

However, "open captions" were considered a hindrance by the general population who didn't like the visual distraction. In 1971, a conference sponsored by the Captioned Films for the Deaf was held at the University of Tennessee. The National Bureau of Standards demonstrated Line-21 technology that made it possible to show captions to viewers whose television sets were equipped with decoders, removing the "visual distraction" for those who didn't want the captions. Thus closed captioning technology was born.

In 1976, the Federal Communications Commission (FCC) consented to reserving the Line 21 television signal for captions. The approval was a breakthrough, and captions were then made readily available because of this dedicated use. In 1979, federal funds were provided to establish the National Captioning Institute (NCI), which produced captions and sold decoders. NCI established its office in suburban Virginia and later a second office in Los Angeles. The first decoders, costing $300 each, were sold on March 15, 1980, at Sears, Roebuck and Company. The day following NCI's opening, the first television program was broadcast with pre-written closed captions. Initially, only 15 hours of captioned programs were available each week. Even with this small number of programs, deaf people everywhere rejoiced at this new world of accessible information.

Less than 50,000 decoders were sold during the first two years. In 1984, after the first 100,000 decoders were sold, NCI improved the decoders and added a remote control. The number of captioned programs increased to 60 hours of captioning in 1985. Most of the captioning was for national news through major networks and several weekly entertainment programs. Continued demand led to the establishment of several firms that competed with WGBH and NCI for captioning contracts. It is believed that today, there are over a hundred firms producing captions for television along with providing live transmission of classroom lectures and similar functions.

In 1980, Zenith was the first and only firm to manufacture television sets with a built-in computer processor chip that made it possible to show captions without decoders. Called TeleCaption, most of the 19-inch sets with internal decoders were labeled with the Sears brand and sold through catalogues or in Sears stores. Sears charged $266 for decoders and $553 for TV sets with internal decoders. The built-in decoders made it possible to turn on and off the captions by turning a switch on the front of the set. "Mostly advertisers and not broadcasters paid for early captioning. Proctor & Gamble, for instance, thought it would help them reach senior citizens. As a result, they captioned many of their ads for products such as laxatives."[14]

Closed captioning received a big boost from the Commission on Education of the Deaf in 1988. The commission's "Toward Equality" report discussed the limited number of programs with captions and the high cost of decoders. In 1990, as a part of the Americans with Disabilities Act (ADA) signed by President George Bush, a decoder chip act was passed, mandating that by July 1, 1993, all television sets with screens 13 inches or larger would be required to have built-in captioning capability.

The Telecommunications Act of 1996 provided for additional requirements of broadcasting closed captions; for example, by January 1, 2006, all television programs were to be captioned. The FCC ensures that legislation such as this is enforced. In addition, television stations in the nation's largest 25 markets are required to produce live captioning of news. Smaller stations typically pre-record captions on a teleprompter and synchronize the captions with the news feed. However, the captions and pictures are frequently out of sync, and the live local weather and sports segments are usually not captioned.

Interestingly, with the advantages of modern communication technology, a news captioner does not have to be physically in a television newsroom. Live captioning can be done remotely. A home-based stenographer can receive the commentary from a television studio in New York, type it, and send the data back to an encoder located at the studio. The studio then broadcasts the narration with the video, with approximately a five-second delay. This can be confusing at times, though, especially if the captioner is not familiar with the unique names of localities. For example, Takoma Park is a suburb of Washington, D.C., but the oblivious stenographer usually types Tacoma Park.

The federal mandate does not apply to the captioning of videotapes and DVDs. Regardless, a high percentage of movies on DVDs are now captioned or subtitled, yet the special features on the DVDs are not always captioned.

Although deaf people were the primary audience for captioning, studies have indicated that closed-captioned TV and movies help foreigners learn English. More American movies and TV shows are now captioned in Spanish and sometimes in French. Senior citizens who have progressive hearing loss have also discovered that they can benefit from the captions. More frequently, captions are shown at noisy spots, such as bars or restaurants, where the spectators would otherwise not be able to hear the TV.

CAPTIONING SPIN-OFFS

The field of captioning has led to additional technologies, such as Communication Access Real-time Translation, or CART. Like television captioners, CART captioners are trained stenograph reporters who instantaneously convert spoken words into printed text. The printed text appears on a computer and often is projected onto a screen, sometimes as huge as ten feet wide.

CART is regularly used in court or at meetings in large lecture rooms, providing equal access for those who may prefer written English, especially hard of hearing or late-deafened persons. It should be mentioned that real-time captioners must be more proficient than court stenographers. In court, stenographers can make corrections when requested by the court and usually can edit their transcripts at the end of the day after the court sessions. The product of real-time captioners is seen immediately on the screen, leaving very little room for error.

Another technology, similar to CART, that costs much less and requires less equipment is known as C-Print. The difference is that the captioner — not necessarily a stenographer — types the audio narration into a laptop computer instead of a stenograph machine. Like a word processing program, the C-Print program stores a list of words and uses phonetic rules as shortcuts. The system may have a dictionary of more than ten thousand words, and the captioners may add some specialized words of their own. The viewer can watch the computer screen on his desk, or the printed narration could be projected on the screen. C-Print was developed at National Technical Institute for the Deaf and has been used in classrooms since the 1990s.

An important by-product of TV captioning is the increased need for captioners who are trained stenograph reporters. To convert spoken or signed words into printed text, and to keep up with the audio output, stenographers need to type as many as 200 words per minute. With the passage of the Twenty-First Century Communications and Video Accessibility Act in 2010, the job outlook for stenographers or court reporters is projected to grow by 18 percent by 2018.[15]

IN-THEATER CAPTIONING

There are more and more movie theaters that feature movies with captions. There are three basic types of captioning at those theaters:

1. Open captioning — the captions are "burned on" the film, so the captions are shown to all in the theater.
2. Rear window captioning — captions are projected on transparent screen units mounted on seat cup holders. Captions are reflected from the back of the theater and seen on the transparent screens. Deaf moviegoers generally are not fond of this technology; they prefer open captioning. However, a plus of this technology is that it is more readily available, which means more viewing choices than open captioning.
3. Personal-size captioning — Personal Captioning Systems, Inc., of Illinois, offers palm-size captioning. Using a wireless radio transmission, the palm-sized device shows captioning and is similar to a text pager in appearance. It is available on a limited basis. On a related note, the

company also offers eyeglasses featuring a captioning unit attached via clip-on eyeglasses. The words "crawl" in front of the eyes.

PRINTED TELEPHONE COMMUNICATION

Robert Weitbrecht, a charter member of the Alexander Graham Bell Association of the Deaf's Oral Deaf Adults Section, invented the acoustic coupler that enabled Western Union teletypewriters (TTYs) to send messages over telephone lines. This came about in the early 1960s, when Western Union was replacing its old Baudot-technology TTYs — used to send telegrams — with a newer eight-byte technology. The older machines were disposed of and Weitbrecht created the coupler, or modem, that enabled TTYs to send or receive typed messages over the telephone lines. The modem was first publicly demonstrated at the 1964 Alexander Graham Bell Association biennial meeting.

It appears that with the TTY, communication access of deaf people came full circle. Matt Daigle's humorous illustration suggests that deaf Native Americans had equal communication access through smoke signals. The eventual obsolescence of this visual-based communication put deaf people at a disadvantage until the invention of TTYs.

Now almost obsolete, TTY machines were at that time recycled by a group of interested technicians. They overhauled each TTY and connected it to a modem so that TTY-to-TTY calls could be made. The TTY machines were then "loaned" to families and individuals at no charge. It was the first time that deaf people could communicate with each other without eye-to-eye contact. The experience was enormously beneficial for deaf people, who then didn't have to walk or drive to other people's homes. The authors, like many others, felt peculiar when they used the TTY

SMOKE SIGNALS WERE THE EARLIEST "TTY" FOR DEAF INDIANS

Smoke signals © 2010 Matt Daigle, *Adventures in Deaf Culture.*

Model 15 TTY (it was bulky and noisy). Photograph by the author.

for the first time, not seeing the other party.

Also, with TTYs, it was the first time that deaf persons possessed telephone numbers. To meet the demand for a comprehensive directory of numbers, Telecommunications for the Deaf, Inc. (TDI), was incorporated to publish an annual telephone directory for nationwide use. The first directory had 145 listings, and the latest directory, now commonly known as *The Blue Book*, contains over 500 pages. The 2010 edition also lists historical notes, listings for both TTY and VRS numbers, and yellow pages.

Many recall, not so fondly, how TTY users were unable to make longdistance telephone

The 2010 TDI Directory. Photograph by the author.

calls. It so happened that around that time, the telephone companies in larger cities changed over to direct dialing. However, people living in smaller communities could not use TTYs to call their friends without going the long distance route. Those who had a hearing person living in the same household (or neighbors) could ask the hearing person to call the local telephone office or the switchboard operator to initiate long distance calls to connect to the calling party. After the connection was made, the parties could then talk to each other on a TTY.

In 1974, I. Lee Brody developed the first Braille TTY for deaf-blind users. Currently, apparently only one manufacturer produces Braille TTYs with prices for a unit ranging from $5,900 to $8,700.

TTY RELAY SERVICE

Eventually, it was realized that the TTYs, instead of being used solely between TTY users, could expand to communicating with a person without a TTY, through an intermediary. This is how the first relay service was established. A communication assistant, or CA, was a hearing person in possession of a TTY and a telephone. The CA received a typed message from a TTY user, dialed the number, spoke the message to the hearing receiver at the other end, and typed everything that was spoken back.

Telecommunications relay services got their start in the late 1960s. One of the earliest known relay services was in St. Louis when Paul Taylor helped set up a message relay system with 20 families. At the beginning, the relay service served the local population only. Later, relay services were established, mostly in large cities, often on a volunteer basis. Some cities had more than one relay service, and sometimes the relay service served a special group of clientele, such as a church's members.

Unskilled volunteers and minimum wage workers mostly operated early relay services, and the services were often limited to weekday hours. As the number of TTY owners grew, relay services were often overwhelmed with calls. It was not unusual to dial the relay service several times before finally getting an answer. Later, when it was possible for the relay services to form a queue, a caller might have to wait in line as long as an hour before his turn arrived — and even then had to limit his calls to ten minutes or less.

South Dakota's relay, with California and Connecticut closely following, was one of the earliest statewide relay services. "State programs had limited funding, restricted hours, and most limited the user to calls of 10 or 20 minutes or so. The relay staff often had weak typing, poor grammar, and there was no confidence in confidentiality. Despite these shortcomings, the volume of calls skyrocketed."[16]

In the late 1980s, relay services were viewed by the industry as a public welfare program. The national attention of the 1988 Deaf President Now protest at Gallaudet University helped push the FCC into action on relay service funding.[17] In 1990, the Americans with Disabilities Act's Title IV not only improved existing relay services but also required all telephone companies to provide relay services by March 1, 2001. Each state had a different phone number for its relay services, and a campaign was set up for a national 800 number. However, the access to relay services by both deaf and hearing parties was greatly facilitated by the single three-digit number — 711 — that became effective on October 1, 2001. The 711 number is similar to 911 for emergency calls or 411 for information.

It was not until the availability of broadband Internet transmission that video transmission became a reality. Early in the twenty-first century, it became possible to have video relay services through webcams and voice-over Internet protocol (VoIP) technology. Several firms were established to handle VoIP calls, and the best part was that the entire call, to anywhere in the nation, was free of charge. The project was sponsored with federal funding.

VIDEOPHONES (SIGNED COMMUNICATION VIDEO)

For many years, people dreamed of videophones. Since the Picturephone was first introduced at the 1964 World Fair in New York City, the barrier was always the narrow bandwidth of telephone lines preventing huge amounts of transmitted data. Deaf persons, including the authors who witnessed the demonstration at the World Fair, talked endlessly about the futuristic device in their local clubrooms. They fantasized how the Picturephone could change their lives.

When Sorenson Communications mass-distributed its videophone in 2003 to deaf people at no charge, many people realized that the futuristic dream was finally here. Video communication is enabled through a dedicated video camera, situated on top of a TV set, with both parties seeing each other onscreen. High-speed Internet access is a requirement as well.

The concept of video relay interpreting had its beginnings in Texas in the early 1990s. Ed Bosson, a deaf man who was affiliated with the Texas Public Utility Commission, suggested the possibility of using existing video technology for relay calls. A deaf person could call the relay service and see a live interpreter onscreen; the interpreter would function like a CA, but would sign and speak instead of typing and speaking.

After studying the feasibility of the system, the Texas commissioners authorized a trial run of the video relay system in the state. In 1995, four public call centers were part of the first trial, run by Sprint, under Bosson's management. The second trial was expanded to ten cities and was called video relay interpreting (VRI). In 1998, when VRI was tested in Texas and Washington, the term was changed to video relay services (VRS).

VIDEO RELAY SERVICES

In 2002, VRS became a reality nationwide when the FCC provided nationwide funding to reimburse VRS providers for the cost of providing such services. The United States was the second nation, after Sweden, to subsidize VRS nationwide. Since then, at least ten firms have been authorized to provide VRS.

Most VRS providers have the capability to accept messages and forward them to deaf users by sending text messages to the users' computers or pagers. Another feature, introduced in April 2004, is video mail, in which the video interpreter records the hearing caller's message via sign language and e-mails the video to the deaf caller.

Another technology, video remote interpreting (VRI), is not to be confused with the old term of video relay interpreting as described above. VRI is similar to on-site interpreting, such as at work, in a medical setting, in police stations or in schools, except that the interpreter is off-site or located remotely. A VRI call might originate at a doctor's office and be handled through a qualified interpreter in a remote location such as Alaska, for example, and relayed to the Deaf patient in the office. Some hospitals offer VRI capabilities via a mobile video cart. The cart can be deployed to multiple locations at the hospital, e.g., a patient's room. The patient can communicate with the attending medical personnel instantly via VRI, viewing the interpreter on a TV screen mounted on the cart. It should be emphasized that an on-site interpreter is usually the best solution; however in less-than-ideal conditions, VRI may be a suitable, temporary alternate.

Phone conversations through VRS and VRI are effortless as compared to text-based relayed conversations, because signed messages are translated faster and are more natural. Hearing persons have been said to prefer VRS and VRI as well, given the speed of such conversations. Videophones and webcams have become a staple in homes of deaf people to the point where some have gotten rid of their TTYs, although that step is not advisable at this present time, given the need for emergency calls. Generally, 911 centers cannot identify callers' locations through broadband systems. However, it is now possible for the 911 centers to accept emergency calls through VoIP protocol. VRS users are required to list their addresses with their VRS providers for that reason.

Through a two-year effort of a coalition of national deaf organizations, which included Telecommunications for the Deaf, Inc. (TDI), Deaf and Hard of Hearing Consumer Advisory Board (DHHCAN), National Association of the Deaf (NAD), Association of Late Deafened Adults (ALDA), and Hearing Loss Association of America (HLA, formerly SHHH), several comments and petitions were filed with the FCC for service improvements. On July 14, 2005, FCC issued unprecedented regulations to improve VRS services.

One rule stipulated a mandatory speed-of-answer requirement for VRS providers. Furthermore, in order to be eligible for compensation from the Interstate TRS fund, VRS must be available 24 hours, seven days a week. Additional rules also covered VRS Mail and translation of ASL into spoken Spanish or vice versa.

The Interstate TRS fund is managed by The National Exchange Carriers Association, Inc., (NECA), which administers reimbursement to telecommunication service providers that provide relay services. Its statistics demonstrate the changing trends of use of various devices during the last eight years. In the year 2002, TTY usage was the most active, with 3,000,000 minutes logged in during the month of May, but it has been reduced to approximately 500,000 minutes during the month of May 2010. Conversely, the monthly use of VRS was zero in 2010, but rose to 9,000,000 minutes in early 2009 and has leveled down to 8,500,000 minutes in the month of May 2010. The NECA report also showed the changing trends of communication via internet protocol (VoIP), with approximately 700,000 minutes recorded in May 2002, with a peak usage of over 7,500,000 minutes in May 2006. The use of webcams with computers has decreased to approximately 4,800,000 minutes in May 2010.

TRS, VRS, IP Monthly Usage Minutes Recorded by NECA
Length of usage, in minutes

	May 2002	*May 2006*	*May 2010*
Telecom Relay Service	3,000,000	1,800,000	500,000
Video Relay Service	0	3,800,000	8,500,000
Internet Protocol (VoIP)	700,000	7,500,000	4,800,000

The statistics indicate the high usage of TTY relay in 2002, and the high usage of Internet Protocol in 2006. In 2010 most relay service calls were made through video.

So many of the new technologies emerged almost simultaneously at the end of the twentieth century, creating unprecedented access for deaf people. In addition to closed captioning, TTYs, relay services, visual alert devices, fax machines, e-mail, and the Internet, new devices include pagers (or smart phones) and cochlear implants.

FOOD FOR THOUGHT

Will Deaf culture survive in the modern era with all the new technologies? In the past, deaf clubs and schools for the deaf were major gathering places for deaf people and, in turn, were where most traits of Deaf culture were nurtured and passed on. In today's changing world, there are fewer places for Deaf people to congregate other than public places. With modern technologies, deaf people possess a multitude of communication and networking methods. Nowadays, churches with services for deaf people and existing social and political organizations are relatively modern places for maintaining culture, in addition to the time-tested schools for deaf students. Thus, with new technologies and new places to gather, Deaf culture is not (and cannot be) dying anytime soon.

Padden and Humphries[18] also made an interesting, yet practical, observation when they advised that sign language has moved into public places and that our voice has literally moved with it. They referred to, as an example, deaf actors who now perform before audiences with voice actors accompanying them on the stage. Moreover, deaf people have overcome the challenge of being voiceless by having access through sign language interpreters in a range of settings such as medical, legal, business, and education. They also stated that, with the management of voice technology, Deaf people have made themselves less an invisible community, and more a public one.

NINE

Personalities Through the Years

People are the backbone of history. The events as pointed out in the annals of deaf history are the results of the contributions of dedicated people who shaped the world and the American deaf community. This chapter presents the numerous individuals who have left, and continue to leave, their legacies in molding not only the deaf world but also the non-deaf world.

Profiles of Deaf Leaders

Journey into the DEAF-WORLD[1] identified two groups of great leaders who have played a disproportionately large role in leading in the Deaf community. The first group consists of intercultural leaders — leaders who were born hearing to hearing parents and became Deaf after learning to speak English and after having extensive contact with the larger and hearing society, benefiting the Deaf community. The second group consists of culturally centered (or grassroots) Deaf leaders — leaders who were born to Deaf parents and whose cultural knowledge of Deaf culture and fluency in ASL are particularly valuable. They are predominantly found in positions within education, Deaf organizations, or athletic organizations.

The authors wish to avoid further categorizing and further stereotyping between the two groups. However, it should be pointed out that there are children who are born deaf to hearing parents or become prelingually deaf and do not fit into either group. Furthermore, there are instances of children being born hearing to deaf parents but becoming deaf after acquiring language (postlingually deaf).

At any rate, it is interesting to note that the 22 NAD presidents, from NAD's inception in 1880 through 1978, were postlingually deaf. Since then, all of the nine presidents — with the exception of Larry Newman, who lost his hearing at the age of five — were born to deaf parents.

The authors believe there are several main reasons for the cultural shift. First, a great majority of deaf individuals in early days lost their hearing due to a number of factors, mostly through serious illnesses such as measles, spinal meningitis, scarlet fever, and whooping cough. Those deafened individuals heard spoken language and were fluent in spoken English before losing their hearing. Often they retained the use of speech even after becoming deaf. In fact, many of them were partially deaf. They were called hard of hearing, or "semi-mutes," as some old-timers would call them.

With the disappearance of childhood diseases through immunization, there are fewer occurrences of children who become deaf at later ages. Instead, there is a higher occurrence of children who are born deaf, mostly due to hereditary causes even within hearing families. As a result, there are more deaf children who do not hear spoken language even in infancy. Since they become deaf before learning language, they are prelingually deaf.

The fact that several NAD presidents in more recent years have come from deaf families is believed to be an outcome of the increased assertiveness of deaf people through recent generations. After the 1960s when deaf people became more involved in their own causes, they gained self-confidence and possessed a stronger cultural identity. Deaf parents were then able to share experiences and lessons with their deaf children. Using their parents as role models, the younger generations then became more proactive in the fostering their peers' interests.

Networking by Deaf People

For deaf people, social gatherings and publications were the main sources of contact with their peers. Many deaf-school graduates maintained updated connections with their alma maters through school publications. The "Little Paper Family" was a vital network where schools exchanged publications with other schools. The publications usually contained a section or a page devoted to alumni doings on social, family and other affairs and were read by students and faculty.

There were several national publications. The larger ones — most of which do not exist now — were *Silent Worker*, *Cavalier*, *The Frat* (for National Fraternal Society of the Deaf members), and *Silent News*. Current publications are *Deaf Life*, *New Horizons* (for Deaf Seniors of America members), and *SIGNews*. Some state associations for deaf people also print newsletters.

In the present age of convenient Internet access, news sharing among deaf people has not only proliferated geometrically but has also become more updated. When a noteworthy deaf person dies, the news is known all over the globe within a day. In 1996, the late Phil Moos of New Jersey began distributing *USA-L News*, an online mailing list of announcements and articles about deaf-related events or individuals within the deaf community. The venture has been taken over by DeafTimes, which sends out *DeafTimes News* and other state-level mailings. Two editions of *DeafDigest*, compiled by Barry Strassler, are sent out weekly. He also distributes *DeafDigest Sports*.

The 2006 Gallaudet University protest is an excellent example of how news was instantly made available to interested parties, not only across the country but also all over the world. Even though the deaf population may be fragmented, deaf people immediately got together to show their endorsement of the protest. Over 70 tent cities were held all over America within two weeks of the protest, mostly by Gallaudet alumni. This support was further reinforced by national, state, and local organizations that offered monetary contributions to "Tent City" at Gallaudet for food and other necessities. This was accomplished mostly through a great number of blogs and vlogs. Although some people disagreed with the protest, Internet postings were overwhelmingly in support of the protest.

Some Prominent Deaf Leaders

There is a life-size oil painting of Frederick Schreiber (1922–1979) hanging at the NAD headquarters. The unique advocate was a giant among his contemporaries.

Schreiber lost his hearing at the age of six years in New York. He attended the New York School for the Deaf and then graduated from Gallaudet College (now University) at an early age. He taught for a while in Texas before relocating to Washington, D.C. While employed at a full-time night job as a printer at the *Washington Evening Star*, followed by a position as a compositor in the United States Government Printing Office, he labored feverishly, pushing legislation for more deaf rights. In 1966, he became the executive director of the newly established NAD home office. Confident of the NAD's future, he mortgaged his home, and with additional money from colleague Albert Pimentel, he bought an office building in Silver Spring, Maryland, in the early 1970s.

Schreiber is remembered for his fights and advocacy for deaf people's rights. Garretson[2] remembers him this way: "Brilliant, articulate, aggressive, and yet sensitive and blessed with a gift of humor, warmth, and peopleness, this human dynamo began early to gain those experiences which provided meaning and substance to his eventual national and international contributions." Even after his unexpected death in 1979 at the age of 57 after working for NAD for 13 years, Schreiber's legacy is forever honored and cherished. Among his well-known sayings are:

"What is between the ears is more important than what is in the ears."

"There are only two kinds of people: Those that can't hear and those that won't listen."

"Deaf people can do anything except hear."

"As far as deaf people are concerned, our civil rights are violated daily."

Andrew Foster, deafened at the age of 11 and educated at the Alabama School for the Deaf, was the first known African American to graduate from Gallaudet College and the same from Eastern Michigan University. After receiving a degree from Christian Mission College in Washington, he became a minister. He went to Africa and helped establish over 30 schools for deaf children, most of them affiliated with churches in Western African countries including Benin, Cameroon, Central African Republic, Congo, Chad, Ghana, Kenya, and Zaire. He died in a plane crash in 1987.

I. King Jordan, Ph.D., the eighth president of Gallaudet University, lost his hearing in a motorcycle accident as a young adult while serving with the U.S. Navy in Washington, D.C. He attended Gallaudet College as an undergraduate. He then earned both a master's degree and a doctoral degree in psychology from the University of Tennessee. In 1973, he joined the Gallaudet faculty in the psychology department and later served as the dean of the College of Arts and Science. His family moved to House One on the Gallaudet University campus after his inauguration as the first Deaf president of Gallaudet University in March 1988. He retired in December 2006.

Robert Davila, Ph.D., of Hispanic descent, was a vigorous, tireless educator and administrator. He has held numerous positions within the education field, including teaching in the graduate school at Gallaudet University before being promoted to university vice president. He was later selected by President George H.W. Bush to become the Assistant Secretary for Special Education and Rehabilitation Services in the U.S. Department of Education, the highest government position ever held by a Deaf person. He was also the headmaster at the New York School for the Deaf (Fanwood) and then the vice president for the National Technical Institute for the Deaf at Rochester Institute of Technology before his retirement in 2004. He is also the first person to have served as president for all three deaf education professional organizations: the Convention of American Instructors of the Deaf, the Conference of Educational Administrators Serving the Deaf, and the Council on Education of the Deaf. In January 2007, he became the ninth president of Gallaudet University. He retired in January 2010.

Marilyn J. Smith is the founder and executive director of the non-profit

Abused Deaf Women's Advocacy Services (ADWAS). Founded in 1986, ADWAS was the only program of its kind in the nation until 1999, when the agency received a grant from the U.S. Department of Justice; today, the program has been replicated in 15 cities. In March 2005, ground was broken for "A Place of Our Own." The 19-unit affordable housing complex opened in July 2006 and serves deaf and deaf-blind victims of domestic violence and sexual assault. She retired in January 2011.

In 1975, South Dakota native Ben Soukup founded Communication Service for the Deaf (CSD) as a part of the South Dakota Association of the Deaf. The original purpose of CSD was to secure and schedule sign language interpreters and provide TTY repair service. Later, the agency, based in Sioux Falls, became an agent for the statewide relay service.

The organization expanded when CSD signed with several other states to run their relay services. Soukup's leadership and persistence paid off with services in several states, employing over a thousand workers and supporting more than 20 satellite offices. These programs reach deaf and hard of hearing consumers from cradle to grave through a variety of services and functions. CSD also publishes the monthly *SIGNews* newspaper. In late 2010, CSD was awarded a $14.9 million federal grant to create high-speed Internet access for low-income Deaf and hard of hearing people. Through Project Endeavor, the individuals will receive laptop computers with mobile broadband cards and be eligible for a year of high-speed wireless Internet access.

Ruth Seeger, a well-known teacher and athlete at Texas School for the Deaf, not only started the girls' athletic program at the school but also coached many of her protégés to participate in world competitions. As a young athlete, Seeger won several gold medals for the U.S. track and field team at the Deaflympics. Later on, she coached the U.S. women's track and field teams for two decades. After retiring from the school, she decided to return to her true love, which was to compete again. The fitness buff competed in five field events — javelin, shot put, discus, long jump and high jump. From 1991 to 2005, Seeger garnered a total of 304 medals, including at least 280 gold medals. She also holds a national record in javelin, hurling it for 50 feet and 8 inches.[3] As a young lady, Seeger admired Babe Didrikson Zaharias, who was named Top Woman Athlete of the Century by the Associated Press in 1999. As a result, Seeger is often referred to as the Deaf Babe Zaharias.

Seeger has the unique distinction of being inducted into at least ten halls of fame as an athlete, coach and sports leader, including being the first deaf female to be inducted into the USA Deaf Sports Federation Hall of Fame in recognition of her 20 years as track coach. In 1988, Texas Governor William P. Clements inducted Seeger into the Texas Women's Hall of Fame as athletic coach, and in 1999, Seeger was honored as the newest member of the Texas

Senior Games Hall of Fame. TSD named its gymnasium after her, a testimony to Seeger's love for her "girls," athletics, sports equality, and healthy living. A highly unusual award for the octogenarian was made when, in 2006, she was awarded the Austin Female Amateur Athlete of the Year.

Robert and Michelle Smithdas, both deaf-blind, are leading remarkable lives. Robert, or Bob as he is known, lost his hearing and sight at the age of four from illness. In 1950, he earned a bachelor's degree from St. John's University and became the first known deaf-blind man to finish college. In his graduate studies, he majored in vocational guidance and rehabilitation of the handicapped at New York University and in 1953 was the first deaf-blind person to earn a master's degree. He began his career at Industrial Home for the Blind, now known as the Helen Keller School for the Blind, in New York as director of services. The Helen Keller National Center for Deaf-Blind Youths and Adults (HKNC) was established in Long Island, New York, after Bob helped to obtain federal funding in 1967. He was affiliated with HKNC as its director of community education until his retirement in December 2008. Bob has been awarded four honorary doctorates from colleges and universities and was named "Handicapped American of the Year" in 1965 by the President's Committee on Employment of People with Disabilities.

Bob married Michelle Craig in 1975. Originally from California, she was blinded in a snowmobile accident during her senior year at Gallaudet University. Later, she earned her master's degree in the education of blind and visually impaired at Columbia University. She entered the training program at HKNC in 1972 and subsequently became an instructor.

Barbara Walters, a well-known ABC TV commentator, interviewed Bob on the *Today Show* in the 1970s, and in 1998 interviewed the couple for *20/20*. Walters spoke at Bob's retirement luncheon and stated that, in her 30 years of interviews with notables, Bob was the most memorable.

Forgotten Deaf Contributors

Additional deaf people with noteworthy contributions include:

- Thomas Edison (1847–1931), deafened at the age of 14, brightened the world with his invention of a light bulb and obtained a total of 1,097 U.S. patents under his name.
- John Gregg (1867–1948) was the brainchild of shorthand writing.
- Juliette Gordon Low (1860–1927), deafened at the age of 20, founded the Girl Scouts organization in 1912.
- Ludwig Van Beethoven (1770–1827), deafened at the age of 30, was an internationally renowned musician.

- Nanette Fabray (1920–), although possessing hearing loss, was well-known as a comedienne, singer, dancer, and actress. She was one of the earlier advocates for the rights of deaf and hard of hearing people.

The list could go on and on. There are deaf or hard of hearing firefighters, morticians, lawyers, dentists, doctors, chemists, inventors, artists, sculptors, writers, architects, poets, newspaper editors, clergy, actors, and teachers — to mention just a few!

SOME DEAF FIRSTS

Some notable Deaf "firsts" include interesting individuals.

Betty Lou Beets— First Deaf person to be executed. She was sentenced to die by lethal injection in 2000 for the murder of her fifth husband. Home state: Texas

Thomas Coughlin— First Deaf Catholic man to become a priest, in the 1970s. Home state: New York.

Eugene Hairston— First Black Deaf professional middleweight boxer, who won 60 bouts and lost one as an amateur in New York. He turned professional in 1947 and won a total of 45 matches (24 by knockouts) and lost only 13 times with five draws in the 1950s. He was known as The Deaf Wonder and was ranked as a top middleweight contender for two consecutive years. Home state: New York.

William Hoy— First Deaf Major League baseball player, for the Cincinnati Reds and the Washington Senators (1886–1901). Home state: Ohio. Other players include Luther Taylor, Richard Sipek and Curtis Pride (who was the first Black Deaf major league baseball player).

Christy Smith— First Deaf woman to appear on the TV series, *Survivor: The Amazon*, in 2000. Home State: Colorado.

Erastus Smith— First Deaf soldier to spy against Mexico in 1821. Home state: Texas.

Luke Adams— First Deaf person to participate in *Amazing Race*, a TV series. He and his mother, Margie Adams, competed with ten other couples and placed third.

Nellie Willhite— First female Deaf pilot, she flew in many air shows and races in the late 1920s. Home state: South Dakota.

Boyce Williams— First Deaf person to serve in the U.S. Office of Vocational Rehabilitation, in 1945. Home state: Wisconsin.

Heather Whitestone— First Deaf female to be crowned Miss America, in 1995. Home state: Alabama.

Notable Deaf Writers

Alice Cogswell's impressive composition in the first chapter is an example of the work of many excellent deaf writers throughout the years. Some of them owned newspapers and wrote their own news and editorials. Some of them were nationally acclaimed poets. Some of them earn their living as technical writers for the government or industry. Most of the Little Paper Family publications, described earlier in this chapter, were composed and edited by deaf wordsmiths, who often taught English full-time in the classrooms.

Several persons who are known for making fun of themselves as deaf persons through words, or write extensively about deaf people are listed below.

- Steve Baldwin is known for his well-researched and documented study of *Pictures in the Air: The Story of the National Theatre of the Deaf.* He also authored countless cultural, historical, and professional articles. He also writes scripts for television, movie and stage; among them are *T. H. Gallaudet and Monsieur Clerc: Coming to Terms* and *Deaf Smith: The Great Texan Scout.*

- Mark Drolsbaugh grew up with progressive hearing loss and resided four blocks from Pennsylvania School for the Deaf's (PSD) Mt. Airy campus. He attended hearing schools and had his first intensive exposure to Deaf culture when attending Gallaudet University. With a master's degree, he returned to Philadelphia where he has become a school counselor at PSD. He dabbled in writing, with articles for several deaf national publications and other journals. Since he could not "shut up" as he described himself, he has ventured into books and has published *Deaf Again* and *On the Fence: The Hidden World of the Hard of Hearing.* Drolsbaugh, using the best of his humor and insight, gave flavor to his compilation of thought-provoking articles in *Anything But Silent.* His latest work is now in progress — *The One Hundred Dollar Hearing Aid Battery* — a children's book based on a true story.

- Jack Gannon has written extensively about deaf heritage for almost 30 years. In *Deaf Heritage: A Narrative History of Deaf America,* he presented a comprehensive account of deaf legacy throughout the two centuries since the founding of American School for the Deaf in Hartford. He has also authored *The Week the World Heard Gallaudet* and was one of the designers of the *History Through Deaf Eyes* exhibit and book. He is nearing completion of his latest venture, which records the history of the World Federation of the Deaf and its national organizations.

- Comedian Ken Glickman created many humorous "deaf" definitions, published in *Deafinitions* and *More Deafinitions.* An example deafinition is of the word "lens-propelment," which is described as the sudden act of hurling one's glasses accidentally while signing.

- Roy K. Holcomb (1923–1998) authored several books in relation to Deaf culture, through humorous anecdotes. Misdeeds, such as using a vacuum cleaner and later realizing that it was not plugged in to an electric outlet, are described in books like *Hazards of Deafness* and *Silence is Golden ... Sometimes*. His last book, *Deaf Culture ... Our Way*, was written with his two sons Samuel and Thomas.
- Raymond Luczak's first novel, *Men with Their Hands*, won first place in the Project: QueerLit 2006 contest. Since graduating from Gallaudet University in 1988, he has written seven novels and 13 stage plays, of which one — *In Love and Lust We Trust* — was performed in London.
- Damara Goff Paris was the owner of a publishing company, Paris Publications. A descendant of a Cherokee/Blackfoot family, she co-edited, with the late Sharon Kay Woods, *Step into the Circle: The Heartbeat of American Indian, Alaska Native, and First Nations Deaf Communities*. Her company published titles such as *Deaf Culture Behind Bars* and *Deaf Esprit: Inspiration, Humor and Wisdom from the Deaf Community*.
- Maxwell Schneider published *Do You Hear Me*, in which she demonstrated the humorous ways of hard of hearing people. A sample snippet: "I know a man who is hard of hearing who has the grip of a trapeze artist. Naturally, he hangs on to your every word!"
- Bernice Singleton collected breast cancer stories from 50 women and one man from all over the United States. The book, *Signs of Courage: Deaf Survivors of Breast Cancer,* contains real-life experiences, including the victims' prognosis and treatment, Most of them are still living.

NOTEWORTHY ENTREPRENEURS

To give a general picture of what deaf people in the nation can do in various types of business that they founded and operated:

- David Birnbaum, of Birnbaum Interpreting Services in Silver Spring, Maryland, and Eric and Moon Feris, are owners of two of four deaf-owned interpreting/videophone firms. Being deaf, they have a unique perspective in the field of interpreting as compared to the many firms owned by hearing persons.
- Skiqwaqui, a nine-hole golf course in Morganton, North Carolina, was designed and is owned by Charles Crowe.
- Joe Dannis founded DawnSignPress in San Diego, with a focus on ASL

and Deaf culture publications. The firm, established over 25 years ago, is well known for its *Signing Naturally* ASL curriculum. In 1997, Dannis received the Small Businessperson of the Year award for the state of California.

- Bob Harris, of Minnesota-based Harris Communications since 1982, runs an Internet and mail order business that sells various hearing loss equipment, novelties and books/DVDs.

- James Macfadden owned Macfadden and Associates, Inc., a computer-consulting firm that earned $12 million a year in revenue through federal government contracts in Washington, D.C. In 2007, he sold the company to his 80 employees through its Employee Stock Ownership Plan Trust Fund. He is now a freelance entrepreneur and serves on the Gallaudet University board of trustees.

- Technical Computer Services (TCS) designs and repairs computer systems and provides assistive technology in federal government, in Maryland. Established in 1982, it is owned by Myrna Orleck-Aiello, the president and chief executive officer, and Phil Aiello, the chief technical officer.

- Louis Schwarz's Schwarz Financial Services provides financial planning and tax preparation services. It was founded in 1983 and is operated out of Maryland. An avid collector, Louis Schwarz has a unique hobby: the collection of Deaf Americans' business cards. His binders of over 700 business cards are found in a sitting room area in his office for clients or visitors to browse through.

- Trudy Suggs, a prolific writer, established T.S. Writing Services in 2003 and provides writing, editing and design services in ASL and English. Her firm works with individuals and businesses all over the world. Working from home in a log house surrounded by open countryside outside Faribault, Minnesota, she and her staff conduct business predominantly via the Internet and video technology.

DEAF WAX MUSEUM

One of the top attractions at the 2005 Deaf Seniors Conference in San Francisco was a room where conference participants came face-to-face with famous deaf individuals of bygone decades. They exclaimed at William Hoy's demure 5'5", attired in his Washington baseball uniform as the first deaf player in the major leagues. Other notable figures included Girl Scouts of America founder Juliette Gordon Low, American School for the Deaf founder Thomas Hopkins Gallaudet, and the first Deaf teacher in America, Laurent Clerc.

Three figures in the traveling Deaf Heritage Wax Collection. *Left:* William E. "Dummy" Hoy, 1862–1961, "Deaf Major League Ballplayer." Hoy was a fixture in the Major Leagues for 14 years (1888–1902) with five teams. He had a lifetime batting average of .288 with a total of 2,054 hits and 1,004 walks in 1,798 games. The five-foot-five speedster ranks 17th among the all-time leaders in stolen bases with 607. He is credited with inventing hand signals for "strike" and "ball," which are still being used today. *Middle:* Juliette Gordon Low, 1860–1927, "Founder, Girl Scouts of the USA." Low, deafened at the age of 26, founded two Girl Scout troops in her hometown, Savannah, and it was the beginning of the Girl Scouts movement in the USA. She was also a skilled artist, painter, sculptor, and writer. She was buried in her Girl Scout uniform. *Right:* Frederick C. Schreiber, 1922–1979, "Deaf Rights Advocate/Activist." Schreiber became deaf at the age of six and a half from spinal meningitis and entered Gallaudet College at the age of 15. His early career included teaching, tutoring, counseling and work as a printer. He entered community service when he became the first executive secretary of the National Association of the Deaf in 1966, and he expanded NAD to a million-dollar association with 40 employees. He was well known all over the world for his advocacy efforts for deaf people. Photographs by the author.

The eight life-size, three-dimensional wax figures on display were so realistic that visitors were tempted to shake hands or chat with them in ASL. A look-alike figure of Fred Schreiber with his ever-present enticing smile and his assertion, "Ears are not important. It's what's between them that counts," was unveiled at the conference.

Don Baer, a native Californian and the founder of the Deaf Heritage Wax Collection, was present to share his apprenticeship experience at Hollywood Wax Museum and his desire to preserve Deaf heritage and culture by creating a collection of at least a hundred wax figures representing individuals who have influenced the lives of the Deaf throughout the years.[4] Don has continued to add to his collection; the latest is of Bernard Bragg performing mime. During the last ten years DEAFWAX, a non-profit organization, exhibited in at least 25 local and national events.

EXCEPTIONAL DEAF PEOPLE

In reviewing the contributions of deaf people in America, there are so many who deserve to be mentioned. Space does not permit discussing each notable person. Instead, a brief outline discusses the contribution each Deaf person has made.

Art

Hillis Arnold, North Dakota (1906–1988) Many of his sculptures are in St. Louis and Midwest states, and his work was exhibited at the New York World's Fair in 1939. In 1938, he was appointed to a private junior college for women (now known as Lewis and Clark Community College in Godfrey, Illinois) as professor of sculpture and ceramics. Upon his retirement from the college after 34 years, he was awarded the rank of Professor Emeritus of Sculpture.

John Brewster, Maine (1766–1854) Renowned as a portrait painter in New England, Brewster's works continues to be exhibited today. At the age of 51, he interrupted his work to attend American Asylum for the Deaf as one of its first pupils and stayed there for three years. Early in 2007, his two portraits *Daniel Coffin* and *Elizabeth Stone Coffin* were auctioned to an unidentified buyer for $801,600.[5]

Morris Broderson, California (1928–) Broderson's oil paintings, watercolors, pastels and lithographs are part of permanent collections at Hirshhorn Museum in Washington, D.C., and Whitney Museum of American Art in New York City. His works were exhibited at the M. H. De Young Museum in San Francisco, the University of Arizona in Tucson, and several others, including some universities.

John Carlin, Pennsylvania (1813–1891) As an artist, Carlin painted portraits of personalities such as William Seward, Horace Greeley, and Jefferson Davis. He was an inexhaustible writer; his articles on architecture, geology, and ecology were published in leading newspapers. He was the first deaf poet whose work was praised by William Cullen Bryant. A dormitory building at Gallaudet University is named after him.

George Catlin (1796–1872) Catlin spent eight years traveling to document in painting every Native American tribe in America. He was the first artist to travel to the west with the purpose of learning more about Native Americans. Over 500 of his paintings and sketches recorded the "manners and customs" of American Indians, and he was also a writer and documented how the government treated the Native Americans. His paintings were exhibited in one of the Smithsonian museums recently.

Louis Frisino, Maryland (1934–) Often called Deaf John James Audubon, Frisino is well known for his realistic detailed paintings of animals. His work has won several Duck Stamp contests and Trout Stamp contests. His dog and waterfowl paintings have also earned several federal and state awards.

Kathleen Giddens, Florida (1949–) Giddens' surrealism and humor art in oils, acrylics, colored pencils and mixed media have been exhibited all over the country for the past 40 years. Her creations have won many awards.

William B. Sparks, North Carolina (1937–) As an oil portrait painter, Sparks is known for capturing his subject's personality in creating lifelike and almost photographic reproductions. His works have been exhibited in the Eastern United States, Brazil and Mexico. He painted formal portraits for the last four Gallaudet University presidents.

Douglas Tilden, California (1860–1935) Several of Tilden's sculptures adorn the streets of San Francisco; the best-known ones are the *Mechanics*

Left: Sculpture: *Mechanics* by Douglas Tilden, 1901, located at Market, Battery, and Bush streets, San Francisco. *Right:* Sculpture: *California Volunteers* by Douglas Tilden, 1906, located at Market and Dolores streets, San Francisco. Photographs by the author.

and the *California Volunteers*. The *Mechanics,* completed before 1900, survived the infamous San Francisco earthquake in 1906 and is still standing. He is often called the "Michelangelo of the American West."

Cadwallader Washburn, Minnesota (1866–1965) An adventurer, Washburn interviewed revolutionary foreign leaders and taught cannibals sign language. He was well known for developing dry point etchings, and he created over 1,000 etchings, in addition to oil paintings and watercolors. Most of his collections are now at the Library of Congress and Metropolitan Museum of Art in New York City. The art building on the Gallaudet campus is named for him.

Those interested in art might like to read Debbie Sonnenstrahl's outstanding book, *Deaf Artists in America*. It contains profiles of over 60 artists' lives and selections of their work with vivid descriptions. Jack Gannon's book *Deaf Heritage* also contains an excellent collection of artists and other notable deaf individuals in American history.

Athletics

Shelley Beattie, Oregon and California (1967–2008) In 1990, Shelley won the National Physique Committee USA title as a body builder. She participated in the *American Gladiators* television show for three seasons as "Siren."

Lou Ferringo, New York and California (1951–) Ferringo is most recognized for his role as the green giant in *The Incredible Hulk* television series between 1976 and 1981. At the age of 20, he was the youngest ever to win the Mr. Universe title — by a unanimous decision over 90 experienced contestants. He later lost the Mr. Olympia world title to Arnold Schwarzenegger.

LeRoy Colombo, Texas (1905–1974) As a lifeguard for 40 years for the city of Galveston, he saved the lives of 907 persons. A strong swimmer, he won many long-distance races.

Marsha Wetzel, New York (1963–) In 2002, Marsha Wetzel secured a position as a referee in the NCAA Division I men's basketball, becoming the first Deaf female to do so. She had been refereeing for more than a decade in high school and Division III basketball before going over to work in the Atlantic 10 and Patriot League conferences; she still officiates at Division III and high school games. Wetzel is currently a teacher at the National Technical Institute for the Deaf.

Aviation

Rhulin Thomas, Missouri and Maryland (1910–1999) In 1947, Thomas was the first deaf aviator to fly across the nation — from the Atlantic Coast to the Pacific Ocean. It took him 12 days and, because of his deafness, he flew without any radio equipment.

Business

Olof Hanson, Minnesota (1862–1933) Hanson was one of the first Deaf Americans to become an architect. He designed a total of 48 homes, 28 buildings, 18 schools and institutional buildings, churches and other structures. The United States Court House in Juneau, Alaska, is one of his famous works. State Route 299 circles the campus of Minnesota State Academy of the Deaf and is named Olof Hanson Drive.

Thomas Scott Marr, Tennessee (1866–1935) Marr's architecture firm designed many buildings in Nashville, among them the post office building, three modern luxury hotels, large apartment buildings, and two theaters. His last project was the State Supreme Court building. He was known as the "Dean of Nashville's Architects."

Thomas J. Posedly, Arizona (ca. 1940–) In 2007, Posedly was awarded the Arizona Architect's Medal, the highest honor given by the Arizona American Institute of Architects. He is one of five known professional deaf architects in the United States and is licensed in all 50 states. In his 35-year career, he has been involved with over 100 projects including commercial buildings, shopping centers, educational facilities, and churches.

Education

Frank G. Bowe, New York (1947–2007) After receiving a doctorate in educational psychology from New York University, Bowe became a disability-rights advocate. He was involved in many activities and wrote over 25 books on disability rights and other topics. He was a professor at Hofstra University's School of Education from 1989 until his death in 2007.

Entertainment

Heather Whitestone, Alabama and Georgia (1973–) Best known as the first deaf lady to be crowned Miss America in 1995, Whitestone had a cochlear implant surgery in 2002. Married to a politician, with whom she had two children, she tours as a motivational speaker.

France Woods, Ohio (1907–2000) Married to a hearing man, Woods was one of the professional dancers known as "Frances Woods and Billy Bray." They performed all over the nation and in Europe for over 55 years. Ripley's museum contains a wax replica of the couple as "The Wonder Dancers."

Inventions

John R. Gregg, Illinois (1866–1948) Gregg invented the Gregg Shorthand system and started the Gregg School, which became a business school. At the age of 19 he was considered a world authority on shorthand writing.

Anson R. Spear, Minnesota (1860–1917) Spear invented and patented a merchandise mailing envelope and secured two patents. He established the Spear Safety Envelope Company, which prospered for many years and employed many deaf workers.

Robert Carr Wall, Pennsylvania (1858–1939) In 1900, Wall built the first gas-powered automobile in Philadelphia and sold it for $1,800. He also developed the first bicycle that had both wheels of the same size. His firm made rattle-proof windshields for the Packard automobile company.

Law

Michael A. Chatoff, New York (1946–) While in law school during the late 1960s, Chatoff became deaf. He graduated from the New York University School of Law with a Master of Laws degree. He is known to be the first deaf lawyer to argue a case before the Supreme Court, and it was the first time that the Court permitted the use of technology (real-time captioning) in its hallowed halls of justice.

Lowell Myers, Chicago (1930–2005) A certified public accountant, Myers finished law school in 1956 ranking second in his class although he did not have an interpreter. He handled both deaf and hearing clients. He successfully defended a black young man who was accused of murder (this case was eventually the topic of a book and made into a 1979 television movie starring LeVar Burton). Myers represented at least a thousand deaf persons in court. In 1979, he was honored with the Distinguished Alumnus Award by the John Marshall Law School.

Bonnie Poitras Tucker, Massachusetts and Arizona (1939–) After majoring in journalism, Tucker married a hearing man. After 17 years, he divorced her because she was deaf. She finished law school at University of Colorado Law School. After several years of private practice, she became a tenured law professor at Arizona State University College of Law.

Media

William W. Beadell, New Jersey (1865–1931) Beadell was a weekly newspaper publisher in Illinois and later owned a run-down daily newspaper in Arlington, New Jersey. *The Observer* later became successful, and Beadell was credited with developing the "Want Ad" page or classified ads.

Edmund Booth, Massachusetts and Iowa (1810–1905) A pupil of Laurent Clerc at American School, Booth taught there for nine years. He moved to Iowa where he helped found the Iowa School for the Deaf. Later he became a gold prospector during the Gold Rush of 1849. Returning to Iowa in 1854, he bought a weekly newspaper and became its editor. He helped found the

National Association of the Deaf. In 1880 he was awarded an honorary Master of Arts degree by Gallaudet University.

Laura Redden Searing, Missouri (1840–1923) A journalist and poet who was recognized by her peers in literary world, Searing was a Civil War correspondent for the *St. Louis Republican* and wrote for two New York newspapers. She also wrote about people, places, politics and books under the pen name of Howard Glyndon.

David Pierce, Texas (1965–) A 1988 graduate of Rochester Institute of Technology, Pierce is the owner and CEO of Davideo Productions, a motion picture film and broadcast television production in Seguin, Texas. He is also the inventor of an editing technique for cutting video to audio by deaf editors, known as the "Pierce Method for Deaf Editors."

Henry Kisor, Illinois (1940–) A retired book editor of the *Chicago Sun-Times*, he is known for authoring *What's That Pig Outdoors?*, a humorous account of his life as a deaf man growing up in a non-deaf world. He lost his hearing at age three and a half. After earning a master's degree from Northwestern University, he began his writing career. Instead of relying on lipreading skills, he audiotaped his interviews and had his wife transcribe the tapes. Retired in 2006 after five years with the old *Chicago Daily News* and 28 years with *Sun-Times*, he has written two other nonfiction books and three mystery novels.

Medicine

Donald L. Ballantyne, China and New York (1922–2006) As the director of the Microsurgery Training Program at New York University Medical Center, he was a pioneer in the field and trained surgeons in the United States and Europe. He co-authored over 75 journal articles and two books on the technique. After his retirement in 1990, NYU designated him Professor Emeritus of Surgery.

Frank Peter Hochman, New York and California (1935–) Hochman was the first born-deaf American to become a physician. At the age of 37, he entered Rutgers University medical school. He now practices in the Bay Area; 90 percent of his patients are hearing.

Movies and TV

Kitty O'Neil, Texas and California (1946) As a stuntwoman in movies, O'Neil substituted for Lindsay Wagner in *The Bionic Woman* and Linda Carter in *Wonder Woman*. By 1981, she had set 26 world records on land, among them a speed record for a woman at 513 miles per hour in a three-wheeled rocket car, beating the old record by 200 mph.

Science

Regina Olson Hughes, Nebraska and District of Columbia (1895–1993) Hughes started with the U.S. Department of Agriculture in 1930 and later was its botanical artist. In 1969, she moved to the Smithsonian Institute and worked as a contract illustrator for both offices. Her works are exhibited in several botanical museums and published in at least a dozen books, including one titled *Common Weeds of the United States.*

Service

Juliette Gordon Low, Georgia (1860–1927) Deafened in her 20s, Low founded Girl Scouts in Savannah in 1912. The organization later grew nationwide. After the death of her husband, Low traveled alone all over the world.

Erastus Smith, Texas (1787–1837) Smith was a spy for General Houston in the Texan army that beat Mexico in a revolution. Deaf Smith County in Texas is named after him.

Boyce R. Williams, Wisconsin (1910–1998) Williams served 38 years in the Office of Vocational Rehabilitation and retired in 1983 as Chief, Deafness and Communication Disorders Branch, Rehabilitation Services Administration in the U.S. Department of Education. During his tenure, he helped start programs for deaf people, including the National Theatre of the Deaf, Registry of Interpreters for the Deaf, and Captioned Films for the Deaf.

Sports

Tamika Catchings, Indiana (1979–) Her father was an 11-year National Basketball Association player, so she grew up in a basketball family. She played college basketball at University of Tennessee on the Lady Volunteers team. She was drafted by Indiana Fever of the Women's National Basketball Association and has been named to WNBA All-Star Selection six times and All-WNBA Team six times.

William E. Hoy, Ohio (1862–1961) In 1887, Hoy was the first deaf person to play baseball professionally. He was the first and only outfielder to throw out three players at home base in one game and the first player to hit a grand slam home run in the newly founded American League. He is better known for inventing the signals now used by umpires.

Ronda Jo Miller, Minnesota (1978–) As an outstanding basketball player for Gallaudet University from 1997 to 2000, she was named to the NCAA Division III All-Decade Team. Scoring 2,656 points during her college career, she ranks third place on the Division III all-time scoring list. She was drafted by the Kansas City Legacy of the National Women's Basketball League.

She also played professionally for the Dallas Fury and Washington Mystics teams in the Women's National Basketball Association.

Curtis Pride, Maryland (1968–) In high school, Pride was a *Parade* All-American selection and was the only American to be named as one of the top 15 soccer players in the world. He has been a professional baseball player for at least 17 years; most of his career was with the New York Mets. He is currently Gallaudet University's baseball coach.

William Schyman, Illinois and Maryland (1930–) In 1950, as the most-feared player on the DePaul University basketball team, 6'5" Schyman was the first deaf hoopster to play on a major college varsity team. After signing with the Baltimore Bullets, he was the first deaf person to play professional basketball. He also played three years for the team that traveled with the Harlem Globetrotters.

Luther H. Taylor, Kansas (1876–1954) Taylor pitched for the famed manager John McGraw as a member of the New York Giants. His fastball helped the Giants win the National League pennant in 1904 and 1905. His ten-year ERA (earned run average) of 2.75 ranks favorably with today's best pitchers. He was also a crowd-pleaser with his antics. Taylor, then working as a houseparent at the Illinois School for the Deaf (ISD), helped bring ISD student Richard Sipek into professional baseball.

Kenny Walker, Colorado and District of Columbia (1967–) After starring in high school football, Walker received a scholarship to attend the University of Nebraska. As a defensive end, he was the first deaf player named to AP's All-America first team. He played for the Denver Broncos for two years and then in the Canadian Football League. At present he is the defense line coach at Gallaudet University.

The Football Huddle

Many football buffs are not familiar with the origin of the football huddle. Paul Hubbard, a star quarterback for Gallaudet College (1892–1895), did not want the opponents to see him sign plays to his teammates. He got his players to huddle around him, preventing any possible sighting of his visibly signed plays. The rest is history.

EPILOGUE

Today and Beyond

The well-being of deaf people has improved tremendously through the centuries, especially in the twentieth century. Education gave deaf children the tools to use what they learned, and the opportunity to associate with their peers gave them the tools to function in society. Through research and empowerment, deaf people have broken down the barriers of what they perceived to be a misleading picture of helpless souls who were deprived of the advantages of a productive life.

The future of deaf individuals may be enhanced by a deeper understanding of the exciting venture into deaf people's visual properties through a major research project funded by the National Science Foundation (NSF). The Visual Language and Visual Learning (VL^2) project started in 2007 to gain a greater understanding of the biological, cognitive, linguistic, socio-cultural, and pedagogical conditions that may influence language and knowledge acquisition through the visual modality. VL^2, located at Gallaudet University, is one of six NSF Science of Learning Centers across the nation and is the only research center focusing on learning through vision.

Through its research projects and six ongoing programs, the project will explore further how deaf people acquire visual language and learn to read. VL^2 will challenge current theories on learning through hearing for language acquisition and literacy development. The center hopes that findings on visual learning will benefit both deaf and hearing learners. Needless to say, understanding of teaching and learning of ASL will also be enhanced. It is confident that whatever the VL^2 research reveals, ASL will remain as a linguistically-based language, way beyond "formation of signs."

Deaf people's lives continue to make headway at a rapid rate. A main consequence has been trying to keep up with the changes in technology. As an example, Line 21 closed captioning and the law requiring built-in decoders in TV sets, mandated with the adoption of the Television Decoder Circuitry Act of 1990, was believed to be the answer to Deaf people's need for information. However, gaps were created with the new generation of TVs, such as high definition TV, and with Internet-based film streaming and cell phone video capabilities.

Thanks to a strong push from individuals and especially from organizations such as the Coalition of Organizations for Accessible Technology (COAT), Congress passed the Twenty-First Century Communications and Video Accessibility Act in 2010. The law makes it possible to receive captioned television on the Internet, provides for closed caption buttons on TV remote controls and makes available communications equipment for deaf-blind individuals.

The year 2010 marked the twentieth anniversary of the Americans with Disabilities Act (ADA). A celebration was held at White House on July 26, the anniversary of President George H. W. Bush's signing the bill into law. Guests included representatives from national disability advocacy organizations and several federal agencies. President Obama signed an executive order at the event to improve enforcing the ADA and to make the federal government a model employer.

Recognition of deaf filmmakers was boosted through a four-day WORLDDEAF Cinema Festival held in October 2010 at Gallaudet University. More than 170 films were submitted by 132 filmmakers from 30 countries. Over 250 attendees witnessed the Lifetime Achievement Award presentation to Marlee Matlin. Other notable professionals attending were Shoshannah Stern, upcoming actor Russell Harvard, and longtime Hollywood producer Samuel Goldwyn, Jr.

More recently, Marlee Matlin was part of a high-rating television show that got people talking at the water cooler. She made it to the very final episode of *Celebrity Apprentice*'s fourth series and survived the dreaded words, "You're fired," out of entrepreneur Don Trump's mouth. Incidentally Trump learned how to sign these words. Matlin also proved her mettle by challenging other renowned cast members, and raised a season-high amount of $1.05 million for Starkey Hearing Foundation.

Matlin then appeared on another popular show, *Switched at Birth*, shown on the ABC Family channel. The first season in 2011 unveiled outstanding newcomers Katie LeClerc and Sean Berdy. Both represented the faces of typical teenagers who happened to be Deaf. Berdy was born Deaf and grew up in a Deaf family. For his boisterous acting, Berdy was dubbed the Deaf James Dean. The hit drama had been renewed for a second season at the time of this book's printing.

On the federal level, 1989 Gallaudet University graduate Greg Hilbok was appointed to head the Federal Communications Commission (FCC) Office of Disability Rights (DRO). As an attorney who came from a Deaf family he had been with the DRO office since 2001, and his appointment marked the first time a Deaf person managed the FCC rulemaking body on telecommunications access for persons with disabilities.

Last, but not least, a major event in July 2010 took place at the International Congress on Education of the Deaf (ICED) in Vancouver, Canada. "A New Era: Deaf Participation and Collaboration" formally rejected the 130-year-old resolution made at the 1880 Milan ICED that banned sign language in education. Nine resolutions included Deaf people's rights "...to treat sign languages as equal to spoken languages, to involve the deaf community in supporting parents of deaf babies, and to refer families with deaf children to deaf schools and organizations...."[1] The document was enthusiastically supported by 750 Deaf and hearing participants in the audience.

In view of the continuous changes in technology and population diversity, the question of how these changes will affect Deaf culture in the future remains. Will Deaf culture morph into a different image, requiring a different set of cultural characteristics, or fade away into oblivion? Communication technology, captioning, cochlear implants, and remote interpreting may pave the way for increased independence in Deaf people's lives. Will this result in a lesser need for bonding among people of similar interests and likes? In visualizing the future, the authors possess confidence that we will continue to witness barrier-breaking actions performed by the younger generations of Deaf people who are now equipped to meet the demands of their and other people's lives. With increased independence, will there be less need for bonding among people of similar interests and likes?

This book has been, hopefully, an enjoyable and eye-opening journey through the history, culture, and language of deaf people. Once again, the information in this book only scratches the surface of the vast Deaf community and history. To delve further into this wonderfully intricate community, enroll in ASL courses, immerse yourself in ASL with fluent deaf signers, and learn all you can through books, Web sites and other resources.

The authors hope that you have found our heritage, language, and culture educational, entertaining, and enlightening.

Notes

Chapter One

1. Carroll, 1982, p. 6.
2. *Ibid.*
3. Caswell, 1992, p.12.
4. Deaf Time-Line, online.
5. Scouten, 1984, pp. 5–6.
6. *Ibid*, p. 6.
7. Braddock, 1975, pp. 131–133.
8. *Ibid*, p. 132.
9. Moores, 2001, p. 33.
10. *Ibid.*
11. Moores, 2001, p. 32.
12. Giangreco and Giangreco, 1976, p. 5.
13. Scouten, 1984, p. 8.
14. Moores, 2001, p. 35.
15. Van Cleve and Crouch, 1989, p. 6.
16. Deaf Time-Line, online.
17. Giangreco and Giangreco, 1976, pp. 4–5; Eriksson, 1993, p. 21.
18. Scouten, 1984, p. 12.
19. Plann, 1997, p. 19.
20. Bender, 1981, p. 30.
21. Scouten, 1984, p. 16.
22. Eriksson, 1993, p. 28.
23. Bender, 1981, pp. 37–39; Walker, 1994, pp. 10–11.
24. *Ibid*, p. 10.
25. *Ibid*, p. 21.
26. Val, 1985, p. 40.
27. Scouten, 1984, pp. 24–25.
28. *Ibid*, pp. 26–28.
29. *Ibid*, p. 33.
30. *Ibid.*
31. Hodgson, 1953, p. 11.
32. Eriksson, 1993, pp. 48–49.
33. Val, 1985, p. 78.
34. Scouten, 1984, pp. 42–45.
35. Bender, 1981, p. 113.

36. Giangreco and Giangreco, 1976, p. 12.
37. Scouten, 1984, pp. 64–65.
38. Moores, 2001, p. 47.
39. *Ibid*, pp. 68–69.
40. *Ibid*, p. 48.
41. Walker, 1994, pp. 17–18.
42. Fischer, 1993, p. 14.
43. Scouten, 1984, pp. 69–70.
44. Karacostas, 1994, pp. 162–163.
45. Scouten, 1984, p. 72.
46. *Ibid*, p. 73.
47. Lane, 1984, p. 27.
48. Weiner, 1987, p. 22.
49. *Ibid.*
50. Lane, 1984, pp. 24–29.
51. Braddock, 1973, p. 56.
52. Lane, 1984, p. 120.
53. *Ibid.*
54. Braddock, 1975, p. 56.
55. Carroll, 1991, p. 18.
56. *Ibid*, p. 60.
57. *Ibid*, pp. 110–111.
58. *Ibid*, p. 134.

Chapter Two

1. Groce, 1980, p. 6.
2. Paris, Wood, and Miller, 2002, p. 38.
3. Groce, 1985, pp. 23–25.
4. *Ibid* p. 23.
5. Banks, 2007, online.
6. Riggs, 2007, online.
7. Bahan and Nash, 1995, pp. 19–20.
8. Raymond, 2001.
9. Kennedy, 2004.
10. Paris, Wood, and Miller, 2002, p. 38.
11. Fox, 2007, pp. 66–69.
12. Reucroft and Swain, 2001.

13. Carroll, 1997, p. 10.
14. Carroll, 1996, pp. 17–19.
15. Van Cleve and Crouch, 1989, pp. 21–28.
16. *Ibid*, pp. 25–26.
17. *Ibid*, pp. 26–27.
18. Boatner, 1959, p. 5.
19. *Ibid*.
20. Braddock, 1975, p.71.
21. Gannon, 1981, p. 19.
22. Lane, 1984, p. 277; Van Cleve and Crouch, 1989, p. 80.
23. Scouten, 1984, p. 141.
24. Boatner, 1959, p. 37.
25. Holcomb and Wood, 1989, p. 17.
26. Giangreco and Giangreco, 1976, p. 25.
27. Bahan, 1989b, p. 86.

Chapter Three

1. Gallaudet, 1983, pp. 182–183.
2. Garretson, 2010, p. 121.
3. *Ibid*, p. 117.
4. Winefield, 1987, pp. 61–62.
5. *The Deaf-Mute Advance*, 1880, p. 2.
6. Boatner, 1959, p. 105.
7. Bender, 1981, pp. 154–156.
8. Van Cleve and Crouch, 1989, p. 122.
9. Walker, 1994, p. 59.
10. Jankowski, 1997, p. 54.
11. Padden and Humphries, 2005, p. 59.
12. *Ibid*, p. 77.
13. *Ibid*, pp.48, 73.
14. Walker, 1994, p. 67.
15. Gallaudet, 1983, p. 166.
16. *Ibid*, p. 179.
17. Burch, 2002, p. 38.
18. Hairston and Smith, 1983, p. 11.
19. Jowers-Barber, 2008, p. 124.
20. Padden and Humphries, 2005, p. 41.
21. Hairston and Smith, 1983, pp. 16–17.
22. Lane et al., 1996, p. 163.
23. Stuart and Gilchrist, 2005, p. 61.
24. McCaskill-Emerson, 2005, p. 34.
25. Padden and Humphries, 2005, p. 55.
26. *Ibid*.
27. Padden, 1999, p. 8.
28. Hovinga, 2010, pp. 639–640.
29. Buchanan, 1999, p. 39; Van Cleve and Crouch, 1989, p. 157.
30. *Ibid*, p. 122.
31. Gannon, 1981, p. 169.
32. Gannon, 1989, p. 37.
33. Padden and Humphries, 2005, p. 72.
34. Garretson, 2006, p. 241.
35. Moores, 2001, p. 318.
36. Gannon, 1998, p. 40.
37. Gannon, 1989, p. 87
38. Bahan, 1989a, p. 192.
39. Lane et al., 1996, p. 159.
40. Bahan, 1989b, pp. 45–48.
41. Dillehay and Arnos, 2002, p. 9.
42. Humphries, 1977, p. 12.
43. Lane, 1992, p. 43.
44. Humphries, 1977, p. 16.
45. Ladd, 1993, p. 211.
46. Ladd, Gertz, and Eberwein, 2006, p. 1.
47. Walker, 1994, p. 71.
48. Van Cleve, 1987, pp. 38–39.
49. Lane, 1995, pp. 309–310.
50. Eastman, 1996, p. 54.
51. Padden, 1999, p. 3.
52. Walker, 1994, p. 71.
53. Moores, 2001, p. 23.
54. Mitchell and Karchmer, 2006, pp. 98–99.
55. *Ibid*, pp. 98–99.
56. Padden, 1999, p. 13.
57. McCaskill, 2005, p. 34.

Chapter Four

1. Harris, 1988, p. 20.
2. Naisbitt, 1982, p. 14–15.
3. Baker and Padden, 1978, p. 4.
4. Lane, Hoffmeister, and Bahan, 1996, p. 127.
5. Gannon, 1981, p. 181.
6. *Ibid*, p. 190.
7. Braddock, 1975, p. 112.
8. Gannon, 1981, p. 157.
9. Buchanan, 1999, p. 79.
10. Kannapell, 1996, p. 112.
11. Gannon, 1981, pp. 221, 223.
12. Padden and Humphries, 1988, pp. 44–45.
13. Baldwin and Suggs, 1998, p. 15.
14. Goldman, 2010, online.
15. Padden and Humphries, 2005, pp. 86–89.
16. Van Cleve and Crouch, 1989, pp. 60–69.
17. Smith and Jacobowitz, 2005, p. 63.
18. *Ibid*.
19. Walker, 1994, p. 102.
20. Fay, 1906, pp. 36–37.
21. Nomeland, 1967, pp. 30–31.

22. Barnard, 1852, p. 107.
23. Brill, 1974, p. 199.
24. Moores, 2010, pp. 231–239.
25. Dolman, 2010, p. 355.
26. Lane et al., 1996, p. 5.
27. Padden, 1980, p. 92.
28. Garretson, 1988, p. 7.
29. Gannon, 1981, p. 320.
30. *Ibid*, p. 322.
31. Stokoe, Cronenberg, and Casterline, 1965.
32. Padden, 1989, p. 1.
33. Corson, 1992, pp. 9–10.
34. Gannon, 1991, p. 55.
35. Kannapell, 1992, p. 108.
36. Padden, 1989, p. 4.
37. Supalla, 1992, p. 16.
38. *Ibid*, p. 7.
39. Meadow, 1977, p. 241.
40. Gannon, 1981, p. 373.
41. Feldman, 2002, p. 23.
42. Andersson, 1991, pp. 90–91.
43. Cohen, 1993, p. 54.
44. Aramburo, 1994, pp. 477–478.
45. McCaskill-Emerson, 2005, p. 29.
46. *Ibid*, 2005, p. 35.

Chapter Five

1. Corballis, 1999, p. 139.
2. Gorilla Sign Language, 2002, online.
3. Stokoe, 2001, p. viii.
4. Harkins, 1984, p. 3.
5. Baker and Cokely, 1980a, pp. 47–48.
6. Stokoe, 1989, p. iv.
7. Carroll, ed., 1994.
8. Bahan and Nash, 1995, p. 18.
9. Frishberg, 1975.
10. Baker and Padden, 1978, pp. 8–9.
11. Adapted from Bahan and Nash, 1995, p. 18.
12. Baker and Cokely, 1980a, p. 53.
13. Woodward, 1978, pp. 333–347.
14. Padden and Humphries, 2005, p. 175.
15. Baynton et al., 2007, p. 114.
16. *Ibid*, p. 115.
17. Padden and Humphries, 2005, p. 125.
18. Bienvenu, 2000, p. 20.
19. Scouten, 1984, p. 362.
20. Baker and Cokely, 1980a, p. 58.
21. Baker and Padden, 1978, p. 2.
22. Baker and Cokely, 1980a, p. 47.
23. Markowicz, 1977, p. 7.
24. Battison, 1980, p. 42.
25. *Ibid*, p. 38.
26. Siple, 1978, p. 7.
27. Valli et al., 2005, pp. 17–19.
28. Liddell, 1980.
29. Baker and Cokely, 1980b, pp. 121–163.
30. Valli et al., 2005, pp. 127–134.
31. Eastman, 1996, pp. 16–17.
32. Fant, 1993, p. 24.
33. Garretson, 1981, p. 367.

Chapter Six

1. Woodward, 1980, p. 124.
2. Lane et al., 1996, p. 58.
3. *Ibid*, p. 59.
4. Brill, 1974, p. 259.
5. Gannon, 1981, p. 369.
6. Padden and Humphries, 2005, p. 169.
7. Moores, 2001, p. 318.
8. Smith and Jacobowitz, 2005, p. 39.
9. Fleetwood and Metzger, 2007, online.
10. Klossner, 2007, online.
11. Bridges, 1992.
12. Lewis, 2005, p. 227.
13. Fingerspelling, 2006, online.
14. Zinza, 2006, p. xviii.
15. Padden and Gunsauls, 2003, p. 29.
16. Lindholm, 1968, p. 13.
17. Sanderson, 2004, p. 5.
18. Hahn, 2010, p. 7.
19. Carmel, 1982.
20. Corderoy du Tiers, 1996.
21. Lane et al., 1996, p. 440.
22. DawnSignPress, 2005, online.
23. Firkins, 2007, p. 1.
24. Welles, 2004, p. 8.
25. Furman et al., 2007, p. 19.
26. Modern Language Association, 2009, online.
27. Garcia, 1999.
28. Begley, 1999.
29. Harrington, 2006, online.
30. Madsen, 2000, p. 1.
31. Lane et al., 1996, p. 77.

Chapter Seven

1. Bienvenu, 1989, p. 1.
2. Bahan, 1992, p. 153.
3. Carmel, 1987, pp. 428–430.
4. Ryan, 1993, p. 145.
5. Newman, 2006, p. 193.
6. Carmel, 1987, p. 429.

7. Bahan, 1992, p. 153.
8. Bienvenu, 1989, pp. 1–3.
9. *Ibid*, p. 2.
10. *Ibid*.
11. Bienvenu, 1989, p. 3.
12. Jacobowitz, 1992, p. 189.
13. Vicars, 2007, online.
14. Schneider, 1996, p.1.
15. Holcomb et al., 1994.
16. Holcomb, 1985.
17. Moore and Levitan, 2003, pp. 86–87.
18. Strassler, 2005, online.
19. Ortiz, 2004, p. 24.
20. McGann, 2003, p. 38.
21. Dollard, 1988, p. 26.
22. Valli, 1996, pp. 253–263.
23. Miller, 2005, online.
24. Miller, 2007, online.
25. Rosenbaum, 1993, p. 17.
26. *Ibid*.
27. Lane et al., 1996, pp. 144–149.
28. Padden and Humphries, 1988, pp. 77–78.
29. Sonnenstrahl, 2002, pp. 200–207.
30. Moore and Panara, 1996, pp. 148–153; Schuchman, 1988, pp. 13–14.

Chapter Eight

1. Deafness in Disguise, 2007a, online.
2. Deafness in Disguise, 2007b, online.

3. *Ibid*.
4. Lane et al., 1996, p. 386.
5. Pickett, 1987, pp. 193–196.
6. Finley, 2007.
7. FDA, 2007, online.
8. Aiello, 2002, pp. 23–24.
9. National Consortium, 2009, p. 9.
10. Watson and Taff-Watson, 1993, pp. 28–29.
11. AADB White Paper, 2010, online.
12. Padden and Humphries, 2005, p. 101.
13. Heppner, 2005; Boatner, 1980, pp. 7–9.
14. Heppner, 2005.
15. Bureau of Labor Statistics, 2010, p. 6.
16. Heppner, 2005.
17. *Ibid*.
18. Padden and Humphries, 2005, p. 122.

Chapter Nine

1. Lane et al., 1996, p. 172.
2. Garretson, 1981, p. 421.
3. Baldwin, 2004.
4. Nomeland, 2005.
5. Tait, 2007.

Epilogue

1 . Collins, 2010, pp. 3, 16.

Bibliography

AADB White Paper. 2010. http://www.aadb. org/information/ssp/white_paper_ssp.html.

Aiello, Phil. 2002. Quoted in "What's Best for the Child?" *Deaf Life*, vol. 11, no. 8, pp. 22–27.

Andersson, Yerker. 1991. "Some Sociological Implications of Deaf Studies." *Conference Proceedings of Deaf Studies for Educators*, pp. 90–104. Washington, DC: Gallaudet University Press.

Aramburo, Anthony J. 1994. "Sociolinguistic Aspects of the Black Deaf Community." In *The Deaf Way: Perspectives from the International Conference on Deaf Culture*, edited by Carol J. Erting, Robert C. Johnson, Dorothy L. Smith, and Bruce D. Snider, pp. 474–482. Washington, DC: Gallaudet University Press.

Bahan, Ben. 1989a. "The War Is Not Over." In *American Deaf Culture: An Anthology*, edited by Sherwin Wilcox, pp. 189–192. Silver Spring, MD: Linstok Press.

_____. 1989b. "What If ... Alexander Graham Bell Had Gotten His Way?" In *American Deaf Culture: An Anthology*, edited by Sherman Wilcox. Silver Spring, MD: Linstok Press.

_____. 1992. "ASL Literature: Inside the Story." *Conference Proceedings Deaf Studies: What's Up?* pp. 153–164. Washington, DC: Gallaudet University Press.

_____, and Joan Cottle Poole Nash. 1995. "The Formation of Signing Communities." In the conference proceedings of Deaf Studies IV: *Visions of the Past, Visions for the Future*. Washington, DC: Gallaudet University Press.

Baker, Charlotte, and Dennis Cokely. 1980a. *American Sign Language, a Teacher's Re-source Text on Grammar and Culture* (aka "Green Book"). Silver Spring, MD: T.J. Publishers.

_____, and Dennis Cokely. 1980b. "Sign Language in the 20th Century: A Chronology." In *Sign Language and the Deaf Community: Essays in Honor of William C. Stokoe*, edited by Charlotte Baker and Robbin Battison, pp. xv–xx. Silver Spring, MD: National Association of the Deaf.

_____, and Carol Padden. 1978. *American Sign Language, a Look at Its History, Structure and the Community*. Silver Spring, MD: T.J. Publishers.

Baldwin, Stephen C. "What Makes Ruth Run, Jump, and Throw?" *Houston Deaf Senior Citizens Newsletter*, October issue, vol. 5, issue 10.

Baldwin, Steve, and Trudy Suggs. 1998. "Thou Shalt Not Peddle: A Look at Peddling and the Deaf Community...." *Hearing Health*, January-February issue, vol. 14, no. 2, pp. 14–16.

Banks, Charles. 2007. *The History of Martha's Vineyard*. <http://history.vineyard.net/b2 wtres.htm> (accessed 1/2/2007).

Barnard, Henry. 1852. *A Discourse in Commemoration of the Life, Character and Services of the Rev. Thomas H. Gallaudet, LLD*. Hartford, CT: Brockett and Hutchinson.

Battison, Robbin. 1980. "Signs Have Parts: A Simple Idea." In *Sign Language and the Deaf Community: Essays in Honor of William C. Stokoe*, edited by Charlotte Baker and Robbin Battison, pp. 35–52. Silver Spring, MD: National Association of the Deaf.

Baynton, Douglas C., Jack R. Gannon, and Jean Lindquist Bergey. 2007. *Through Deaf*

Eyes: A Photographic History of an American Community. Washington, DC: Gallaudet University Press.

Begley, Sharon. 1999. "Talking from Hand to Mouth." *Newsweek,* March 15. Reprinted from *USA-L News,* March 9.

Bender, Ruth E. 1981. *The Conquest of Deafness*. Third ed. Danville, IL: The Interstate Printers and Publishers.

Bienvenu, M.J. 1989. "Reflections of American Deaf Culture in Deaf Humor." *TBC News,* September issue, no. 17.

_____. 2000. Quoted in "Rebel with a Cause." *Gallaudet Today,* Fall issue, vol. 31, no. 1, pp. 18–21.

Boatner, Edmund Burke. 1980. *Captioned Films for the Deaf*. Washington, DC: Described and Captioned Media Program.

Boatner, Maxine Tull. 1959. *Voice of the Deaf*. Washington, DC: Public Affairs Press.

Braddock, Guilbert. 1975. In *Notable Deaf Persons,* edited by Florence Crammattee, pp. 130–133. Washington, DC: Gallaudet College Alumni Association.

Bridges, Byron W. 1992. *Gender Variations*. A paper presented to Sociolinguistics course. Obtained through personal correspondence.

Brill, Richard G. 1974. *The Education of the Deaf: Administrative and Professional Developments*. Washington, DC: Gallaudet College Press.

Buchanan, Robert M. 1999. *Illusion of Equality: Deaf Americans in School and Factory 1850–1950*. Washington, DC: Gallaudet University Press.

Burch, Susan. 2002. *Signs of Resistance: American Deaf Cultural History, 1900 to World War II*. New York: New York University Press.

Bureau of Labor Statistics. 2010. *Occupational Outlook Handbook, 2010–11 Edition*. <http://online.onetcenter.org/link/summary/23–2091.00> (accessed 1/1/11).

Carmel, Simon. 1987. "Folklore." In *Gallaudet Encyclopedia of Deaf People and Deafness,* vol. 1, edited by John Van Cleve, pp. 428–430. New York: McGraw-Hill.

_____. 1982. *International Hand Alphabet Charts*. Rockville, MD: Studio Printing Incorporated.

Carroll, Cathryn, Editor. 1982. "People's First Language: Sign Language?" *World Around You,* vol. 3, no. 9, p. 6.

_____. 1991. *Laurent Clerc: The Story of His Early Years*. Washington, DC: Gallaudet University Press.

_____. 1996. "A Look at Parents, History, and Deaf Education in the United States." *Perspectives,* vol. 15, no. 2, pp. 16–19. Washington, DC: Gallaudet University Press.

_____. 1997. "Deaf Colonials: Evidence Suggests That Some Were Literate." *Perspectives,* vol. 15, no. 3, pp. 8–11. Washington, DC: Gallaudet University Press.

Carroll, Cathy, Editor. 1994. "What's in a Word?" *World Around You,* March-April issue. Used with permission from Robert Johnson.

Caswell, Paulette. 1992. "In the Eyes of the Law Are We (Really) Equal?" *Deaf Life,* March issue, vol. 4, no. 9, pp. 12–15.

Chan, S. 1994. "Freedom of Speech: Understanding the World's Highest Context Cultures." *Access Silent Asian Conference* proceedings. De Kalb: Northern Illinois University.

Cohen, Oscar P. 1993. "Educational Needs of African American and Hispanic Deaf Children and Youth." *Multicultural Issues in Deafness,* edited by Kathee M. Christensen and Gilbert Delgado. White Plains, NY: Longman.

Collins, Sara. 2010. "The Making of History at 21st International Congress on the Education of the Deaf." *SIGNews,* vol. 8, issue 9, pp. 3, 16.

Corballis, Michael C. 1999. "The Gestural Origins of Language." *American Scientist,* vol. 87, no. 2, pp. 138–144.

Corderoy du Tiers, Fanny. 1996. *Manual Alphabet (American) Alphabet en Dactylologie (francais)*. Private collection.

Corson, Harvey. 1992. Deaf Studies: "A Framework for Learning and Teaching." *Proceedings: Deaf Studies for Educators,* pp. 7–16. Washington, DC: College for Continuing Education.

DawnSignPress. 2005. Press Release on American Sign Language. <www.dawnsign.com>.

The Deaf-Mute Advance, 1880. Vol. 11, no. 20, p. 2.

Deaf Time-Line: 1000 B.C.–1816. <www.aslinfo.com> (accessed 9/14/06).

Deafness in Disguise. 2007a. Washington University School of Medicine. "Timeline of Hearing Devices and Early Deaf Education." <http://beckerexhibits.wustl.edu/did/timeline/index.htm> (accessed 8/2006).

Deafness in Disguise. 2007b. Washington University School of Medicine. "Concealed Hearing Devices of the 19th Century." <http://beckerexhibits.wustl.edu/did/19thcent/spv.htm> (accessed 8/2006).

Dillehay, Jane, and Kathleen Arnos. 2002. "Genetics Research in Deaf Community." Summarized in 2001 Deaf Way conference and printed in *Silent News*, edited by Jonathan Lamberton, vol. 34, no. 8, p. 9.

Dollard, Vincent. 1988. "Visual Poetry: Evolution of an Art Form." *NTID Focus,* summer 1988 issue, pp. 26–27.

Dolman, David. 2010. "Employment Trends in Deaf Education Teacher Preparation Programs, 1973–2009." *American Annals of the Deaf,* vol. 155, no. 3, pp. 353–359.

Eastman, Gilbert. 1989. *From Mime to Sign.* Silver Spring, MD: T.J. Publishers.

_____. 1996. *Just a DEAF Person's Thoughts.* Burtonsville, MD: Sign Media.

"The Education of Koko." 2002. <http://koko.org/world/> (accessed 9/6/2007).

Eriksson, Per. 1993. *The History of Deaf People: A Source Book.* Translated from the Swedish by James Schmale. Orebro, Sweden: SIH Laromedel.

Fant, Louie. 1993. Quoted in "William Stokoe, Part 2." *Deaf Life,* vol. 5, no. 8, pp. 19–26.

Fay, Edward Allen. 1906. "Tabular Statement of American Schools for the Deaf, November 10, 1905." *American Annals of the Deaf,* vol. 51, no. 1, pp. 36–37.

FDA. 2007. Medical Devices: Recalls and Safety. Food and Drug Administration. <http://www.fda.gov/MedicalDevices/ProductsandMedicalProcedures/Implantsand Prosthetics/CochlearImplants/ucm062892.htm> (accessed 12/30/2010).

Feldman, Shane, Editor. 2002. "What Is Deaf Culture?" *NADmag,* vol. 2, issue 1, pp. 23–24.

Fingerspelling. 2006. Answers.com <www.answers.com/topic/fingerspelling> (accessed Feb. 7, 2007).

Finley, Don. 2007. "Seminar Celebrates Godsend for the Deaf." *San Antonio Express-News.* February 17.

Firkins, Katherine. 2007. "Most States Recognize American Sign Language." *SIGNews,* vol. 5, issue 7, p. 1.

Fischer, Renate. 1993. "Abbé de l'Épée and the Living Dictionary." In *Deaf History Unveiled: Interpretations from the New Schol-arship*, edited by John Van Cleve, pp. 13–26. Washington, DC: Gallaudet University Press.

Fleetwood, Earl, and Melanie Metzger. 2007. "What's the Difference Between Cued Speech, Cuem, Cued English, and Cued Language?" Language Matters, Inc. <http://www.language-matters.com/difference.php3>.

Flynt, Suzanne L. 2002. *The Allen Sisters: Pictorial Photographers (1885–1920).* Deerfield, MA: Pocumtuck Valley Memorial Association.

Fox, Margalit. 2007. "Village of the Deaf." *Discover.* July issue, pp. 66–69.

Frishberg, Nancy. 1975. "Arbitrariness and Iconicity: Historical Changes in American Sign Language." *Language*, vol. 51, no. 3, pp. 696–719.

Furman, Nelly, David Goldberg, and Natalia Lusin. 2007. "Enrollments in Languages Other Than English in United States Institutions of Higher Education, Fall 2006," p. 19. Modern Language Association. <http://www.mla.org/2006_flenrollmentsurvey>.

Gallaudet, Edward M. 1983. In *History of the College for the Deaf 1857–1907.* Edited by Lance J. Fischer and David L. de Lorenzo. Washington, DC: Gallaudet College Press.

Gannon, Jack R., Editor. 1974. *The Gallaudet Almanac.* Washington, DC: Gallaudet College Alumni Association.

_____. 1981. *Deaf Heritage: A Narrative History of Deaf America.* Silver Spring, MD: National Association of the Deaf.

_____. 1989. *The Week the World Heard Gallaudet.* Washington, DC: Gallaudet University Press.

_____. 1991. "The Importance of a Cultural Identity." *Perspectives on Deafness: A Deaf American Monograph*, edited by Mervin Garretson. Silver Spring, MD: National Association of the Deaf, pp. 55–58.

_____. 1998. "And Finally..." *Gallaudet Today,* vol. 28, no. 3, p. 40.

Garcia, W. Joseph. 1999. *How to Communicate with Infants Before They Can Speak.* Seattle: Northlight Communications.

Garretson, Mervin. 1981. Quoted in Jack Gannon. *Deaf Heritage.* Washington, DC: Gallaudet University Press.

_____. 1988. "Results of the Original 1961 Fort Monroe Conference." *The Proceedings of the National Conference on Deaf and*

Hard of Hearing People, edited by Richard G. Brill. Publisher not identified.

_____. 2006. *Sands of Time: NAD Presidents 1880–2003*, edited by Larry Newman, pp 233–246. Silver Spring, MD: National Association of the Deaf.

_____. 2010. *My Yesterdays: In a Changing World of the Deaf.* Bloomington, IN: Xlibris.

Giangreco, C. Joseph, and Marianne Ransom Giangreco. 1976. *The Education of the Hearing Impaired.* Springfield, IL: Charles C. Thomas.

Goldman, David. 2010. "Descent into Slavery, and a Ladder to Another Life." *The New York Times*, June 22. Reprinted in *DeafTimes*. <http://deaftimes.com/usa-l/descent-into-slavery-and-a-ladder-to-another-life/>.

Groce, Nora Ellen. 1980. "Martha's Vineyard: Everyone Speaks Sign Language Here." *The Deaf American*, vol. 33, no. 2, pp. 3–6. Silver Spring, MD: National Association of the Deaf.

_____. 1985. *Everyone Here Spoke Sign Language: Hereditary Deafness on Martha's Vineyard.* Cambridge, MA: Harvard University Press.

Hahn, Ernie. 2010. "Ernie's Ramblings." *New Horizons*, vol. 15, no. 4, p. 7.

Hairson, Ernest, and Linwood Smith. 1983. *Black and Deaf in America: Are We That Different?* Silver Spring, MD: T.J. Publishers.

Harkins, Judith, Editor. 1984. "An Interview with Dr. Stokoe." *Gallaudet Research Institute Newsletter*, Fall issue.

Harrington, Tom R. 2006. FAQ: Sign Languages of the World, by Name. <http://library.gallaudet.edu/Library/Deaf_Research_Help/Frequently_Asked_Questions_%28FAQs%29/Sign_Language/Sign_Languages_of_the_World_by_Name.html>

Heppner, Cheryl. 2005. "Birth of Civil Rights." *USA-L News*, copyrighted by Northern Virginia Resource Center.

Hodgson, Kenneth. 1953. *The Deaf and Their Problems.* New York: Philosophical Library, p. 106. Quoted in C. Joseph Giangreco and Marianne Ransom Giangreco. 1976. *The Education of the Hearing Impaired*, p. 11. Springfield, IL: Charles C. Thomas.

Holcomb, Mabs, and Sharon Wood. 1989. *Deaf Women: A Parade through the Decades.* Berkeley, CA: DawnSignPress.

Holcomb, Roy. 1985. *Silence Is Golden.* San Diego, CA: DawnSignPress.

_____, Sam Holcomb, and Tom Holcomb. 1994. *Deaf Culture, Our Way: Anecdotes from the Deaf Community.* San Diego, CA: DawnSignPress.

Hovinga, Sharon Kay. 2010. *A Proud Tradition: Texas School for the Deaf Sesquicentennial.* Austin, TX: Historical Publications.

Humphries, Tom. 1977. *Communicating Across Cultures (Deaf-Hearing) and Language Learning.* Doctoral Dissertation, Union Graduate School. Ann Arbor, MI: University Microfilms. No. DP10817.

Jacobowitz, E. Lynn. 1991. "Humor and Wit in the Deaf Community." *Conference Proceedings of Deaf Studies: What's Up?* pp. 187–191. Washington, DC: Gallaudet University Press.

Jankowski, Katherine A. 1997. *Deaf Empowerment.* Washington DC: Gallaudet University Press.

Jowers-Barber, Sandra. 2008. "The Struggle to Educate Black Deaf School Children." *A Fair Chance in the Race of Life: The Role of Gallaudet University in Deaf History*, edited by Greenwald and Van Cleve. pp. 113–131. Washington, DC: Gallaudet University Press.

Kannapell, Barbara. 1992. "The Relationship of Deaf Studies and Deaf Identity." In *Deaf Studies for Educators*, pp. 105–116. Washington, DC: Gallaudet University College for Continuing Education.

_____. 1996. "The Forgotten People: Deaf People's Contributions During WWII." *Conference Proceedings of Deaf Studies IV: Visions of the Past, Visions of the Future*, pp. 111–123. Washington, DC: Gallaudet University College for Continuing Education.

Karacostas, Alexis. 1994. "The Deaf Population During the French Revolution." In *The Deaf Way's Perspectives from the International Conference on Deaf Culture*, edited by Carol J. Erting, Robert Johnson, Dorothy Smith, and Bruce Snider, pp. 162–166. Washington, DC: Gallaudet University Press.

Kennedy, Louise. 2004. "Vineyard's Deaf Past Is Retold in Drama of Signs and Speech." *The Boston Globe*, June 6.

Klossner, Claire. 2007. "Why Cued Language Is a Great Thing for Cued Speech." Language Matters, Inc. <http://www.language-matters.com/claire.php3>.

Ladd, Paddy. 1993. "Deaf Consciousness— How Deaf Cultural Studies Can Improve the Quality of Life." *Proceedings of Deaf Studies III: Bridging Cultures in the 21st Century*, pp. 199–223. Washington, DC: College for Continuing Education, Gallaudet University.

_____, Genie Gertz, and Dave Eberwein. 2006. "Deafhood: New Term Gains Popularity." *SIGNews*, vol. 4, no. 6, pp. 1, 8.

Lane, Harlan. 1984. *When the Mind Hears: History of the Deaf.* New York: Random House.

_____. 1995. "Are Deaf People Disabled? Disability and Cultural Models of Deaf People." Closing speech presented at the Deaf Studies IV Conference, in Woburn, MA, April 27–30. *Proceedings of Deaf Studies IV Conference*, pp. 309–322.

_____, Robert Hoffmeister, and Ben Bahan. 1996. *A Journey into the DEAF-WORLD.* San Diego, CA: DawnSignPress.

Levitan, Linda. 1992. "ASD Celebrates Its 75th Anniversary." *Deaf Life*, vol. 4, no. 11, pp. 18–25.

Lewis, John G. 2005. "Ebonics in American Sign Language: Stylistic Variation in African American Signers." *Black Perspectives on the Deaf Community*, edited by Jennifer Fuller, Beverly Hollrah, John G. Lewis, and Carolyn McCaskill-Henry. Washington, DC: Gallaudet University Press.

Liddell, Scott K. 1980. *American Sign Language Syntax.* The Hague: Mouton.

Lindholm, Toivo. 1968. "Humor Among the Deaf." *The Deaf American*, April issue, vol. 20, no. 8, pp. 13–14.

Madsen, Willard. 2000. *Gestuno: International Signs.* March-April Class Notes. Washington, DC: Gallaudet University.

Markowicz, Harry. 1977. *American Sign Language: Fact and Fancy.* Washington, DC: Gallaudet University Press.

McCaskill-Emerson, Carolyn. 2005. "Multicultural/Minority Issues in Deaf Studies." *Black Perspectives on the Deaf Community*, edited by Jennifer Fuller, Beverly Hollrah, John G. Lewis, and Carolyn McCaskill-Henry, pp. 29–38. Washington, DC: Gallaudet University.

McGann, Rich. 2003. Untitled. *The Deaf-Blind American*, vol. 42, no. 4, p. 38.

Meadow, K. 1977. "Name Signs as Identity Symbols in the Deaf Community." *Sign Language Studies*, vol. 16, fall issue, pp. 237–245.

Miller, Betty. 2005. *Deaf View/Image Art: The Manifesto's Introduction.* <http://bettigee. purple-swirl.com/DeVIA/DeVIA.html> (accessed 1/1/11).

_____. 2007. Biography as printed in <http://www.deafart.org/Biographies/Betty _G__Miller/betty_g__miller.html> (accessed 1/1/11).

Mitchell, Ross E., and Michael A. Karchmer. 2006. "Demographics of Deaf Education: More Students in More Places." *American Annals of the Deaf*, vol. 151, no. 2, pp. 95–104.

Modern Language Association. "New MLA Survey Report Finds That the Study of Languages Other Than English Is Growing and Diversifying at US Colleges and Universities." <http://www.mla.org/pdf/2009 _enrollment_survey_pr.pdf> (accessed 11/1/2010).

Moore, Matthew S., and Linda Levitan. 2003. *For Hearing Only: Answers to Some of the Most Commonly Asked Questions about the Deaf Community, Its Culture and the "Deaf Reality."* Rochester, NY: Deaf Life Press.

_____, and Robert F. Panara. 1996. *Great Deaf Americans.* Rochester, NY: Deaf Life Press.

Moores, Donald F. 2001. *Educating the Deaf: Psychology, Principles, and Practices, 5th ed.* Boston, MA: Houghton Mifflin.

_____, Editor. 2010. *American Annals of the Deaf Reference Issue,* vol. 155, no. 2, pp. 231–239. Washington, DC: Gallaudet University Press.

Naisbitt, John. 1982. *Megatrends: Ten New Directions Transforming Our Lives.* New York: Morrow.

Nash, Joan Cottle Poole. 2002. "The Island That Spoke by Hand." *Deaf Life*, vol. 11, no. 10. Rochester, NY: MSSM Productions.

National Consortium on Deaf-Blindness. 2009. "The National Child Count of Children and Youth Who Are Deaf-Blind." <http://www.nationaldb.org/documents/ products/2009-Census-Tables.pdf>.

The National Exchange Carriers Association, Inc. (NECA). http://www.neca.org.

Newman, Larry, Editor. 2006. *Sands of Time: NAD Presidents 1880–2003.* Silver Spring, MD: National Association of the Deaf.

Nomeland, Ronald E. 1967. *Beginnings of Vocational Education in Schools for the Deaf.* Research paper submitted to University of Maryland.

_____. 2005. "Deaf Wax Museum Expands." Deaf Seniors of America. <deafseniorsofamerica.org>.

Ortiz, Alyssa. 2004. "The Wind." *SIGNews,* vol. 2, no. 7, p. 24.

Padden, Carol. 1980. "Deaf Community and the Culture of Deaf People." *Sign Language and the Deaf Community,* edited by Charlotte Baker and Robin Battison. Silver Spring, MD: National Association of the Deaf.

_____. 1989. "The Deaf Community and the Culture of Deaf People." *American Deaf Culture: An Anthology,* edited by Sherman Wilson, pp. 1–16. Silver Spring, MD: Linstok Press.

_____. 1999. "The Future of Deaf People." *Conference Proceedings: Deaf Studies IV: Making the Connection,* pp. 1–15. Washington, DC: College for Continuing Education, Gallaudet University.

_____, and Darline Clark Gunsauls. 2003. "How the Alphabet Came to Be Used in a Sign Language." *Sign Language Studies,* vol. 4, no. 1, pp. 10–33.

_____, and Tom Humphries. 1988. *Deaf in America: Voices from a Culture.* Cambridge, MA: Harvard University Press.

_____, and Humphries, Tom. 2005. *Inside Deaf Culture.* Cambridge, MA: Harvard University Press.

Paris, Damara Goff, Sharon Kay Wood, and Katrina Miller. 2002. "A Brief Historical Overview of the Contributions of AISL to ASL." *Step Into the Circle: The Heartbeat of American Indian, Alaska Native, and First Nations Deaf Communities,* pp. 37–42. Salem, OR: AGO Publications.

Pickett, James M. 1987. "Cochlear Implants." In *Gallaudet Encyclopedia of Deaf People and Deafness,* vol. 1, edited by John Van Cleve, pp. 193–196. New York: McGraw-Hill.

Plann, Susan. 1997. *A Silent Minority: Deaf Education in Spain, 1550–1835.* Berkeley, CA: University of California Press.

Raymond, Midge. 2001. "A Silent Culture with a Strong Voice." *Bostonia,* Spring 2001 issue.

"Rethinking the Possibilities: A Brief History of the Deaf." http://www.deafchurch.com/ note_from_president/history.html (accessed 9/14/06).

Reucroft, Stephen, and John Swain. 2001. "Deaf Children Invent Language." *The Boston Globe.* Reprinted in *USA-L News.*

Riggs, Cynthia. 2007. *A Short History of Martha's Vineyard.* <http://marthasvineyard.com/html/penn/history.htm> (accessed 1/19/1999).

Rosenbaum, David. 1993. "Witty Cartoonist Wants Deaf Cartoons to Be Commonplace!" *Deaf USA,* January issue, p. 17.

Ryan, Stephen. 1993. "Let's Tell an ASL Story." In *Proceedings, Deaf Studies III: Bridging Cultures in the 21st Century,* pp 145–150. Washington, DC: College for Continuing Education, Gallaudet University.

Sanderson, Robert C. 2004. "Whatever Happened to Our Beloved 'E'?" *SIGNews,* vol. 2, no. 10, p. 5.

Sayre, Maggie Lee. 1955. '*Deaf Maggie Lee Sayre': Photographs of a River Life,* edited by Tom Rankin. Jackson: University of Mississippi Press.

Schneider, Maxwell. 1996. *Do You Hear Me?: Laughs for the Hard of Hearing by Hard of Hearing.* Eau Claire, WI: Thinking Publications.

Schuchman, John S. 1988. *Hollywood Speaks: Deafness and the Film Entertainment Industry.* Urbana: University of Chicago Press.

Scouten, Edward L. 1984. *Turning Points in the Education of Deaf People.* Danville, IL: The Interstate Printers & Publishers.

Shroyer, Edgar H., and Shroyer, Susan P. 1984. *Signs Across America: A Look at Regional Differences in American Sign Language.* Washington, DC: Gallaudet College Press.

Siple, Patricia, Editor. 1978. *Understanding Language through Sign Language Research.* New York: Academic Press.

Smith, Adonia K., and E. Lynn Jacobowitz. 2005. *Have You Ever Seen...? An American Sign Language (ASL) Handshape DVD/Book.* Frederick, MD: ASL Rose.

Sonnenstrahl, Deborah M. 2002. *Deaf Artists in America: Colonial to Contemporary.* San Diego, CA: DawnSignPress.

Stokoe, William C. 1989. Foreword. *From Mime to Sign.* Silver Spring, MD: T.J. Publishers.

_____. 2001. *Language in Hand: Why Sign Came Before Speech.* Washington, DC: Gallaudet University Press.

_____, Carl Cronenberg, and Dorothy Cast-
erline. 1965. *A Dictionary of American Sign
Language on Linguistic Principles.* Silver
Spring, MD: Linstok Press.

Strassler, Barry, Editor. 2005. "A Deaf Riddle." *Deaf Digest*, June. http://deafdigest.net.

Stuart, P., and A. Gilchrist. 2005. "A Sense
of Identity." *Black Perspectives on the Deaf
Community*, edited by Jennifer Fuller, Bev-
erly Hollrah, John G. Lewis, and Carolyn
McCaskill-Henry, pp. 61–71. Washington,
DC: Gallaudet University.

Supalla, Samuel J. 1992. *The Book of Name
Signs.* San Diego, California: DawnSign-
Press.

Tait, Stephen. 2007. "Port Paintings Hit
$800k at Auction." *The Daily News* of
Newburyport, MA. January 23.

Val, Sarah. 1985. *None So Deaf.* Washington,
DC: Pre-College Programs, Gallaudet College.

Valli, Clayton. 1996. "Poetics of ASL Poetry."
*Conference Proceedings of Deaf Studies for
Educators IV: Visions of the Past, Visions for
the Future.* Washington, DC: Gallaudet
University Press.

_____, Ceil Lucas, and Kristin Mulrooney.
2005. *Linguistics of American Sign Language: An Introduction.* Washington, DC:
Gallaudet University Press.

Van Cleve, John V., Editor. 1987. *Gallaudet
Encyclopedia of Deaf People and Deafness.*
New York: McGraw-Hill.

_____, and Barry A. Crouch. 1989. *A Place of
Their Own: Creating the Deaf Community
in America.* Washington, DC: Gallaudet
University Press.

Vicars, Bill. 2007. "Deaf, HOH, and ASL
Jokes." <http://www.lifeprint.com/asl101/
pages-layout/jokes.htm> (accessed 1/1/11).

Walker, Lou Ann. 1994. *Hand, Heart, &
Mind: The Story of the Education of America's Deaf People.* New York: Dial Books.

Watson, Douglas, and Myra Taff-Watson,
Editors. 1993. *A Model Service Delivery System for Persons Who Are Deaf-Blind.* Fayet-
teville: University of Arkansas.

Weiner, Dora B. 1987. "Abbé Roch Ambroise
Cucurron Sicard." In *Gallaudet Encyclopedia of Deaf People and Deafness*, vol. 3, edited by John Van Cleve, p. 22. New York:
McGraw-Hill.

Welles, Elizabeth B. 2004. "Foreign Language
Enrollments in United States Institutions
of Higher Education, Fall 2002." *ADFL
Bulletin*, vol. 35, no. 2–3.

Woodward, James. 1978. "Historical Bases of
American Sign Language." *Understanding
Language Through Sign Language Research*,
edited by P. Sigle, pp. 333–347. Rochester,
NY: Academic Press.

_____. 1980. "Sociolinguistic Research on
American Sign Language: A Historical Per-
spective." *Sign Language and the Deaf
Community: Essays in Honor of William C.
Stokoe*, edited by Charlotte Baker and Rob-
bin Battison, pp. 117–134. Silver Spring,
MD: National Association of the Deaf.

World Federation of the Deaf. Unification of
Signs Commission. 1975. *Gestuno: international sign language of the deaf = langage
gestuel international des sourds: the revised
and enlarged book of signs agreed and
adopted by the Unification of Signs Commission of the World Federation of the Deaf = le
livre révisé des signes acceptés et adoptés par
la Commission d'unification des signes de la
Federation mondiale des sourds.* Carlisle,
England: British Deaf Association [for] the
World Federation of the Deaf. (Distributed
in USA through the National Association
of the Deaf.)

Zinza, Jason. 2006. *Master ASL! Fingerspelling, Numbers, and Glossing.* Burtonsville,
MD: Sign Media.

Index

Numbers in **bold italics** indicate pages with photographs.

access 1, 4, 35, 76, 124, 135, 175–177, 185, 187; communication 28, 30, 60, 78, 92, 174, 180, 182; deaf-blind 175; information 100, 136, 168, 179; Internet 185, 190, 193; interpreting 136, 188; movie 177; signing 30; telephone 35, 174–175; visual 93
Adams, Luke 195
African American 56–58, 60, 63, 99, 129, 160, 162, 165, 168, 192
Agricola, Rudolph 11
Aiello, Phil 173, 198
Alexander Graham Bell Association 47, 49, 182
Allen, Frances 167
Allen, Mary 167
Al-Sayyid Bedouin Sign Language 30
altering device 174, 176, 187
Amann 50
Amelish 119
American Annals of the Deaf 62, 88
American Association to Promote the Teaching of Speech to the Deaf 49
American Asylum for the Deaf 28, 45–46, 59, 86
American Asylum for the Deaf and Dumb 103, 200
American Athletic Association of the Deaf 83–84
American School for the Deaf 35, 38–39, 43–45, 58, 86, 127, 161, 196, 198, 204
American Sign Language (ASL) 1, 3, 28–29, 38, 45, 53, 63, 69, 76–77, 83, 89–93, 95, 100, 101–104, 107, 109–116, 119, 122–125, 127–128, 131–134, 139–140, 149, 152, 155, 158, 168, 187, 189, 197–199, 209; *see also* ASL
Americans with Disabilities Act 1, 136, 180, 185, 210
Ameslam 119
Ameslish 119
Amman, Johann 16, 19–20
ancient times 5–6, 9, 67
Anthony, David 121–122
Aristotle 7, *7*, 12, 50

Arnold, Hillis 200
Asian 60
Asian American 60, 76, 99
ASL classes 151; course 211; curriculum 198; film 168–169; humor 151; jokes 145; learning 209; linguistics 68, 110, 112, 139, 156 (*see also* linguistics); morphology 107, 111, 113; phonology 107, 111–112; play 162; poetry 142, 156; storytelling 142 (*see also* Deaf storytelling; storytelling); syntax 107, 111–113
ASL, increasing demand 132–134
ASL parameter: handshape 96, 103–104, 109–110, 112 (*see also* handshape); location 96, 106–110, 112 (*see also* location); movement 96, 109–110, 112 (*see also* movement); parameter, non–manual signs 113 (*see also* facial expression; non–manual signs); parameter, palm orientation 112 (*see also* palm orientation)
ASL Poetry: Selected Works of Clayton Valli 156
Association of Late Deafened Adults 187
asylum 9
audism 65–66
Austria 18, 22

Baer, Don 200
Bahan, Ben 28, 47, 62, 64
Baker, Henry 16–17
Baker and Cokely 102, 104, 111, 114
Baker and Padden 103, 111
Baldwin, Steve 196
Ballantyne, Donald L. 205
Banks, Michelle 165
Barwacz, M.E. 86
Battiste, Hume Le P. 56
Beadell, William W. 204
Beam, Fred 162
Beattie, Shelley 202
Beethoven, Ludwig van 194
Beets, Betty Lou 195
behavior 9, 65, 93, 96
Bell, Alexander Graham 46–47, 48–53, 65, 106, 108, 136

Bellugi and Klima 110
Benedictine monks 10–1, 15
Berdy, Sean 120
Betts, Wayne, Jr. 168
Biblical times 6, 67
Bienvenu, M.J. 110, 145
Bilingual Act 125
bilingual approach 107, 123, 125, 158
bilingual education 107, 125
Birnbaum, David 137, 197
black 43, 56–58, 99, 129, 160, 163, 165, 195, 204
Black Deaf culture 58
Bolling, John 32
Bolling, Thomas 31
Bolling, William 31–32
Bonet, Juan Pablo 12, 14, 50
Booth, Edmund 204–205
Bornstein, Harry 122
Bosson, Ed 185
Boston School for Deaf Mutes (Horace Mann School) 46
Boston University 29, 46, 168
Boston WGBH TV 178–179
Bove, Linda 164–165
Bowe, Frank G. 203
Bragg, Bernard 119, 161–162, 200
Braidwood 50
Braidwood, John, I 17–18
Braidwood, John, II 18, 31–32
Braidwood, Thomas, I 17–18
Braidwood Academy 17, 31, 34–35
Braidwood method 18, 72
Bravin, Jeffrey 165
Bray, Deanne 165
Brewster, John 157, 200
Bridges, Byron 128
Brill, Richard 121
British sign language 131
Broderson, Morris 200
Brody, I. Lee 184
broken English 111–112
Brown v. Board of Education 57–58
Bryan, Ann Marie 168
Bullard, Douglas 86
Bulwer, John 14
Burges, Gaspart 11
Burnes, Byron B. 143

C-Print 181
California School for the Deaf, Berkeley 143
California School for the Deaf, Fremont 158, 165
California School for the Deaf, Riverside 120–121
California State University, Northridge 89, 168
California Volunteers **201**
Caplan, Kimby 168
captioned films 77, 84, 142, 161, 169, 177–178

Captioned Films for the Deaf 177–179, 206
captioned movies 60, 77, 93, 161, 177, 178; programs 179; television 84, 93, 178, 180;
captioning 137, 162, 169, 178–181, 210
captioning, closed 179–180, 187, 209–210; Internet 210; in-theater 181–182; live 178, 180; real-time 137, 204; videos and DVDs 180
captions 177–181
captions, decoder 83, 85, 179–180, 209; non-English viewers 180; open 60; pre-recorded 180
Cardano, Girolamo 11
Carlin, John 42, 157, 200
Carmel, Simon 132
Carroll, Cathryn 4
Casterline, Dorothy **108**, 109
Catchings, Tamika 206
Catlin, George 201
cemeteries 59
A Century of Difference **75**, 160
Charles Thompson Memorial Hall 77
Chatoff, Michael A. 204
Children of Deaf Adults 97, 133, 135
Chilmark 27–28
Christianity 7
church 7, 9, 11, 24, 35, 43, 67, 78–79, 100
Chushim 6
Cistercian monks 21
Civil War 57–59, 106, 205
Clarke School for the Deaf 46
Clerc, Rev. Francis J. 79
Clerc, Laurent 33–35, 37–38, 53, 72, 79, 86, 196, 198, 204; in France 24–26, 33–35, 37; as mentor 53, 204; name sign 95–96; sign language 104, 119; vocational training 88
clubhouse 77, 84, 100
Cobbs School **32**, 32
cochlear implant 58, 130, 147, 170–173, 187, 203, 210
coffee shops 85
Cogswell, Alice 32–34, 39, 56, 196
Cogswell, Mason 32–35, 39
Colombo, LeRoy 202
colored 56–58
Columbia Institution for the Deaf and Dumb and Blind 40, 42–45, 50, 56
Columbia Institution for the Instruction of Deaf and Dumb 72
combined 58
combined method 35, 43, 45, 49, 53–55, 120–121
combined schools 121
combined system 51, 53, 120
communication access
Communication Access Real-time Translation (CART) 180–181
community 1–2, 28, 76, 86, 89, 91, 93, 111, 176–177, 188
community, African-American 76; Black Deaf 99; college 134, 159; education 194; educa-

tional 61; Gallaudet 108; hearing 76, 78, 99, 142, 163; Hispanic 76; Latino 76; Paris 22; signing 28, 30
community, Deaf 1–3, 23, 62, 65–66, 72, 74, 76, 81, 84, 89–92, 95–97, 100, 106, 108–109, 115, 122, 134–135, 141–142, 145, 149–150, 156, 163–164, 169, 173, 189, 191, 197, 210–211; *see also* Deaf Community
Conference of Executives of American Schools for the Deaf 124, 192
Connecticut Asylum for the Education and Instruction of Deaf and Dumb 33, 35, *36*, 37–39, 41
Connexin 26 (Cx26) 65
Convention of American Instructors of the Deaf 49
Corballis, Michael 101
Corson, Harvey 61, 91
Coughlin, Thomas 79, 195
Council of Organizations Serving the Deaf 90
Couthen, Albert 58
Croesus, King of Lydia 7
Cronenberg, Carl *108*, 109
Crowe, Charles 197
Cued Speech 125–126, 139
culture 1–2, 5, 77, 91–93, 98–99, 111, 124, 135, 137, 144–145, 169, 188
culture, American 141; black 58; diverse 106; ethnic 99; European American 70; free-thinking 110; minority 146; non-deaf 135; *see also* Deaf culture
culture, deaf 4, 47, 69–71, 90–93, 97–100, 110, 115, 125, 135, 141–142, 144–147, 157–158, 161, 173, 188–189, 196–198, 200, 210–211; *see also* Deaf culture

Daigle, Matt 4, *151*, 157–158, 157, *182*, 185
Dalgarno, George 15
Dannis, Joe 197–198
Davila, Robert 63, 192
deaf and dumb 50–51
The Deaf and Dumb Asylum *18*
Deaf and Hard of Hearing Consumer Advisory Board 187
deaf-blind 99, 146, 148, 175–176, 184, 193–194, 210
Deaf cartoons 151–158, 160; clubs 76–77, 83–85, 100; folklore 142, 145 (*see also* folklore); history 3, 5, 38, 53, 69, 103, 125, 189; identity 91–92, 99, 142, *160*; norms 94; rules of behavior 93, 98; storytelling 93, 142–143 (*see also* ASL storytelling; storytelling); teachers 49, 51–52, 54, 121, 125; traditions 86, 93, 98; values (belief) 70, 76, 92–93, 98–99; world 63, 89–91, 157–159, 189, 205
The Deaf Community 72, 74, 76, 89–90, 92, 95, 97, 99–100
Deaf culture 4, 69, 71, 90–93, 97–100, 110, 115, 125, 141–142, 144–147, 149, 157–158, *159*, 161, 173, 188–189, 196–198, 210

Deaf Identity Crayons *98*, 160
Deaf Life 173, 190
Deaf Mosaic 169
Deaf President Now 1, 62, 185
Deaf Seniors of America 78, 80, 132, 190
Deaf Studies 71, 91, 99, 110, 149
Deaf Studies Conference 69, 91, 103
Deaf Way Conference 91
Deaf-World 63, 89–90, 132, 140, 189
deafened 33, 46, 190, 192, 194, 206; *see also* late deafened
deafhood 66–67
Deaflympics 84
Deafvision Filmworks, Inc. 169
de Carrión, Manual Ramirez 12, 50
Defoe, Daniel 17
de Leon, Ponce 11–12, *13*, 50
de l'Épée, Charles-Michel 17, 19–23, *20*, 25, 31, 50–51, 69
Delgado, Gilbert 177
Denison, James 50
Department of Education 49
de Priego, Marquis 12
Described and Captioned Media Program 177–178
Detmold, George 49
de Velasco, Francisco 12
de Velasco, Juan 11
de Velasco, Luis 14
de Velasco, Pedro 12
A Dictionary of American Sign Language 90, 109
Digby, Sir Kenelm 14
discrimination 60–61, 63, 65
Drolsbaugh, Mark 196

Eastman, Gilbert 69, 102, 115, 161, 169
Edge, John 30
Edge, Samuel 30
Edinburgh Institute 18
Edison, Thomas 194
Egyptians 6
Emperor Justinian 9, 67
Engelsman, Bernard 45
England 10, 14, 16–17
ephthatha 8
eugenics 65; research 47

Fabray, Nanette 195
facial expression 102, 113–115, 120, 142, 144, 147, 156–157
Fant, Lou 49, 115, 119
Father of American Sign Language Linguistics 110
Fay, Edward M. 53
Federal Communications Commission 179–180, 185–187
Feris, Eric 137, 197
Feris, Moon 62–63
Fernandes, Jane 62–63

Ferringo, Lou 202
Fingerspelling 34, 60, 93, 96, 123–124, 126,
    131–132, 148, 150; in Europe 10, 12, 14–16;
    history 131–132; humor 146, 150; names 96;
    106–107; Rochester method 120; in schools
    52–54, 106–107
Florida School for the Deaf and Blind 57, 120,
    159
Florida School for the Negro Deaf and Blind
    57
Flournoy, John James 86
folklore 93, 141–142, 144–145, 167
football huddle 207
For Hearing People Only 150
Forester, Jane 17
Foster, Andrew J. 56, 192
France 16–17, 19–26, 34–36, 38, 69, 72, 95,
    119, 132, 162, 167, 172
Frelich, Phyllis 164–165
Frishberg, Nancy Jo 103
Frisino, Louis 201

Gallaudet, Edward Miner 36, 38, 40–45, *43,*
    48–50, 53, 56, 78, 95–96, 168
Gallaudet, Sophia Fowler 36, 41, *41,* 43–45, 48
Gallaudet, Rev. Thomas 78–79
Gallaudet, Thomas Hopkins 33–37, 39–41,
    43–45, 67, 72, 78, 88–89, 91, 95–96, 120,
    198
Gallaudet College 44, 48, 50–51, 53, 56, 81,
    159, 161, 166, 191–192, 207
Gallaudet University 4, 37–39, 41, 122, 137,
    142, 149, 162, 164–166, 185, 194; Archives 4,
    81; artists 156, 158, 160, 196–197, 200–201;
    board of trustes 62, 164, 198; conferences
    69, 91, 103, 156; Deaf Mosaic 169; dramatics
    161, 165; faculty 70, 75, 87, 108, 110, 158–
    159, 207; history 44–46; linguistic research
    90, 108, 110; president 42–45, 53, 56, 62–
    63, 192, 201; protests 62–63, 185, 191; Vi-
    sual Language and Visual Learning 209–210
Galloway, Sue 38, *38*
Gannon, Jack 62, 92, 196, 202
Garcia, Joseph 134
Garretson, Mervin 4, 49, 61, 115, 191
gay/lesbian 63, 99
Georgia School for the Deaf 59
Germany 18–19
Gertz, Genie 4
Gestuno 138–139
gestures 5, 14, 18, 91, 101–102, 109, 111, 118,
    124, 134, 138–139, 142–144, 150–151
Giddens, Kathleen 201
Gilbert, James 56
Gillett, Philip 49–50
Giordano, Tyrone 165
Glickman, Ken 196
Gough, John 177
Graybill, Patrick 156, 161
Greek 6–7, 67

Green, Francis 31, 34
Gregg, John 194, 203
Groce, Nora Ellen 28, 105
Gustason, Gerilee 122

Hahn, Ernie 132
Hairston, Ernest 58
Hairston, Eugene 195
Hall, Percival 56
handshape, cued speech 125
handshape, fingerspelling 96, 131–132, 144
handshape, sign 14, 94–95, 105–106, 109, 117–
    118, 121–123, 126, 139, 142, 144, 156, 162
Hanson, Olof 77, 203
hard of hearing 10, 47, 55, 62, 69–70, 72–74,
    76, 89, 98–99, 126, 136, 146–147, 151, 159,
    166, 168, 170, 173–175, 181, 187, 190, 193,
    195–197
Harrington, Thomas 137
Harris, Bob 198
Harrow, John 30
Harvard, Russell
Hazards of Deaf Culture **94**, 159
hearing aid 73, 147–148, 159, 170–171, 196;
    history 171–172
Hearing Aid Tree **149**, 159
hearing impaired 47, 72–74
hearing loss 5, 10, 48, 66, 70, 74, 76, 91–92,
    171–172, 180, 196, 198
Hearing Loss Association of America 187
hearing teachers 49, 52, 54, 142
hearing world 55, 61–62, 64, 158
Hebrews 6–7, 9, 67
Heinicke, Samuel *19*, 19, 22, 50
Hermogenes 7
Herodotus 7
Hewes, Gordon 5, 101
Hispanic 63, 76, 99, 192
Hispanic-American 63, 99
Hlibok, Greg 210
Hochman, Frank Peter 205
Hodgson, Kenneth 16
Holcomb, Roy K. 4, 124, 149, 197
Holcomb, Tom 64
Holder, William 14–16
Holland 16, 19
Holt, Laurent Clerc 38
Horace Mann School 46
Hotchkiss, John B. 53
Houston Association of the Deaf 77, 84
Hoy, William 195, 198, *199,* 206
Hubbard, Gardiner 46
Hubbard, Mabel 46
Hubbard, Paul 207
Hughes, Regina Olson 206
Humphries, Tom 65–66
Hurwitz, T. Alan 63

Identity, Black 59
Identity, ethnic 99

ILY Handshape **97**, 159
International Congress on Education of the
  Deaf 50–51, 210
international sign language 138–139
international signs 137, 138, **138**
Internet 84–85, 94
interpreted 64, 79
interpreter 49, 54, 79, 83, 85, 87, 89, 93,
  134–137, 139, 146, 149–151, 158, 160, 176,
  186, 197, 204, 210; certificate 136; jokes
  150–153; training program 89; video relay
  137, 185–186
interpreting agency 137; field 137; profession
  89; program 136; service 87, 137; sign language 110, 149, 197; video relay 185–186;
  voluntary 136
Invisible Hands, Inc. 162

Jacobowitz, Lynn 4, 147
Johnson, Bob 102
Jones, C.J. 163
Jordan, I. King 62, 192

Kannapell, Barbara 4, 92
Kannapell, George 166
Kansas School for the Deaf 59, 161
Keller, Helen 15, 47, 108
Kendall, Amos **40**, 39–42, 44, 72
Kendall Green 41, 44, 56, 72
Kendall School 44–45, 56–57
Kentucky School for the Deaf 39, 59, 167
King Louis XVI 22, 24
Kisor, Henry 205
Klusza, Maureen 4, **153**, 158
Kovacs, Jonathan 162

Ladd, Paddy 66
Lane, Harlan 66, 69
late deafened 99, 133, 172, 181, 187; *see also*
  deafened
Latino 63, 76, 99
Latino-American 99
Laurent 86
Laurent Company 86
Laurent Institute 86
Leadership Training Program 88
LeClerc, Katie 210
Leviticus 6
Lexington School for the Deaf 45–46, 83, 96
Liddell, Scott 113
linguistics 2, 15, 90, 92, 96, 99, 107, 111, 115,
  120, 126, 145, 156, 209
Linguistics of Visual English 122
Linguistics Research Laboratory 108, **108**
lipreading 16, 34, 53–54, 146–148, 151–152,
  205
Little Paper Family 190, 196
location, cued speech 125
location, sign 95–96, 109, 112, 117, 123, 156
Lois Misunderstanding **152**, 159

The London Asylum for the Deaf and Dumb
  17–18
Louisiana School for the Deaf 59, 61, 120
Low, Juliette Gordon 194, 198, **199**, 206
Lucazk, Raymond 197
Luhn, Arthur 168

Macfadden, Jim 198
mainstreamed settings 69–70
mainstreaming 30
Mangiardi, Adrean 168
Mann, Horace 46
manual alphabet 14, 18–19, 34, 82, 115, 131–
  132, **132**; French 132, **133**
manual class 54
manual department 54
manual language 52, 61
manual program 51
manualism 51, 58
Marr, Thomas Scott 203
Marshall, Ernest 168
Martha's Vineyard 27–29, 76, 86, 103, 105
Maryland School for Colored Deaf-Mutes 56
Maryland School for the Deaf 81
Massieu, Jean 23–26, 34–35, 37
Matlin, Marlee 164–165, 210
Maucere, John 163
McCaskill-Emerson, Carolyn 58, 70
McGregor, Robert 53
Mechanics **201**
medical 11, 19; aspect/perspective 68, 92, 97;
  profession 66, 74
Meyers, Lowell 204
Michaels, John W. 78
Michigan School for the Deaf 80
Middle Ages 9–11
Milan conference 50–51, 53, 67, 120, 210
Milan resolution 51, 53, 120–121, 210
Miller, Betty 156, 158, 160
Miller, Marvin 86
Miller, Ronda Jo 206
Miller v. D.C. Board of Education 56–57
Minnesota School for the Deaf 53, 61
Mississippi School for the Deaf 59, 120
Missouri School for the Deaf 59, 163
Mitchell and Karchmer 69
Model 15 TTY **183**
Moore, Mindy 169
Moores, Donald 62
Moos, Phil 191
Morse, Samuel 39–40
Mt. Airy School for the Deaf 56; *see also*
  Pennsylvania School for the Deaf
movement, body 111, 114; fingerspelling 120;
  mouth 147; sign 96, 103–104, 109, 116–117,
  120, 122–123, 126, 156

name signs 94–96, **95**
Nash, Poole 28–29
National Association of the Deaf 37, 52–53,

61, 63, 80–82, 97, 132, 143, 168, 187, 189–192, 205
National Captioning Institute 179
The National Exchange Carriers Association, Inc. 187
National Fraternal Society of the Deaf 80–81
National Institute for Deaf-Mutes 21, 23–26
National Technical Institute for the Deaf 88, 97
National Theatre for the Deaf 161–164, 196, 206
Native Americans 27, 29, 60, 63, 99, 105, 182, 201
Navaretta, Juan Fernandez 12
Nebraska School for the Deaf 52
New Horizons 132, 190
New York Institute for the Deaf 40, 45, 78–79
New York Institution for the Improved Instruction of Deaf Mutes (Lexington School) 45
New York Institution for the Instruction of the Deaf and Dumb 40
New York School for the Deaf 161, 168, 191–192
New York University 160, 168, 194, 203–205
Nicaraguan Sign Language 30
Nomeland, Melvia 2, 54, 57–58, 64–65, 77–78, 94, 143, 175
Nomeland, Ronald 2, 49, 53–55, 57–59, 61–62, 77–78, 81–82, 87, 106, 120, 136, 143, 175, 177
non-deaf world 141
non-manual signs 113–114, 156
normal training 43, 48
Norris, Carolyn B. 86
North Carolina School for the Negro Deaf and Blind 57
Northeastern University 110
Norwood, Malcolm 177–178
Novitsky, Mary Lou 169

Ohio School for the Deaf 56
Oliva, Gina 70
O'Neil, Kitty 205
open captions 60, 77, 177–179
oppression 63
oral advocates 52; approach 55; department 54; education 51–53; failures 52; history 57; influence 52; method 31, 34, 42, 45–46, 50–51, 53, 55; movement 54; program 51–55; schools 49, 53; system 51; training 55
oralism 49–54, 58
Orleck-Aiello, Myrna 198
O'Rourke, Terry 119

Padden, Carol 4, 30, 89, 93
Padden and Humphries 54, 57–58, 84–85, 176, 188
palm orientation 103, 112, 123, 156

Panara, Robert 161
parameter 110, 112–113, 117, 122; handshape 110, 112; location 110, 112; movement 110, 112; non–manual signs 113; orientation 112; *see also* ASL parameter
Paris, Damara Goff 197
paternalism 50, 60, 66, 68
peddlers 82–83
Pedius, Quintus 9
Peet, Harvey 40–41
Pennsylvania School for the Deaf 56, 59; *see also* Mt. Airy School for the Deaf
Pereire, Jacob Rodriguez 20, 22
Perrier, Abbé 25
Peterson, Ruth 4, *97, 152*, 159
Pfetzing, Donna 122
Picnic Alert **135**, 159
Pidgin Sign English 119, 122
Pierce, David 205
Popham, Admiral 14
Posedly, Thomas J. 203
Possible Historical Sources of Modern ASL **104**
postlingually deaf 6, 14, 48, 189
prelingually deaf 6, 189–190
The Preservation of the Sign Language 167–168
Pride, Curtis 207

Quinones, Heriberto **94, 149**, 154, **155**, 159

Rathskellar 162
Red Hat Society 78
Redmond, Granville 163
Registry of Interpreter for the Deaf 136, 206
rehabilitation 1–2
Rehabilitation Act of 1973 136
relay service 135, 175–176, 185, 187; TTY 184–185, 187, 196; video 137, 186–187
religion 11, 20, 68, 78, 89
Renaissance 11–12
Rennie, Debbie 156
residential school 52, 56, 59–60, 69–70, 76, 83, 85, 88, 100
revival preacher **64**
Richardson, Shawn 4, *152*, 153–154, **154**, 160
Rochester Institute of Technology 88, 97, 157–159, 168, 192, 205
Rochester Method 120, 123
Rochester School for the Deaf 120
Roman 9, 50, 67
Rose Cottage **42**
Royal National Institution for the Deaf-Mutes **21**, 31, 34–35, 37
Ryan, Stephen 146–147

Saint Augustine 9, 50
St. John of Beverly 10
Salaway, Tracey 168
Salk Institute 110
Sayre, Maggie Lee 167
Schneider, Maxwell 197